KT-547-899

SS REF

FOR REFERENCE
ONLY

The College of Law, Bloomsbury

S09373

Practical Corporate Governance

For Smaller Quoted Companies and Private Companies

Practical Corporate Governance

For Smaller Quoted Companies and Private Companies

Dr John Mellor

Published by
Jordan Publishing Limited
21 St Thomas Street, Bristol BS1 6JS

Copyright Jordan Publishing Limited 2008

All rights reserved. No part of this publication may be reproduced, stored in a retrieval system, or transmitted in any way or by any means, including photocopying or recording, without the written permission of the copyright and database right holder, application for which should be addressed to the publisher.

British Library Cataloguing-in-Publication Data

A catalogue record for this book is available from the British Library.

ISBN 978 1 84661 126 1

Typeset by Letterpart Limited, Reigate
Printed in Great Britain by CPI Antony Rowe, Chippenham, Wilts

PREFACE

Throughout my career as a banker and then in corporate governance, I have experienced over some 30 years the circumstances and challenges that are faced by smaller companies and, in particular, their boards of directors. By smaller companies I include listed companies, those preparing for listing, and other private companies.

If I were to identify one feature common to all these companies it is that their success and sustainability over the long term depends upon how they are directed and controlled. Furthermore, I do not recall any client or company I have had the opportunity to be in contact with disagreeing with this proposition. The same goes for investors in these companies.

However, when 'direction and control' was applied to define corporate governance, and in some minds corporate governance became associated with 'rules' and 'paperwork' (often grouped together as 'bureaucracy'), some smaller companies resisted corporate governance as a business imperative. I have sympathy with this perception of corporate governance, but this is not to imply any abrogation of a board's responsibility for the governance of a company on my part. The consequence of this perception has probably been that corporate governance has not been taken seriously enough by some smaller companies.

In my view corporate governance has to be presented in a more 'user-friendly' way to help smaller companies realise the value of good governance, with guidance given on the application of the principles of good governance tailored to their particular circumstances. And this, in a nutshell, is the purpose of this book.

Hitherto much of the focus of corporate governance has been on much larger companies, in spite of the fact that smaller companies are a vital component of the economy. Smaller companies make a significant contribution to national income and employment as well as being a source of larger companies through organic growth and acquisition, with the scale and reach to penetrate global markets.

Practical Corporate Governance for Smaller Quoted Companies and Private Companies brings focus to the corporate governance of smaller companies.

This book applies mainly to smaller quoted companies, but it is also relevant for private companies. Smaller quoted companies covers those quoted on the main list of the London Stock Exchange but not included in the FTSE 350 index, and those quoted on the Alternative Investment Market. The former are usually referred to as FTSE small caps and the latter as AIM companies. Together they aggregate some 2,500 companies ranging in size based on turnover from a very few to hundreds of millions of pounds sterling.

This book is written for practical use by smaller companies. It does not theorise on corporate governance but provides explanation where necessary. It contains guidance for boards and directors in particular on how to apply corporate governance. As its source of the principles of corporate governance, it takes the Combined Code on Corporate Governance, coupled with my own experience of the Code which includes being a contributor to its continuing development. It aims to put the principles of the Code to work for smaller companies, always having in mind that a Code, and any accompanying regulation of smaller companies, should have as a basis the vision of a thriving and competitive smaller company sector of the economy. Codes and regulations are not an end in themselves, but a means to an end.

As a practical guide, the book is therefore deliberately not of undue length and the headings and sub-headings of each chapter have been selected to describe the practical content of what follows. Each chapter is self-contained to the extent that the reader can expect to find within it comprehensive explanation and guidance on the chapter topic. The Appendices with each chapter have also been carefully selected so as not to include unnecessary detail.

The book is divided into six chapters.

Chapter 1 explains the Combined Code from the perspective of the smaller company and therefore lays the groundwork for the application of its principles of good governance.

Chapter 2 provides the rationale and guidance on applying the principles to AIM companies, notwithstanding that AIM companies, unlike FTSE small caps, do not fall under the Code. The relevance of the principles and how they might be applied to private companies is also explained in this chapter.

Chapter 3 considers the duties of directors as contained in the Companies Act 2006 from the perspective of a practising director. This lays down the groundwork for Chapters 4 and 5.

Chapters 4 and 5 present guidance for the non-executive director, company boards and their committees respectively.

Chapter 6 is the final chapter for good reason. Corporate governance is a model of two parts – companies and shareholders – and at its heart is communication between these two parties. The chapter provides guidance on corporate governance reporting, and on engagement between smaller company boards and their institutional shareholders. Both reporting and engagement play a crucial role in making corporate governance work effectively. The link between corporate governance and raising capital, which is considered from time to time throughout the book, is also brought together in this final chapter.

Corporate governance is about the management of a business, and management is the more robust and effective if the principles of good governance are applied, tailored to meet the particular circumstances of the smaller company. 'No one size fits all' is a useful mantra for both companies and investors to keep continually in mind when considering or evaluating corporate governance arrangements for smaller companies.

Corporate governance is also about people – their behaviours, attitudes and abilities. People are central to corporate governance and the effectiveness of any corporate governance arrangement is dependent upon them. Structures, processes and well sounding words do not of themselves qualify as good corporate governance.

The ultimate purpose of corporate governance is the preservation and creation of value for shareholders. Applying the principles of good governance practice increases the probability of business success and the avoidance of business failure. At the same time, and just as important, good governance generates confidence and trust from shareholders to provide the capital for investment and growth.

These statements combined provide the riposte to the question – why bother with corporate governance? – which in my experience is sometimes heard from smaller companies.

The aim of this book will have been achieved if, by bringing focus to the corporate governance of smaller companies, and hopefully doing so in a 'user-friendly' way, it provides both practical and easily accessible guidance for their boards of directors in particular, and also for their investors and advisors.

Dr John Mellor
October 2008

CONTENTS

ACKNOWLEDGMENTS

As the author I would like to acknowledge and thank the following organisations for permission to reproduce certain materials: Financial Reporting Council, Quoted Companies Alliance, National Association of Pension Funds, Institute of Chartered Accountants of Scotland, Institute of Chartered Secretaries and Administrators, Institutional Shareholders' Committee, Hermes Pensions Management, Alexandra plc and Ricardo plc.

I would also like to express my appreciation and thanks to my colleagues at the Foundation for Governance Research and Education for the inclusion of certain aspects of the Foundation's work and the opportunity for stimulating and thought-provoking discussion. I am particularly grateful to the Foundation's President, Professor Ian Percy CBE, and Chris Hodge, both members of the Foundation's Board of Trustees, for their interest and support.

In the spirit of saving the best till last, this book would never have been written without the commitment, the application of her outstanding professional skills including that of reviewer and critic, and the enduring patience of my wife Anne. It is to her that I dedicate this book.

ABBREVIATIONS

AGM	Annual General Meeting
AIM	Alternative Investment Market
CEO	chief executive officer
CFO	chief financial officer
DWP	Department of Work and Pensions
FGRE	Foundation for Governance Research and Education
FRC	Financial Reporting Council
HEOS	Hermes Equity Ownership Services
HMRC	Her Majesty's Revenue and Customs
ICAS	Institute of Chartered Accountants for Scotland
ICSA	Institute of Chartered Secretaries and Administrators
IMA	Investment Management Association
NAPF	National Association of Pension Funds
NOMAD	Nominated Adviser
PWC	PricewaterhouseCoopers
QCA	Quoted Companies Alliance
UKLA	United Kingdom Listing Authority

INTRODUCTION

How companies are governed has been a matter of interest for a very long time. Intuitively, the better a company is governed the more likely it is to survive and prosper. However, this cannot be the one determining factor of corporate success. Other things come into play such as economic and market conditions, competition, commercial and financial strategy, resources, and other risks to success. Nevertheless, good governance, meaning how well a company is directed and controlled, is an important ingredient of business success and at the same time mitigates the risk of failure. Business history is littered with examples of business failure which can be put down to poor corporate governance. It is self-evident that governance matters for both listed and private companies.

The focus of this book is smaller quoted companies in particular, but also private companies. Smaller quoted companies includes companies on the main list of the London Stock Exchange outside the FTSE 350 index and those listed on the Alternative Investment Market (ie AIM companies). Smaller quoted companies also include those listed on alternative exchanges such as PLUS markets. Private companies include owner-managed as well as private equity-owned companies.

Corporate governance fell under the microscope at the time of the Cadbury Report in December 1992. This report followed notable failures amongst some larger quoted companies and led in due course to the Combined Code on Corporate Governance. The origins of the Code, its status, contents and application are explained in the chapters that follow.

At this point it is relevant to point out that the Code was established to apply to companies on the main list of the London Stock Exchange, so excluding AIM listed and private companies. Those outside the main list are encouraged to take note and apply those principles of the Code relevant to their circumstances. However, they are not required to comply with its contents. For these companies the Code is a useful framework and reference point for good governance practice, in particular so far as the composition and operation of the board of directors is concerned. This applies equally to companies on the main list.

Up until fairly recently corporate governance was taken to mean embracing the Combined Code. More enlightened thinking in recent times has taken governance to also include strategy (corporate and financial) as well as risk management. This broader meaning better reflects its importance to a company's prosperity.

CHAPTER 1

THE COMBINED CODE ON CORPORATE GOVERNANCE – THE CODE

1.1 PURPOSE OF THIS CHAPTER

The purpose of this chapter is to view the Combined Code from the perspective of the smaller quoted company and from there to interpret its contents for both AIM listed and private companies. A key point to note from the outset is that the Code should be understood as a framework or set of guidelines for good governance and not a straitjacket into which companies of all shapes and sizes, be they listed or private, must and need to fit. Much frustration with the Code, particularly amongst smaller quoted companies, arises because this basic and simple point is missed. Corporate governance codes and connected regulation of smaller companies should be driven by a vision of a thriving and competitive smaller company sector of the economy. This vision should determine the objectives for Code and regulatory developments. Codes and regulations are not an end in themselves, but a means to an end.

To assist in keeping the Code in perspective as far as its application to those companies which are the focus of this book are concerned, namely smaller quoted companies, AIM listed and private companies, the following diagram will prove helpful.

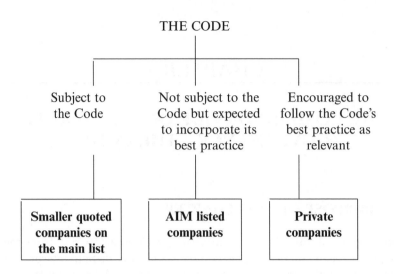

1.2   THE CODE

The Code is a governance code of best practice which, as has already been pointed out, applies from a regulatory point of view only to UK companies listed on the main market of the London Stock Exchange. The Code is not of itself a statutory instrument and is therefore not enshrined in legislation. The Code also applies to institutional shareholders.

1.3   PUBLICATION OF THE CODE

In July 2003, the Financial Reporting Council (FRC) published the Combined Code on Corporate Governance. The document included the Code itself, supporting schedules on respectively performance-related remuneration, the liability of non-executive directors and the disclosure of corporate governance arrangements, related guidance on internal control and audit committees, and various pieces of good practice guidance from a report on non-executive directors. The Code was updated in June 2006 with only minor changes, but with more developed guidance on internal control and audit committees.

The FRC, established by the Government, is the UK's independent regulator responsible for promoting confidence in corporate reporting and governance. The FRC's functions are exercised principally by its operating bodies (the Accounting Standards Board, the Auditing Practices Board, the Board for Actuarial Standards, the Financial Reporting Review Panel, the Professional Oversight Board and the Accountancy and Actuarial Discipline Board) and by the Council. The Committee on Corporate Governance, whose members are drawn from the Council, assist it in its work on corporate governance.

1.4 ORIGINS OF THE CODE

In December 1992, a committee headed by Sir Adrian Cadbury ('the Cadbury Committee') reported on the financial aspects of corporate governance. The Committee had been set up in May 1991 by the FRC, the London Stock Exchange and the accountancy profession. The Committee's terms of reference were:

> 'To consider the following issues in relation to financial reporting and accountability and to make recommendations on good practice:
>
> (a) the responsibilities of executive and non-executive directors for reviewing and reporting on performance to shareholders and other financially interested parties, and the frequency, clarity and form in which information should be provided
>
> (b) the case for audit committees of the board, including their composition and role
>
> (c) the principle responsibilities of auditors and the extent and value of the audit
>
> (d) the links between shareholders, boards, and auditors
>
> (e) any other relevant matters.'

Its sponsors were concerned with the perceived low level of confidence both in financial reporting and in the ability of auditors to provide the safeguards which the users of company reports sought and expected. The underlying factors were seen as the looseness of accounting standards, the absence of a clear framework for ensuring that directors kept under review the controls in their business, and competitive pressures both on companies and on auditors which made it difficult for auditors to stand up to demanding boards.

These concerns about the working of the corporate system were heightened by some unexpected failures of major companies (eg the Maxwell group of companies) and by criticisms of the lack of effective board accountability for such matters as directors' pay.

In the course of the work the Cadbury Committee recognised that boards must be free to drive their companies forward, but should exercise that freedom within a framework of effective accountability. The Committee therefore drafted a corporate governance Code of Best Practice, underpinned in the case of listed companies by a 'comply or explain' rule and not by legislation. In June 1998, the Code of Best Practice was updated by a further committee, headed by Sir Ronnie Hampel (then chairman of ICI plc), so that it embraced Cadbury, the committee's own work, and recommendations on directors' remuneration set out by a third committee headed by Sir Richard Greenbury (then chairman of Marks and Spencer plc). This gave rise to the Combined Code.

The 2003 Code, published in July 2003 by the FRC, arose from revisions to this Combined Code following a period in which investor confidence had continued to be badly shaken, both by lapses in corporate governance and by the high-profile failure of some corporate strategies. These revisions resulted from reviews of the role and effectiveness of non-executive directors ('the Higgs Review') and of the existing Combined Code provisions on audit committees. Both reviews were clear that the fundamentals of corporate governance in the UK were sound, but suggested amendments to the Combined Code to advance and reflect best practice.

1.5   STRUCTURE OF THE CODE

The Code is divided into two sections. Section 1 applies to companies and is set out under four main headings: 'Directors'; 'Remuneration'; 'Accountability and Audit'; and 'Relations with Shareholders'. Under each heading are: 'Main Principles'; 'Supporting Principles'; and 'Code Provisions'. For companies there are a total of 14 Main Principles, 21 Supporting Principles and 48 Code provisions.

Section 2, which is much shorter, applies to institutional shareholders and contains only three 'Main Principles' and five 'Supporting Principles', grouped under three main headings: 'Dialogue with Companies'; 'Evaluation of Governance Disclosures'; and 'Voting'.

The three 'Supporting Schedules' also included, and integral to the Code, are:

A   Provisions on the design of performance related remuneration;

B   Guidance on liability of non-executive directors; and

C   Disclosure of corporate governance arrangements.

The refined guidance on internal controls and audit committees, namely the Revised Turnbull Guidance and Smith Guidance, is also referenced.

1.5.1   Regulatory status

The Code is annexed to the Listing Rules for UK listed companies. The UK Listing Authority (which administers the London Stock Exchange listing regulations under the aegis of the Financial Services Authority) requires that the Code applies to all listed companies and was in effect for financial years commencing on or after 1 November 2003. At the same time listed companies are also required to satisfy Listing Rule 9.8.6R which provides that in the annual report and accounts the following must be included:

(a)   A statement of how it has applied the Main Principles set out in Section 1 of the Code, (the section applying to companies), in a manner that enables its shareholders to evaluate how the principles have been applied. (Listing Rule 9.8.6R(5))

The form and content of the narrative statement are not prescribed; the intention being that companies should have a freehand to explain their governance policies in the light of the principles, including any special circumstances applying to them which have led to a particular approach.

(b)   A statement as to whether or not it has complied throughout the accounting period with all relevant Code provisions set out in Section 1 of the Code. A company that has not complied with the provisions of the Code or complied with only some of the provisions (in the case of provisions whose requirements are of a continuing nature), or complied for only part of an accounting period, must specify the Code provisions with which it has not complied, and (where relevant) for what part of the period such non-compliance continued, and give reasons for any non-compliance. (Listing Rule 9.8.6R(6))

In other words, companies have either to confirm that they comply with the Code's provisions, or, where they do not, provide an explanation. It is for shareholders in particular to evaluate companies' explanations for non-compliance. The Code is therefore based on the 'comply or explain' principle and it stands or falls depending upon how effectively this principle is applied.

Listing Rule 9.8.10R also requires that the provisions compliance statement described under (b) above must be reviewed by the auditors before publication insofar as it relates to certain provisions of the Code. This is explained in Chapter 6 under reporting of corporate governance.

Listing Rule 9.8.11R also requires that the auditors review the following disclosures:

•   the amount of each element of remuneration packages and information on share options;

•   details of long-term incentive schemes for directors;

•   defined benefits schemes; and

•   money purchase schemes.

The auditors must state in their report if, in their opinion, the company has not complied with any of the foregoing requirements and, to the extent possible, provide a statement giving details of non-compliance.

1.5.2   Sanctions

To summarise, the Code is therefore in itself not part of the Listing Rules but an account of its application, and compliance is required to be set out in the annual report by reason of the Listing Rules. The consequence is that the sanctionable breach which arises is breach of Rule 9.8.6R, not breach of the Code. In other words, if a listed company fails to insert a disclosure statement in its annual report which complies with Rule 9.8.6R, then the sanctions which apply are those which would apply for breach of any other Listing Rule. The Financial Services Authority (FSA) as Listing Authority makes no judgment on the accuracy or adequacy of the compliance statements made by listed companies. These are matters for the judgment of the directors and shareholders. If a company is in breach of Rule 9.8.6R, sanctions available to the FSA range from:

*   a fine on a director, or former director, or on the company; or

*   a suspension of share dealings or a de-listing of the company's shares; or

*   a private warning or public censure by the UK Listing Authority; or

*   censure by the FSA either publicly or privately to the board of any company which falls under the control of the FSA; or

*   possible removal of an offending director by the relevant FSA regulatory authority.

In reality, however, personal sanctions against directors of defaulting companies are infrequent and possibly insufficient. For this reason the FSA announced, in October 2003, a review of the Listing Rules, which led to the FSA being given powers under fresh regulations to disqualify directors of companies which break the Listing Rules similar to the powers given to the Department of Trade and Industry (now the Department for Business Enterprise and Regulatory Reform).

It is unlikely that a company would overtly and deliberately refuse to comply with Rule 9.8.6R. The FSA monitors compliance with the Rules by sampling a number of annual reports on a routine basis.

1.6   THE 'COMPLY OR EXPLAIN' PRINCIPLE

It has already been emphasised above that the Code without 'legislative teeth' is based upon a 'comply or explain' regime. This 'comply or explain' approach has been in operation in the UK for over 10 years and the flexibility it offers has been widely welcomed both by company boards and by investors. Its effectiveness rests upon disclosure (by companies) and evaluation (by shareholders – and institutional shareholders in particular as the major owners of shares). Without both sides playing their proper part, and being seen to do so, the threat of legislation is ever present. An overburdensome legislative regime is considered by many, companies and institutional shareholders alike, to be detrimental to business enterprise. For this reason it is considered most important that the 'comply or explain' regime persists.

As a front-runner in establishing a code of best practice on a 'comply or explain' basis, the UK has been a pointer to other parts of the world. Across Europe the 'comply or explain' approach is becoming accepted. On the other hand, the UK regime is in marked contrast to that of the US which has always favoured, and continues to favour, legislation and regulation, including the use of fines and prison as sanctions against companies and directors. This approach has most recently been enshrined in the Sarbane-Oxley Act 2002, enacted in response to the corporate disasters at Enron and Worldcom in particular.

There is, however, one notable exception to 'the regime of self-regulation' underpinning the Code and that is the Directors' Remuneration Report Regulations 2002. In essence these require listed companies to publish an annual remuneration report which has to contain comprehensive information on the pay and benefits of directors. The report has to be put to shareholders for approval at the AGM, but there is no legislative sanction as to what happens if the vote is against the report.

1.6.1   Disclosure by companies

Because the 'comply or explain' regime is so fundamental to the effectiveness of the Code, it is worthwhile exploring further. It has been pointed out that the Code's effectiveness rests on two 'pillars': disclosure (by companies) and evaluation (by shareholders). In the Code, disclosure may be taken to cover the statement by a company of how it has applied the Code principles and its record of compliance and explanations for any non-compliance with the Code provisions. Whilst listed companies, especially those in the FTSE 350, may be expected to comply with the Code's provisions most of the time, departures from those provisions may be justified in particular circumstances. It is for each company to review each provision carefully and give a considered explanation if it departs from the Code provisions. The crucial point here, therefore, is that the Code allows for some flexibility, and tailoring, properly justified to meet particular companies' circumstances, is acceptable.

For this reason the Code is better viewed as a framework for business conduct and accountability, and this is most probably better conveyed by changing the 'comply or explain' to 'apply or explain'. Viewed in this light, and without in any way undermining the integrity of the Code, some companies might be helped to overcome their resistance to the Code on the grounds that it is merely 'another layer of bureaucracy'. Smaller listed companies, in particular those new to listing, may judge that some of the provisions are disproportionate or less relevant in their case. Indeed some of the provisions do not apply to companies below FTSE 350. But the Code, viewed and applied in the way it is meant to be, is responsive to the circumstances of smaller listed companies.

Assuming listed companies of all sizes take a considered approach to disclosure and explanation, it then rests with institutional shareholders in particular (as the major owners of shares) to take a similarly considered approach to evaluation.

1.6.2   Evaluation by institutional shareholders

The Preamble to the July 2003 Code put the position succinctly:

> 'Whilst recognising that directors are appointed by shareholders who are the owners of companies, it is important that those concerned with the evaluation of governance should do so with common sense in order to promote partnership and trust, based on mutual understanding. They should pay due regard to companies' individual circumstances and bear in mind in particular the size and complexity of the company and the nature of the risks and challenges it faces. Whilst shareholders have every right to challenge companies' explanations if they are unconvincing, they should not be evaluated in a mechanistic way and departures from the Code should not be automatically treated as breaches. Institutional shareholders and their agents should be careful to respond to the statements from companies in a manner that supports the "comply or explain" principle. As the principles in Section 2 (that section which applies to institutional shareholders) make clear, institutional shareholders should carefully consider explanations given for departure from the Code and make reasoned judgements in each case. They should put their views to the company and be prepared to enter a dialogue if they do not accept the company's position. Institutional shareholders should be prepared to put such views in writing where appropriate.'

1.7   MONITORING AND REVIEW BY THE FRC

In March 2004 the FRC set up a new committee to lead its work on corporate governance. The committee's terms of reference were:

*   to keep under review developments in corporate governance generally, reflecting the FRC's objective of fostering high standards of corporate governance; to undertake reviews, either directly or by overseeing the work of others, and then to consider whether any actions by the FRC would be desirable; and to put proposals to the Council where appropriate;

- to monitor the operation of the Combined Code on Corporate Governance and its implementation by listed companies and by shareholders; and

- where significant doubts are raised about the appropriate interpretation of part of the Code, to consider the case for issuing a clarification and, if appropriate, to do so after any suitable consultation.

The point to be made here is that the Code should be regarded as continually evolving in response to what is best practice and 'works' for both companies and institutional shareholders.

The FRC conducted a review of the 2003 Code in 2005 and found that the Code was settling down well and that no significant changes were required. However, the Code had been devised with larger companies (ie above the FTSE 350) mainly in mind. This review, therefore, caused the FRC to consider paying more attention to the Code's impact on smaller quoted companies in subsequent reviews. This aspect was incorporated into the FRC's next Review of the Code, the results of which were published in November 2007 and are contained in the following:

'Executive Summary

The Combined Code continues to have a broadly beneficial impact, and is seen as having contributed to higher overall standards of governance among UK listed companies and to more professional boards. Preoccupation with following the Code should not, and in general does not, undermine the board's ability to provide entrepreneurial leadership, although it will be necessary to keep under review the impact of the Code and regulation more generally on how boards spend their time and on the supply of potential non-executive directors.

While there are many positive indicators to suggest that the "comply or explain" approach is working fairly well, such as the increase in resources devoted to engagement by institutional investors, there is also a good deal of frustration with its day-to-day operation. In particular, investors are concerned by what they consider to be the poor quality explanations provided by some companies, while companies consider some investors and voting advisory services to be guilty of "box-ticking" and failing to give sufficient weight to explanations. *This view was held most strongly by smaller listed companies who perceive themselves to be of lower priority to investors.*

While it appears that there is currently a critical mass of institutional investors who devote the necessary time and resource to constructive engagement needed to make "comply or explain" work, it will be necessary to keep the health of the engagement process under review in the light of changes in ownership patterns and increased outsourcing of voting and engagement activities. Action may also be needed to address structural barriers to constructive engagement.

There is little support for widespread derogations from the full Code to apply to smaller companies.

There has been a gradual but discernible improvement in the overall quality of disclosure, although the general perception among investors and other observers is that there remains scope for considerable further improvement. Better communication will be an important element in improving the effectiveness of "comply or explain".' (Author's emphasis)

Only two changes were made to the Code as a result of the FRC's 2007 Review. Importantly, because it applies to smaller quoted companies, was that the chairman can be a member of, but not chair, the audit committee provided he or she is considered independent on appointment.

A new edition of the Code, published in June 2008, applied to accounting periods beginning on or after 29 June 2008. In practice this means that most companies will begin to apply the updated Code in 2009, and will report against them for the first time in 2010. In the normal course of events the next review of the Code will take place in 2010.

1.8   CONTENTS OF THE CODE

1.8.1   Introduction

To date the focus of corporate governance has been large companies, in spite of the fact that smaller companies are vital to European economies. Smaller companies make a significant contribution to national income and employment as well as being a source of larger companies through organic growth and acquisition to build the scale and reach to penetrate global markets. For smaller companies to prosper, good governance and investment are vital. Without these, companies stagnate or fail with serious knock-on effects for economic development and society.

Policy-makers need to put in place corporate governance regimes that are effective, well understood and applied by these companies. They need to avoid over-regulation that hinders innovation and sensible risk taking. Corporate governance needs to establish confidence in the capital markets for investment to be forthcoming and sustained, but as investment markets become more global a 'one-size-fits-all' model of corporate governance is unlikely to be effective.

The Main and Supporting Principles underlying the Code are carefully crafted and so are reproduced in full to obtain an overall picture of the Code framework and its intended application. Code provisions are necessarily more detailed, both amplifying and providing guidance on implementation of the principles. Many of the provisions have particular relevance for non-executive directors.

Following each combination of Main and Supporting Principles is a commentary tailored to focus on smaller quoted companies, with references to certain provisions.

In the text, Code provisions are categorised as a subset of that part of the Code to which they refer; in other words, A.1.1 is a provision relating to 'A.1 The board'.

1.8.2   Section 1 – Companies

A Directors

Under 'Directors', the Code lays out best practice for:

- the unitary board and its role;

- the roles of chairman and chief executive;

- the balance of executive and non-executive directors on the board and addresses the issue of independence;

- appointments to the board;

- information to be supplied to the board and professional development of directors;

- performance evaluation of the board, board committees and individual directors;

- the re-election of directors.

In summary, this part of the Code encapsulates a framework and guidelines for effective operation of a unitary board.

A.1 The Board

The Main Principle, which applies to the board as a whole, is that:

> 'Every company should be headed by an *effective* board, which is *collectively* responsible for the success of the company.' (Author's emphasis)

The Supporting Principles help clarify the application of this principle:

> 'The board's role is to provide *entrepreneurial leadership* of the company within a framework of prudent and effective controls which enables risk to be assessed and managed. The board should set the company's strategic aims, ensure that the necessary financial and human resources are in place for the company to meet its objectives, and review management

performance. The board should set the company's values and standards and ensure that its obligations to its shareholders and others are understood and met. (Author's emphasis)

All directors must take decisions objectively in the interests of the company.

As part of their role as members of a unitary board, non-executive directors should constructively challenge and help develop proposals on strategy. Non-executive directors should scrutinise the performance of management in meeting agreed goals and objectives, and monitor the reporting of performance. They should satisfy themselves on the integrity of financial information and that financial controls and systems of risk management are robust and defensible. They are responsible for determining appropriate levels of remuneration of executive directors and have a prime role in appointing, and where necessary removing, executive directors, and in succession planning.'

The Code provisions give guidance on how the board should conduct itself (A.1.1), including setting out in the annual report the names of senior members of the board and chairmen of board committees (A.1.2).

The Supporting Principles include a useful encapsulation of the role of the non-executive directors on a board.

In the unitary board structure executive and non-executive directors share responsibility for both direction and control of the company. The role and effectiveness of the non-executive director needs to be considered in the context of the board as a whole and the board is collectively responsible for promoting the success of the company by directing and supervising the company's affairs ('All directors must take decisions objectively in the interests of the company.') The benefit of the unitary board derives from the combination of executive knowledge within the board with the wider experience that the non-executive directors can bring to board discussion and decision making. *This wider experience is of particular value to smaller companies.*

Provision A.1.3 states that the chairman should hold meetings with the non-executive directors without the executives present. Led by the senior independent director, the non-executive directors should meet without the chairman present at least annually to appraise the chairman's performance, on such other occasions as are deemed appropriate and on resignation.

Further, where directors have concerns which cannot be resolved about the running of the company or a proposed action, they should ensure that their concerns are recorded in the board minutes. On resignation a non-executive director should provide a written statement to the chairman, for circulation to the board, if they have any such concerns (A.1.4).

With regard to the legal responsibilities and liability of directors, although the law does not apply different duties to executive and non-executive directors, it has been recognised that the knowledge, skill and experience expected will vary between directors with different roles and responsibilities. This applies both to executive and non-executive directors.

The Code, nevertheless, includes very helpful guidance on liability of non-executive directors. This guidance builds on directors' duties in relation to care, skill and diligence by making clear that, although non-executive directors and executive directors have the same legal duties and objectives as board members, their involvement is likely to be different. In particular a non-executive director is likely to be able to devote significantly less time to, and in most cases have less detailed knowledge and experience of, the company's affairs.

In this context the following elements of the Code are particularly relevant:

In order to enable directors to fulfil their duties, the Code states that:

(a)   the letter of appointment of the director should set out the expected time commitment; and

(b)   the board should be supplied in a timely manner with information in a form and of a quality appropriate to enable it to discharge its duties. The chairman is responsible for ensuring that the directors are provided by management with accurate, timely and clear information.

In addition non-executive directors should themselves:

(a)   undertake appropriate induction and regularly update and refresh their skills, knowledge and familiarity with the company;

(b)   seek appropriate clarification or amplification of information and, where necessary, take and follow appropriate professional advice;

(c)   where they have concerns about the running of the company or a proposed action, ensure that these are addressed by the board and, to the extent that they are not resolved, ensure that they are recorded in the board minutes;

(d)   give a statement to the board if they have such unresolved concerns on resignation.

It is up to each non-executive director to reach a view as to what is necessary in particular circumstances to comply with the duty of care, skill and diligence they owe as a director to the company. In considering whether or not a person is in breach of that duty, a court would take into account all relevant circumstances. These may include having regard to the above where relevant to the issue of liability of a non-executive director.

A.2 Chairman and Chief Executive

The Main Principle which applies to the roles of chairman and chief executive is that:

> 'There should be a clear division of responsibilities at the head of the company between the running of the board and the executive responsibility for the running of the company's business. No one individual should have unfettered powers of decision.'

The Supporting Principle focuses on the important role of chairman:

> 'The chairman is responsible for *leadership of the board*, ensuring its effectiveness on all aspects of its role and setting its agenda. The chairman is also responsible for ensuring that the directors receive accurate, timely and clear information. The chairman should ensure effective communication with shareholders. The chairman should also facilitate the effective contribution of non-executive directors in particular and ensure constructive relations between executive and non-executive directors.' (Author's emphasis)

The chairman is pivotal in creating the conditions for overall board and individual non-executive director effectiveness, both inside and outside the boardroom. This is neatly summed up by the supporting principle.

The Code provisions emphasise the different roles of chairman and chief executive and that they should not be exercised by the same person (A.2.1). Further, that on appointment the chairman should be 'independent' (a concept referred to later on in the Code) and that only in 'exceptional' circumstances should a chief executive become chairman of the same company (A.2.2). These two provisions have not always been acceptable to business, but nevertheless, where exceptions have been carefully reasoned and justified to shareholders, they have been accepted. This is an example of the Code's flexibility.

This separation is often inappropriate for smaller companies. A chairman is often close to the executive management of the company for good reason. This situation highlights the need for a strong and independent non-executive presence on the board.

A.3 Board Balance and Independence

The Main Principle which applies to board balance and independence is that:

> 'The board should include a balance of executive and non-executive directors (and in particular independent non-executive directors) such that no individual or small group of individuals can dominate the board's decision taking.'

This is the counterweight referred to above.

The Supporting Principles provide useful guidance:

> 'The board should not be so large as to be unwieldy. The board should be of sufficient size that the balance of skills and experience is appropriate for the requirements of the business and that changes to the board's composition can be managed without undue disruption.
>
> To ensure that power and information are not concentrated in one or two individuals, there should be a strong presence on the board of both executive and non-executive directors.
>
> The value of ensuring that committee membership is refreshed and that undue reliance is not placed on particular individuals should be taken into account in deciding chairmanship and membership of committees.
>
> No one other than the committee chairman and members is entitled to be present at a meeting of the nomination, audit or remuneration committee, but others may attend at the invitation of the committee.'

Whilst all non-executive directors (and of course executive directors) need to be independent of mind, a proportion also needs to be independent in a stricter sense. There is a natural potential for conflict between the interests of executive management and shareholders in a range of instances; for example director remuneration. Although there is a legal duty on all directors to act in the best interests of the company, it has long been recognised that in itself this is insufficient to give full assurance that these potential conflicts will not impair objective board decision making. Much evidence has been accumulated to indicate that a board is strengthened significantly by having a strong group of non-executive directors with *no other connection* with the company. The Code addresses this in two ways:

(1) by including a determination of independence (in the stricter sense); and

(2) by calling for at least half the board, except in smaller companies and excluding the chairman, to be made up of non-executive

directors determined by the board to be independent. A smaller quoted company should have at least two independent non-executive directors (A.3.2).

Hereby rests the problem for smaller quoted companies in that the chairman is often of necessity considered to be one of the two independent non-executive directors. The problem is exacerbated by the composition requirements of the three board committees, namely the audit, remuneration and nomination committees.

On the issue of 'independent' Code Provision A.3.1 states that the board should identify in the annual report each non-executive director it considers to be independent. The board should determine whether the director is independent in character and judgment and whether there are relationships or circumstances which are likely to affect, or could appear to affect, the director's judgment. The board should state its reasons if it determines that a director is independent notwithstanding the existence of relationships or circumstances which may appear relevant to its determination, including if the director:

(a)   has been an employee of the company or group within the last 5 years;

(b)   has, or has had within the last 3 years, a material business relationship with the company either directly, or as a partner, shareholder, director or senior employee of a body that has such a relationship with the company;

(c)   has received or receives additional remuneration from the company apart from a director's fee, participates in the company's share option or a performance-related pay scheme, or is a member of the company's pension scheme;

(d)   has close family ties with any of the company's advisers, directors or senior employees;

(e)   holds cross-directorships or has significant links with other directors through involvement in other companies or bodies;

(f)   represents a significant shareholder;

(g)   has served on the board for more than 9 years from the date of his or her first election.

Notwithstanding the requirement for independent non-executive directors on a board, non-executive directors in addition who are deemed not to be independent (in the stricter sense) may still fill a much valued role on a board.

The appointment of a senior independent non-executive director (senior independent director) is also recommended in the Code (A.3.3).

A.4 Appointments to the Board

The Main Principle applying to appointments to the board is that:

> '. . . there should be a formal, rigorous and transparent procedure for the appointment of new directors to the board.'

The Supporting Principles point out that appointments should be made on *merit and against objective criteria* and also stress the important place for *plans for succession*.

> 'Appointment to the board should be made on merit and against objective criteria. Care should be taken to ensure that appointees have enough time available to devote to the job. This is particularly important in the case of chairmanships.

> The board should satisfy itself that plans are in place for orderly succession for appointments to the board and to senior management, so as to maintain an appropriate balance of skills and experience within the company and on the board.'

The Code provisions focus on the composition and role of the *nomination committee*, which should lead the process for board appointments and make recommendations to the board. *This committee should comprise a majority of members who are independent non-executive directors.* The chairman or an independent non-executive director should chair the committee, but not the chairman when the committee is dealing with the appointment of a successor to the chairmanship (A.4.1).

The nomination committee should evaluate the balance of skills, knowledge and experience on the board, and, in the light of this evaluation, prepare a description of the role and capabilities required for a particular appointment – chairman, executive or non-executive (A.4.2). In the case of the chairman, particular importance is attached to the candidate being able to meet the commitment expected and to availability in the event of crises (A.4.3).

The terms and conditions of appointment of non-executive directors should be available for inspection and non-executives should ensure they have sufficient time to meet their commitments (A.4.4).

A separate section of the annual report should describe the work of the nomination committee and the processes for appointment it has applied (A.4.6).

The calibre and composition of board membership is clearly of fundamental importance to corporate governance and this is reflected in this part of the Code.

The nomination and appointments process is crucial to the securing of the best candidates so that the board has an appropriate mix of skills and experience and the personal characteristics of the individuals complement one another as far as is possible. The whole should constitute an effective decision-making body and board team (the unitary board). To that end a vigorous, fair and open recruitment process with appointments based on merit is essential.

To date this has not always been the case for non-executive directors, where a high level of informality has surrounded the process of appointment, with personal contacts or friendships playing a large part. The 'pool' from which non-executives have been selected has also been too narrow with little or no representation of, for instance, female candidates and those with careers which do not include prior experience on a listed company board. Diversity amongst board members, including amongst the non-executive directors themselves, is recognised as adding strength to board discussion and decision making.

A.5 Information and Professional Development

The Main Principle applying to information and professional development is that

'The board should be supplied in a timely manner with information in a form and of a quality appropriate to enable it to discharge its duties. All directors should receive induction on joining the board and should regularly update and refresh their skills and knowledge.'

The Supporting Principles amplify the role of chairman and company secretary in this regard:

'The chairman is responsible for ensuring that the directors receive accurate, timely and clear information. Management has an obligation to provide such information but directors should seek clarification or amplification where necessary.

The chairman should ensure that the directors continually update their skills and the knowledge and familiarity with the company required to fulfil their role both on the board and on board committees. The company should provide the necessary resources for developing and updating its directors' knowledge and capabilities.

Under the direction of the chairman, the company secretary's responsibilities include ensuring good information flows within the board and its committees and between senior management and non-executive directors, as well as facilitating induction and assisting with professional development as required.

The company secretary should be responsible for advising the board through the chairman on all governance matters.'

Adequate relevant, significant and clear information is vital for directors to be effective and it must be provided sufficiently in advance of meetings to enable them to give issues thorough consideration. The chairman, supported by the company secretary, should assess what information is required. Non-executive directors should continually satisfy themselves that they have the appropriate information of sufficient quality to make sound judgments. They should not hesitate to seek clarification or amplification where necessary, calling on the services of the company secretary if required.

It is for the chairman to ensure that all new directors receive induction on joining the board. Newly appointed non-executive directors quickly need to build their knowledge of the host organisation to the point where they can use their skills and experience gained elsewhere for the benefit of the company. As part of their induction the company should offer major shareholders the opportunity to meet a new non-executive director (A.5.1).

Directors' effectiveness in the boardroom depends not just on their existing capability but on their ability to *extend* their knowledge and skills. To meet the exacting standards of professionalism now required in this complex and demanding role, continuing professional development for directors is a necessity. Provision should be properly structured to meet individual needs.

Further provisions include directors, especially non-executive directors, having access to independent professional advice at the company's expense (A.5.2) and access to the advice and services of the company secretary. Both the appointment and removal of the company secretary should be a matter for the board as a whole (A.5.3).

A.6 Performance Evaluation

The Main Principle on performance evaluation is straightforward:

'The board should undertake a formal and rigorous annual evaluation of its own performance and that of its committees and individual directors.'

The Supporting Principle provides amplification:

'Individual evaluation should aim to show whether each director continues to contribute effectively and to demonstrate commitment to the role (including commitment of time for board and committee meetings and any other duties). The chairman should act on the results of the performance evaluation by recognising the strengths and addressing the weaknesses of the board and, where appropriate, proposing new members be appointed to the board or seeking the resignation of directors.'

The board should state in the annual report how the performance evaluation has been conducted. The non-executive directors, led by the senior independent director, should be responsible for the performance evaluations of the chairman, taking into account the views of executive directors (A.6.1).

A.7 Re-elections

The Main Principle on re-election, which applies to all directors, states that:

> 'All directors should be submitted for re-election at regular intervals, subject to continued satisfactory performance. The board should ensure planned and progressive refreshing of the board.'

There are no Supporting Principles, but the Code provisions provide amplification.

Code Provision A.7.1 states that all directors should be subject to election by shareholders at the first AGM after their appointment, and to re-election thereafter at intervals of no more than 3 years. Sufficient biographical details should accompany submissions for election or re-election.

Non-executive directors should be appointed for specified terms (usually 3 years) but any term beyond 6 years should be subject to particularly vigorous review. The chairman should confirm to shareholders when proposing re-election of a non-executive director that, following performance evaluation, the individual's performance continues to be effective and demonstrates commitment to the role. Non-executive directors may serve longer than 9 years (eg three 3-year terms) subject to annual re-election (A.7.2).

B Remuneration

The remuneration part of the Code is divided into:

- the level and make up of remuneration; and

- the procedure for developing remuneration policy and fixing individual packages.

It is arguable that directors' remuneration, important a subject though it is, has absorbed too much of the debate and discussions on corporate governance. It has certainly received a lot of media coverage, some of which has been justified where cases for unsubstantiated remuneration packages have come to light, for example payment for under performance.

The Directors' Remuneration Report Regulations 2002 are now in effect. These require listed companies to publish an annual remuneration report to be put to shareholders for approval at the AGM.

B.1 The Level and Make Up of Remuneration

The Main Principle on remuneration is that:

> 'Levels of remuneration should be sufficient to attract, retain and motivate directors of the quality required to run the company successfully, but a company should avoid paying more than is necessary for this purpose. A significant proportion of executive directors' remuneration should be structured so as to link rewards to corporate and individual performance.'

The Supporting Principle points to the role of the remuneration committee in setting levels of remuneration:

> 'The remuneration committee should judge where to position their company relative to other companies. But they should use such comparisons with caution, in view of the risk of an upward ratchet of remuneration levels with no corresponding improvement in performance. They should also be sensitive to pay and employment conditions elsewhere in the group, especially when determining annual salary increases.'

The Code provisions amplify remuneration policy. Where performance-related elements of remuneration should form a significant proportion of the total package, guidelines on their design are included in Schedule A of the Code (reproduced in Appendix 2) (B.1.1). Levels of remuneration for non-executive directors should reflect the time commitment and responsibilities of the role (B.1.3). On the issues of service contracts and compensation there are guidelines on avoiding rewarding poor performance (B.1.5) and on directors' notice or contract periods which should be set at one year or less (B.1.6).

B.2 Procedure

The Main Principle on procedure states that:

> 'There should be a formal and transparent procedure for developing policy on executive remuneration and for fixing the remuneration packages of individual directors. No director should be involved in deciding his or her own remuneration.'

The Supporting Principles again point to the role of the remuneration committee in particular:

> 'The remuneration committee should consult the chairman and/or chief executive about their proposals relating to the remuneration of other executive directors. The remuneration committee should also be responsible for appointing any consultants in respect of executive director remuneration. Where executive directors or senior management are involved in advising or supporting the remuneration committee, care should be taken to recognise and avoid conflicts of interest.
>
> The chairman of the board should ensure that the company maintains contact as required with its principal shareholders about remuneration in the same way as for other matters.'

A key provision is the need for the board to establish a remuneration committee (B.2.1). This should comprise at least three members, or in the case of smaller quoted companies two members, who should all be independent non-executive directors. The committee should have delegated responsibility for setting remuneration for all executive directors and the chairman, and also recommend and monitor the level and structure of remuneration for senior management (B.2.2). The board itself will normally be responsible for setting the remuneration of non-executive directors (B.2.3).

C Accountability and Audit

Accountability and audit is divided into three parts:

- financial reporting;

- internal control;

- audit committees and auditors.

C.1 Financial Reporting

The Main Principle on financial reporting states straightforwardly that:

> 'The board should present a balanced and understandable assessment of the company's position and prospects.'

The Supporting Principle simply amplifies the board's responsibility:

> 'The board's responsibility to present a balanced and understandable assessment extends to interim and other price-sensitive public reports and reports to regulators as well as to information required to be presented by statutory requirements.'

Directors should explain in the annual report their responsibility for preparing the accounts, with an accompanying statement by the auditors about their reporting responsibilities (C.1.1), and report that the business is a going concern with supporting assumptions or qualifications as necessary.

C.2 Internal Control

The Main Principle applying to internal control is that:

> 'The board should maintain a sound system of internal controls to safeguard shareholders' investment and the company's assets.'

The board should, at least once a year, conduct a review of the effectiveness of the system of internal controls and should report to shareholders that they have done so (C.2.1).

The Revised Turnbull Guidance (reproduced in Appendix 3) provides guidance for implementing this part of the Code.

C.3 Audit Committees and Auditors

The Main Principle on audit committees and auditors states that:

> 'The board should establish formal and transparent arrangements for considering how they should apply the financial reporting and internal control principles and for maintaining an appropriate relationship with the company's auditors.'

The Code provisions focus on the audit committee, which should comprise at least three members, or in the case of smaller quoted companies two members, who should all be independent non-executive directors. In smaller quoted companies the company chairman may be a member of, but not chair, the committee in addition to the independent non-executive directors provided he or she was considered independent on appointment as chairman. The board should satisfy itself that at least one member of the audit committee has recent and relevant financial experience (C.3.1).

The importance of this issue warrants including the Code provisions, which are self-explanatory, in full:

'Code Provisions

. . .

C.3.2 The main role and responsibilities of the audit committee should be set out in written terms of reference and should include:

- to monitor the integrity of the financial statements of the company, and any formal announcements relating to the company's financial performance, reviewing significant financial reporting judgments contained in them;
- to review the company's internal financial controls and, unless expressly addressed by a separate board risk committee composed of independent directors, or by the board itself, to review the company's internal control and risk management systems;
- to monitor and review the effectiveness of the company's internal audit function;
- to make recommendations to the board, for it to put to the shareholders for their approval in general meeting, in relation to the appointment, re-appointment and removal of the external auditor and to approve the remuneration and terms of engagement of the external auditor;
- to review and monitor the external auditor's independence and objectivity and the effectiveness of the audit process, taking into consideration relevant UK professional and regulatory requirements;
- to develop and implement policy on the engagement of the external auditor to supply non-audit services, taking into account relevant ethical guidance regarding the provision of non-audit services by the external audit firm; and to report to the board, identifying any matters in respect of which it considers that action or improvement is needed and making recommendations as to the steps to be taken.

C.3.3 The terms of reference of the audit committee, including its role and the authority delegated to it by the board, should be made available. A separate section of the annual report should describe the work of the committee in discharging those responsibilities.

C.3.4 The audit committee should review arrangements by which staff of the company may, in confidence, raise concerns about possible improprieties in matters of financial reporting or other matters. The audit committee's objective should be to ensure that arrangements are in place for the proportionate and independent investigation of such matters and for appropriate follow-up action.

C.3.5 The audit committee should monitor and review the effectiveness of the internal audit activities. Where there is no internal audit function, the audit committee should consider annually whether there is a need for an internal audit function and make a recommendation to the board, and the reasons for the absence of such a function should be explained in the relevant section of the annual report.

C.3.6 The audit committee should have primary responsibility for making a recommendation on the appointment, reappointment and removal of the external auditors. If the board does not accept the audit committee's recommendation, it should include in the annual report, and in any papers recommending appointment or re-appointment, a statement from the audit committee explaining the recommendation and should set out reasons why the board has taken a different position.

C.3.7 The annual report should explain to shareholders how, if the auditor provides non-audit services, auditor objectivity and independence is safeguarded.'

The Smith Guidance (reproduced in Appendix 4) provides guidance on implementing this part of the Code.

D Relations with Shareholders

Section 1 of the Code for companies is rounded off with relations with shareholders comprising:

- dialogue with institutional shareholders;

- constructive use of the AGM.

D.1 Dialogue with Institutional Shareholders

The Main Principle on dialogue with institutional shareholders most importantly states that:

'There should be a dialogue with shareholders based on the mutual understanding of objectives. The board as a whole has responsibility for ensuring that a satisfactory dialogue with shareholders takes place.'

The Supporting Principles continue that:

'Whilst recognising that most shareholder contact is with the chief executive and finance director, the chairman (and the senior independent director and other directors as appropriate) should maintain sufficient contact with major shareholders to understand their issues and concerns.

The board should keep in touch with shareholder opinion in whatever ways are most practical and efficient.'

It is fundamental that communication between company boards and shareholders, in both directions, lies at the heart of good corporate governance. There is much progress still to be made on improving communications, particularly with smaller companies.

The importance of this issue warrants including the Code provisions, which are self-explanatory, in full:

'Code Provisions

D.1.1 The chairman should ensure that the views of shareholders are communicated to the board as a whole. The chairman should discuss governance and strategy with major shareholders. Non-executive directors should be offered the opportunity to attend meetings with major shareholders and should expect to attend them if requested by major shareholders. The senior independent director should attend sufficient meetings with a range of major shareholders to listen to their views in order to help develop a balanced understanding of the issues and concerns of major shareholders.

D.1.2 The board should state in the annual report the steps they have taken to ensure that the members of the board, and in particular the non-executive directors, develop an understanding of the views of major shareholders about their company, for example through direct face-to-face contact, analysts' or brokers' briefings and surveys of shareholder opinion.'

D.2 Constructive Use of the AGM

The Main Principle which applies to the constructive use of the AGM is that:

'The board should use the AGM to communicate with investors and to encourage their participation.'

For some years the AGM has been under pressure as an ineffectual forum. With the advent of electronic communications this is changing for the better and should position the AGM in its rightful place in the communications between companies and shareholders and vice versa.

The Code provisions emphasise some aspects of procedure but, importantly, state that the chairman should arrange for the chairmen of the audit, remuneration and nomination committees to be available to answer questions at the AGM and that all directors should attend (D.2.3).

1.8.3   Section 2 – Institutional Shareholders

Section 2, which applies to institutional shareholders, is very much shorter than Section 1 applying to companies, suggesting a lack of balance in the Code. There is some merit in this view, not least because, in order for the Code to be effective, there needs to be commitment from both companies and shareholders. This underpins the 'comply or explain' regime. Evolution of the Code might possibly include a redressing of the existing balance with more emphasis given to a code of best practice for institutional investors.

The Section is divided into three parts:

• dialogue with companies;

• evaluation of governance disclosures by companies; and

• shareholder voting.

There are no provisions included in this section of the Code.

E.1 Dialogue with Companies

The Main Principle on dialogue with companies states that:

> 'Institutional shareholders should enter into a dialogue with companies based on the mutual understanding of objectives.'

The Supporting Principle makes reference to institutional shareholders' own principles statement:

> 'Institutional shareholders should apply the principles set out in the Institutional Shareholders' Committee's "The Responsibilities of Institutional Shareholders and Agents – Statement of Principles", which should be reflected in fund manager contracts.'

The 'Statement of Principles' includes a statement of policy by institutional shareholders requiring investee companies' compliance with the 'core standards' in the Code, as well as their commitment to intervene when an unjustifiable failure to comply with the Code has occurred.

E.2 Evaluation of Governance Disclosures

The Main Principle on evaluation of governance disclosures directs the approach to be taken by institutional shareholders:

> 'When evaluating companies' governance arrangements, particularly those relating to board structure and composition, institutional shareholders should give due weight to all relevant factors drawn to their attention.'

The Supporting Principle provides further amplification:

> 'Institutional shareholders should consider carefully explanations given for departure from the Code and make reasoned judgements in each case. They should give an explanation to the company, in writing where appropriate, and be prepared to enter a dialogue if they do not accept the company's position. They should avoid a box-ticking approach to assessing a company's corporate governance. They should bear in mind in particular the size and complexity of the company and the nature of the risks and challenges it faces.'

A conscientious application of these principles by institutional shareholders is imperative in the case of smaller quoted companies.

The importance of this in preserving and enhancing the 'comply or explain' regime and the effectiveness of the Code has already been highlighted.

E.3 Shareholder Voting

The Main Principle on shareholder voting is again straightforward:

'Institutional shareholders have a responsibility to make considered use of their votes.'

The Supporting Principles provide guidance on best practice:

'Institutional shareholders should take steps to ensure their voting intentions are being translated into practice.

Institutional shareholders should, on request, make available to their clients information on the proportion of resolutions on which votes were cast and non-discretionary proxies lodged.

Major shareholders should attend AGMs where appropriate and practicable. Companies and registrars should facilitate this.'

Sections 1 and 2 of the Code are reproduced in full in Appendix 1.

CHAPTER 2

GOVERNANCE OF AIM LISTED AND PRIVATE COMPANIES

2.1 INTRODUCTION

To what extent does the Code have relevance for AIM companies and private companies? The fact of the matter is that the Code contains a lot of common sense when applied to the running of any company. It is a valuable framework of reference for the board of directors to guide their governance of the company.

This important perspective is quite separate from the need for companies on the main list to apply the Code's principles, comply with its provisions and report thereon.

However, that the Code should be perceived as a source of guidelines and not strict rules to be always followed is as relevant for smaller quoted companies on the main list as it is for companies listed on the AIM market. Any misunderstanding of that point by smaller quoted companies leads to much frustration on their part and annoyance that it is all just a lot of unnecessary bureaucracy getting in the way of doing business.

The 'comply or explain' basis for the Code provides the opportunity for a company to explain and justify non-compliance with any aspect of the Code which is not compatible with the company's prevailing circumstances. This flexibility, which is important for smaller companies on the main list, takes on particular importance for AIM companies, especially those at the very small end of the range.

2.2 ALTERNATIVE INVESTMENT MARKET (AIM) COMPANIES

The Alternative Investment Market for AIM companies is frequently described as 'lightly' regulated by the London Stock Exchange in contrast to the more 'tightly' regulated main market. In addition, and as has already been noted, the Code does not apply to AIM companies in the same way as it does to companies on the main list.

There are currently approximately 1,650 AIM companies ranging in size from a few million to more than £500m in market capitalisation. The market provides an opportunity for young companies, especially, to tap into the public equity market without being subject to the regulatory regime and higher costs of a listing on the main market. However, an AIM listing is frequently the first step along the way to a main listing for a growing company with a significant need for equity capital to fund that growth. It therefore behoves such companies to adopt and apply the principles and provisions of corporate governance enshrined in the Code in order to prepare for their graduation to and acceptance on the main list.

However, following sound corporate governance principles and practice is no less relevant for AIM companies that have no aspirations to graduate to the main market. Not only does this make sound business sense, but weaknesses in corporate governance can be punished by the market causing lack of interest in the shares by the investment community.

2.3   THE LONDON STOCK EXCHANGE RULES FOR AIM COMPANIES

AIM companies are subject to rules drawn up by the London Stock Exchange. The current set of rules – AIM Rules for Companies, February 2007 – may be obtained from the Exchange (see Useful Websites). A private company seeking a listing for the first time is most likely to elect to join the AIM. In order to be eligible for AIM the company must appoint a nominated adviser (shortened to NOMAD) and all NOMADs must be approved by the Exchange.

The NOMAD is responsible to the Exchange for assessing the appropriateness of an applicant for AIM, or an existing AIM company when appointed its nominated adviser, and for advising and guiding an AIM company on its responsibilities under the Rules. NOMADs have a particular role to play in the corporate governance of AIM. The Exchange recognises the importance of:

> ' . . . appropriate corporate governance for AIM companies. However, given the wide range of companies that are admitted to AIM, the Exchange believes that the corporate governance measures to be adopted are a matter for the NOMAD to provide advice about, on a company-by-company basis, both on admission and also on an ongoing basis as the company develops.'

The 'comply or explain' basis for the Code comes into play to provide for the tailoring of corporate governance arrangements to reflect the particular company's circumstances but at the same time ensuring that the integrity of good corporate governance is maintained.

NOMADs are therefore in a pivotal position so far as the governance of AIM companies is concerned. Their current responsibilities are set out in Schedule 3 to AIM Rules for Nominated Advisers, February 2007, and may also be obtained from the Exchange (see Useful Websites).

2.4 NOMINATED ADVISER RESPONSIBILITIES

In Schedule 3 NOMAD responsibilities are presented as a set of principles followed by a list of actions. Whereas the principles must be satisfied in all cases, the actions may vary according to the company's circumstances. The principles which more directly relate to corporate governance (ie admission, ongoing and engagement responsibilities) are covered below:

'Responsibilities on admission to AIM

The applicant and its securities

AR1 – In assessing the appropriateness of an applicant and its securities for AIM, a NOMAD should achieve a sound understanding of the applicant and its business.

Directors and board

AR2 – in assessing the appropriateness of an applicant and its securities for AIM, a NOMAD should (i) investigate and consider the suitability of each director and proposed director of the applicant; and (ii) consider the efficacy of the board as a whole for the company's needs, in each case having in mind that the company will be admitted to trading on a UK public market.'

This principle strikes at the heart of good governance, the board of directors. Listed under actions is the need to consider, with the directors of an applicant, the adoption of appropriate corporate governance measures. The Code provides the framework of reference for the consideration of such measures.

'AIM Rule compliance

AR5 – The nominated adviser should satisfy itself that the applicant has in place sufficient systems, procedures and controls in order to comply with the AIM Rules for Companies and should satisfy itself that the applicant understands its obligations under the AIM Rules for Companies.'

Ongoing responsibilities which apply on a continuing basis are as follows:

'Regular contact between company and NOMAD

OR1 – The NOMAD should maintain regular contact with an AIM company for which it acts, in particular so that it can assess whether (i) the nominated adviser is being kept up-to-date with developments at the AIM company and (ii) the AIM company continues to understand its obligations under the AIM Rules.

Advise the AIM company on any changes to the boards of directors

OR4 – The NOMAD should advise the AIM company on any changes to the board of directors the AIM company proposes to make, including (i) investigating and considering the suitability of proposed new directors and (ii) considering the effect any changes have on the efficacy of the board as a whole for the company's needs, in each case having in mind that the company is admitted to trading on a UK public market.'

Engagement responsibilities apply when a NOMAD is being engaged by an existing AIM company and focus particularly on AR1, AR2 and AR5 above.

The NOMADs ongoing responsibilities and particularly OR4 places it in position to advise the AIM company on the development of its corporate governance arrangements as the company's activities evolve. This is an important role for the NOMAD to undertake.

However, pivotal though they are to providing corporate governance advice to AIM companies, the evidence from the marketplace suggests that NOMADs could be more proactive in giving that advice. This can arise, for example, in cases where a NOMAD is also broker to the AIM company; this dual position can lay the NOMAD open to a conflict of interest with fee generation from broking taking precedence. AIM companies need to be aware of this and respond accordingly. The important point for AIM companies is that they receive independent and good quality advice on their corporate governance arrangements when joining the market and afterwards as they develop, especially if they are seeking progression to the main list of the Exchange.

2.5   PRACTICAL CORPORATE GOVERNANCE FOR AIM COMPANIES

Even without the requirement for AIM companies to comply with the Code as a condition of listing, there is still a need for them to adopt and practise corporate governance principles relevant to their circumstances. This was pointed out previously, and the key therefore is in both company and investor being flexible in the application of the principles, but still retaining the integrity of good corporate governance.

To assist AIM companies with corporate governance the Quoted Companies Alliance (QCA), which represents the interests of companies and their advisers outside the FTSE 350 index, has published a set of guidelines which have met with universal approval by companies, institutional shareholders and the Exchange. These QCA Guidelines are less rigorous than those for companies on the main list under the Code. All AIM companies are expected to comply at least with the QCA Guidelines, with larger AIM companies aiming for higher standards of good governance practice more in line with those contained in the Code.

2.5.1 The QCA Corporate Governance Guidelines for AIM companies

The QCA Guidelines, which take as their basis the Code and apply it to AIM companies, are reproduced in Appendix 5. They contain several sections:

- Matters reserved for the board – there should be a formal schedule of matters reserved for the board's decision.
  This Guideline is considered more fully in Chapter 5, 'Company boards and their Committees'.

- Timely information – the board should be provided with timely information of a quality appropriate to enable it to discharge its duties.

- Internal controls review – the board should carry out a review, at least annually, of the effectiveness of the system of internal controls and report to the shareholders on this.
  Detailed guidance on internal controls is available from the Revised Turnbull Guidance on Internal Controls at Appendix 3.

- Chairman and Chief Executive – the roles should be split but if they are not, then there should be an explanation of what procedures are in place to provide protection against the concentration of power within the company.

- Independent non-executive directors – there should be at least two independent non-executive directors, one of whom may be the Chairman. The board should not be dominated by one person or a group of people.
  The role of the non-executive director is examined in detail in Chapter 4, 'The Non-Executive Director'.

- Re-election – all directors should be submitted for re-election at regular intervals, subject to continued satisfactory performance. There should be planned and progressive refreshing of the board. Performance evaluation of the board and directors is examined in Chapter 5.

- Audit Committee – there should be an audit committee of at least two members who should all be independent non-executive directors.

Detailed guidance on audit committees is available from the Smith Guidance on Audit Committees at Appendix 4.

• Remuneration Committee – there should be a remuneration committee of at least two members who should all be independent non-executive directors.

• Nomination Committee – recommendations for appointments to the board should be made by a nomination committee, or the board as a whole, after due evaluation.
Board committees and their operation are also examined in Chapter 5.

• Dialogue with shareholders – there should be a dialogue with shareholders based on the mutual understanding of objectives. The board as a whole has responsibility for this.
Shareholders as owners have a crucial role to play in corporate governance and are the focus of Chapter 6, 'Shareholders and Corporate Governance'.

Communication between companies and shareholders is pivotal to governance and the sustainability of the 'comply or explain' regime. Reporting on their corporate governance by companies is an important part of this communication and the QCA, therefore, also gives guidance on this. Companies should publish an annual corporate governance statement describing how they achieve good governance which can be published on a company's website and/or in the annual report and accounts. As well as describing how good governance is achieved that report should also include what the QCA term 'basic disclosures' which include, inter alia: a statement of how the board operates, the identity of all the board and board committee members including identifying those directors who are independent, biographical details for all directors, and the number of meetings of the board and board committees and directors' attendance at them. Furthermore, the terms and conditions of appointment of non-executive directors should be made available on the company's website, or available to shareholders on request, as should the terms of reference for the audit, remuneration and nomination committees.

2.5.2   AIM company experience

The Institute of Chartered Accountants for Scotland (ICAS) has recently published some research on corporate governance in AIM companies[1] which provides useful insights into the experience of AIM companies.

---

[1]   C Mallin and K Ow-Yong 'Corporate Governance in Alternative Investment Market (AIM) Companies' (April 2008).

Directors of AIM companies restated that their main reasons for joining AIM were to enable them to raise money for future financing of the business or for acquisitions, and to gain access to institutional investors. They identified one of the main objectives of corporate governance as being to protect the interests of shareholders and other stakeholders. Good governance was generally seen as something that would give investors more confidence in the company and help with the risk management of the business.

From a detailed analysis of corporate governance reporting in the annual report and accounts it was found that the basic elements of good governance practice, such as including a corporate governance statement, the presence of board sub-committees, identifying the directors and their responsibilities, and splitting the role of chairman and CEO, are disclosed by the majority of a sample of 300 AIM companies. The QCA Guidelines on what independence means and having at least two independent non-executive directors were moderately adopted. The level of disclosure was low for aspects of governance that reveal more personal matters like evaluating directors performance and their attendance at board meetings. Corporate governance reporting falls away for AIM companies with small boards.

2.5.3   National Association of Pension Funds (NAPF) Policy and Voting Guidelines for AIM companies

The growing number of companies on AIM and their range by market capitalisation from a few million pounds to over £500m has been the basis for one set of major institutional investors, the pension funds, to also produce a set of corporate governance guidelines for AIM companies. These Guidelines, published by the NAPF, the leading UK body representing the pensions industry, compliment the QCA Guidelines in that they are written from the institutional investor perspective rather than the AIM company perspective. Whilst they are consistent with those of the QCA in all key respects, there are some aspects which are not included in the QCA Guidelines. These arise from taking a more robust view of the application of the Code, but still allow for flexibility based on the 'comply or explain' principle. From an AIM company's perspective, however, the QCA Guidelines provide a particularly practical set of standards.

The NAPF, in its introduction to its Policy and Voting Guidelines for AIM companies, comments:

> 'The substantial growth in the number of companies admitted to AIM in recent years, their increasingly international character and the appearance of larger companies alongside the more traditional smaller capitalisation stocks means that this market is attracting greater interest among institutional investors, including pension funds. Most of these investors take

their voting responsibilities seriously and therefore look to organisations such as the NAPF to provide voting guidelines. We also believe that, by encouraging higher standards of corporate governance, AIM companies will be better able to manage their growth and attract a greater institutional investor following, thereby enabling them to raise fresh capital more easily and on potentially more advantageous terms.

The starting point for these Guidelines has, perhaps inevitably and despite the exemption from compliance, been the Combined Code and the NAPF Policy and Guidelines which are based on it.

The boards of AIM companies should be familiar with the Main Principles of the Combined Code and should seek to apply them as appropriate to each company's circumstances.

The Guidelines do not cover every provision of the Combined Code, they are intended to provide guidance to companies and shareholders on those issues which we believe are of key importance and where practice may reasonably differ from the Code.

Part of the success of AIM derives from its appropriate approach to regulation and any corporate governance guidelines need to be drafted with this in mind. However it is also appropriate that a company's governance structure reflects its size and the complexity of its business and we therefore expect companies at the top end of the AIM market capitalisation range to comply with the provisions of the Combined Code (or to explain non-compliance). Likewise, at the other end of the scale, very small companies can best serve their shareholders by concentrating on growing their business and providing good levels of disclosure in their annual report and accounts, without the burden of compliance with inappropriate guidelines. Between these two extremes, we expect companies to apply the highest standards of corporate governance consistent with the size and complexity of their business. As far as practicable, we expect that shareholders will apply these guidelines with a degree of flexibility suitable to each company's individual circumstances.'

The NAPF Policy and Voting Guidelines for AIM companies are reproduced in Appendix 6, but the most relevant sections are summarised below.

- Disclosure standards – the NAPF Guidelines point out that it is not unusual for smaller companies to publish annual reports that provide little or no explanation of their governance arrangements. This makes it very difficult for shareholders to make an informed evaluation of a company's governance. The NAPF AIM Policy expects a company to disclose its corporate governance policies, including biographical details of its directors and details of board committees.

- Combined roles of chairman and chief executive – the NAPF considers that the functions of chairman and chief executive are different and should be clearly distinguished. However, where this is not the case the company should provide details of the exceptional circumstances underlying the combination of the roles and a forward-looking statement explaining its intentions to separate the roles.

- CEO becoming chairman – this is not addressed in the QCA Guidelines. NAPF AIM Policy, which follows the Code on a CEO not becoming the chairman, states that, if this is the case, the company must disclose its reasons and describe the selection process.

- Appointment of a senior independent director – this is also not addressed in the QCA Guidelines. NAPF Aim Policy requires the appointment of a senior independent director where a company has a combined chairman and CEO, but this is only encouraged in other circumstances.

- Balance of the board – for larger boards NAPF AIM Policy requires at least two independent directors, excluding the chairman, and for smaller boards at least two independent directors, one of whom may be the chairman. These independent directors should comprise not less than one-third of the board.

- Composition of audit, remuneration and nomination committees – NAPF AIM Policy supports the principles enshrined in the Code, but recognises that the lack of independent membership, compounded with the insufficient number of non-executive directors on a board, could make compliance unachievable.

- Director independence – the NAPF recognises that some of the criteria stated in the Code, when applied to AIM companies, require more flexibility due to the particular circumstances faced by these companies. A significant shareholding, option grants and tenure are among the most common.
  The NAPF AIM Policy is that independence may be compromised if a director has a beneficial or non-beneficial shareholding of more than 3% of the company's issued share capital or receives remuneration other than fees paid in cash or shares.
  NAPF AIM Policy is flexible on tenure between 9 and 12 years if tenure is the only factor affecting a director's independence.

2.5.4 A message on governance for AIM companies

For the investment community to have confidence in AIM companies it has already been pointed out how critical it is for these companies to apply corporate governance principles and explain their corporate governance arrangements. Any AIM company that is ambitious to get backing from serious investors cannot afford to cut corners on corporate governance. The QCA Guidelines in particular, based on the Code, are a useful source of practical help for companies listing on the AIM and, once listed, thereafter. However, the record of AIM companies on corporate governance continues to be patchy. An assessment of the governance procedures adopted by AIM companies published in July 2008 by accountants PricewaterhouseCoopers (PWC) provides further evidence.

PWC looked at four categories of AIM companies: the top 100, a sample of companies that have a market capitalisation between £40m and £100m; a sample of those with a market capitalisation of £1m to £40m, and a sample of overseas companies. Of the top 100, 77% were in compliance with some aspect of the Code, with only 3% of this segment choosing to adopt it fully. Only 25% of the £40m to £100m sample had boards where all the non-executive directors were considered independent. The same sample also showed that three out of every ten boards had executive directors serving on their audit committees. Overall the PWC survey revealed that the composition of the board is a particular area of weakness for many AIM companies. The need for strong independent non-executive director representation on the board appears to be something many AIM companies have yet to recognise.

The message for AIM companies is clear if they are to retain the confidence and trust of their investors. Time spent on establishing sound corporate governance arrangements is time well spent.

2.6   PRIVATE COMPANIES

The explanation and guidance on corporate governance contained in this book is largely aimed at companies listed on a public market – the main list in the case of FTSE-small-cap companies below the FTSE 350, and the AIM for AIM companies. The basis for this guidance is the Code on corporate governance. Whereas the small-cap companies fall under the Code and AIM companies do not, it has been pointed out that AIM companies are expected to adopt the principles of governance enshrined in the Code if they are to justify their listing and the confidence of their investors. None of these demands for corporate governance standards which are made on companies whose shares are listed on a public market apply to private companies. Nevertheless, the principles of good corporate governance are just as relevant to the running of a private business, and the Code provides just as much value as a framework of reference, but not on the same scale as for companies on a public market. Furthermore, given the plethora of private companies covering such a wide range of circumstances, the 'no one size fits all' approach should be uppermost when considering governance arrangements.

The governance of private companies which follows is examined primarily from the perspective of owner-managed companies.

2.6.1 Governance of private companies

The practical framework of reference to be used by private companies for their corporate governance is the Code's 14 Main Principles which provide the guidelines for establishing corporate governance arrangements. These principles, which are explained in detail in Chapter 1, are set out below.

The Board	**Every company should be headed by an effective board, which is collectively responsible for the success of the company.**
Chairman and chief executive	**There should be a clear division of responsibilities at the head of the company between the running of the board and the executive responsibility for the running of the company's business. No one individual should have unfettered powers of decision.**
Board balance and independence	**The board should include a balance of executive and non-executive directors (and in particular independent non-executive directors) such that no individual or small group of individuals can dominate the board's decision taking.**
Appointments to the Board	**There should be a formal, rigorous and transparent procedure for the appointment of new directors to the board.**
Information and professional development	**The board should be supplied in a timely manner with information in a form and of a quality appropriate to enable it to discharge its duties. All directors should receive induction on joining the board and should regularly update and refresh their skills and knowledge.**
Performance and evaluation	**The board should undertake a formal and rigorous annual evaluation of its own performance and that of its committees and individual directors.**
Re-election	**All directors should be submitted for re-election at regular intervals, subject to continued satisfactory performance. The board should ensure planned and progressive refreshing of the board.**
Remuneration – the level and make up of remuneration	**Levels of remuneration should be sufficient to attract, retain and motivate directors of the quality required to run the company successfully, but a company should avoid paying more than is necessary for the purpose. A significant proportion of executive directors' remuneration should be structured so as to link rewards to corporate and individual performance.**

Remuneration – **procedure**	**There should be a formal and transparent procedure for developing policy on executive remuneration and for fixing the remuneration packages of individual directors. No director should be involved in deciding his or her own remuneration.**
Financial reporting	**The board should present a balance and understandable assessment of the company's position and prospects.**
Internal control	**The board should maintain a sound system of internal control to safeguard shareholders' investment and the company's assets.**
Audit committee **and auditors**	**The board should establish formal and transparent arrangements for considering how they should apply the financial reporting and internal control principles and for maintaining an appropriate relationship with the company's auditors.**
Dialogue with **institutional** **shareholders**	**There should be a dialogue with shareholders based on the mutual understanding of objectives. The board as a whole has responsibility for ensuring that a satisfactory dialogue with shareholders takes place.**
Constructive use of **the AGM**	**The board should use the AGM to communicate to investors and to encourage their participation.**

Using the Main Principles as a basis, the ICAS has drawn up a checklist of questions for private companies to examine their governance arrangements (see **2.6.5**). ICAS has provided up-to-date, practical and comprehensive guidance on governance for private companies, based on the established principles of the Code and this is reproduced at Appendix 7, 'Avoiding the pitfalls in running a private company – a guide for directors'. It provides a useful basis for discussing the corporate governance of private companies.

For a smaller private company compliance with some or all aspects of the Code will not be practical or even appropriate. This has already been pointed out. Those principles of the Code that are the most relevant to private companies are likely to be the collective responsibilities of the board, the role of each director, and risk management and internal controls. The practical implications of how each principle can be applied also depend on the company's ownership.

Typically the different types of ownership of a private company are:

• 100% private ownership, either start-up or mature situation, ie the owner-managed company;

- 100% private ownership but with external commitment such as bank loans;

- private ownership but with some shareholders who are not involved in management, eg majority ownership by private equity or venture capital funds.

2.6.2   Collective responsibilities of the board

The Code's principle that every company should be headed by an effective board which is collectively responsible for the success of the company is as important for the private company as for any on a public market. The board needs to be clear of its role and responsibilities. Its key responsibilities are to:

- establish clear purpose, vision and values;

- set appropriate strategy and structure;

- delegate day-to-day authority to manage the business to management, monitor management's performance and hold them to account;

- establish proper risk management and internal control frameworks; and

- provide leadership.

In an owner-managed company, especially, the distinction between the board and the management may be blurred or non-existent. Nevertheless, time should be allowed for consideration of purpose, strategy and structure, risks and internal controls. Non-executive directors on the board should first and foremost ensure that the board provides appropriate leadership.

For private companies matters reserved for the board are typically:

- changes to capital;

- payment of dividends;

- corporate objectives, strategies and structure;

- corporate plans and all material changes to corporate plans;

- operating and capital budgets and all material changes to these budgets;

- material transactions;

- the financial statements;

- any borrowings or guarantees;

- relevant external communications;

- the appointment and remuneration of directors;

- any authorities delegated to management;

- company policies; and

- compliance with legislation.

Operational matters need to be delegated in order to ensure the smooth running of the business and to allow the board to focus on its primary role.

The board should meet often enough to complete its statutory and regulatory responsibilities and to exercise its oversight role properly. Good practice should include an agenda prepared by the chairman and company secretary, with any supporting papers, and the complete package circulated with sufficient time to allow directors to prepare for the meeting. At the meeting formal minutes should be taken, ensuring all decisions are recorded, and an action plan included to ensure decisions are followed up within a reasonable timescale. The meeting should monitor progress against the approved plans and budgets and ensure proper coverage of the matters reserved for the board.

Despite the Companies Act 2006 no longer requiring a private company to hold an AGM, companies with shareholders who are not involved in the management of the business may benefit from the discipline of a formal meeting to review the past year's activities and results, and the future prospects of the company.

2.6.3   The role and responsibilities of individual board members

An effective board should have a balance of skills and experience that is appropriate for the size and requirements of the business. In the smallest owner-managed companies it is probable that all responsibilities will fall on one or two people, but as the company grows so should the board. In a private company without external shareholders it is unusual to find the roles of chairman and chief executive as separate appointments. However, the individual fulfilling these two roles should remember that the responsibilities of each are separate and distinct. Having an independent chairman may be best practice but in a small company this is unusual and may not be commercially justifiable. Once a company has external financing and/or shareholders who are not involved in the management, it should have a chairman who is separate from the chief executive. When the chief executive is separated from the chairman he or she is responsible for managing the day-to-day business of the company and should have clear authority from the board to do so. The chairman assumes full responsibility for the leadership of the board.

In an owner-managed company a non-executive director can bring different experiences and an external, more objective, viewpoint to the board. As a company grows, with wider responsibilities and external commitments, this should be reflected by giving consideration to introducing and/or increasing the number of non-executive directors. External investors will frequently insist on a non-executive director(s) and the investor may assist in the appointment.

2.6.4   Risk and internal control

That the board maintains a sound system of internal control to safeguard shareholders' investment and the company's assets is critical. An effective system of internal control is key to robust risk management. In an owner-managed company risk management is generally addressed by the owner, but is rarely documented. This should be corrected. Professional advisers may be of assistance in identifying key risks and controls. In a growing company reporting and monitoring procedures should be in place so that the senior management team, board, and ultimately the shareholders, can be confident that risks are being properly identified and managed. In larger companies the creation of a risk management committee involving senior managers and directors should create the basis for more effective analysis of risks.

Smaller owner-managed companies with few employees may handle risks and controls quite informally, but as a company grows a more formal system of internal control is necessary.

2.6.5   Checklist of questions on the governance of private companies

The Board Role   1.   Is the board clear what the business is supposed to achieve for its owners?

2.   Has it set goals to be achieved?

3.   Has it determined the values and policies that will be adopted by the business?

4.   Has it reviewed the strategic options available, selected those to be followed and decided how they will be implemented and resourced?

5. Does it ensure that policies and plans are
    implemented and reviewed?

Responsibilities of 1. What is the job specification of each director?
Board Members

2. Collectively, what skills do the board require to
    run the company effectively?

3. Are there any skills overlaps? Gaps?

4. Is any training required and how is this
    identified and organised?

5. How are new directors appointed, reappointed
    and, if necessary, removed?

6. Is there a succession plan?

7. Is there a person nominated to understudy key
    functions, as defined in the risk register?

Matters reserved 1. Are corporate plans, operating and capital
for the Board   budgets prepared on a regular basis, for
    example, an annual cycle that ties in to the
    board calendar of meetings?

2. Who is responsible for the instigating,
    preparing, reviewing and authorising of
    corporate plans and budgets?

3. Does the board undertake subsequent
    evaluations of plans to ensure they were
    adequately prepared, and follow up action for
    future plan preparation if necessary?

4. How does the board decide when dividends are
    to be recommended, how much they should be,
    and who organises their payment?

5. What is the board's definition of a material
    transaction, for example, acquisitions,
    disposals, starting or ceasing a business
    activity?

6. Who is responsible for instigating any material
    transaction?

7. How is it evaluated and does the board take a
    collective decision about its final authorisation?

8. Are there subsequent evaluations of material
    transactions?

9. Is there a business plan, a budget, and
    forecasted cash flow for the company and are
    these regularly monitored and, when necessary,
    updated?

10. Are actual results compared to budgets with variances investigated?

11. What are the procedures for preparing the annual financial statements?

12. Is the documentation and related information relating to all borrowings and guarantees up to date, reviewed regularly, and with each board member aware of the company commitments?

13. Are all covenants reviewed regularly to ensure that they are not breached?

14. Are borrowings as cost efficient as possible or should they be renegotiated?

Delegated Authorities

1. Are company policies current, clear and consistent, compliant with legal requirements and derailed in the company manual? Who is responsible for these policies?

2. Who can open bank accounts and sign cheques, and what are the limits on these authorities?

3. Which members of staff have authority for general purchasing, what are the relevant procedures, and what are the limits of their authority?

4. Who can sign regulatory documents and are there procedures in place to check these have been reviewed prior to submission?

5. Who is responsible for authorising the recipients and amounts of political and charitable donations?

6. Who has authority to represent the company or to issue external communications?

7. What are the procedures for recruiting staff?

8. Who has the ability to commit the company to signing of leases?

Board Meetings

1. Is the number of meetings appropriate and is there an annual calendar of board meetings?

2. How many directors are required for a valid (quorate) meeting?

3. Does the chairman set the agenda and can other directors add relevant business?

4. Is the management of meetings satisfactory with agenda papers sent out on a timely basis, sufficient time given to discuss all business, and minutes circulated promptly afterwards?

5. Are there suitable quality control checks in place to ensure that board papers contain appropriate, high quality, timely information to permit discussion and sensible decisions?

6. Do the minutes provide an adequate record of each meeting?

7. Are tasks allocated among directors, and how are these and any action points followed up?

8. What is the process for decision making, and is there a procedure for dealing with decision making between board meetings?

Compliance Schedule

1. Have external advisers and service providers, eg an accountant, pension adviser, auditor, been appropriately appointed with an engagement letter that details the required services, a commencement date, the basis of fees, and reporting requirements?

2. Is there a timetable and project plan in place for producing the annual report and (audited) accounts within the regulatory deadlines for their submission to Companies House and HMRC?

3. Do the timetables and project plans detail what is to be done so that any replacement person could undertake the tasks?

4. Do all the directors have sufficient opportunity to review the draft financial statements before they are signed?

5. Which government departments need to be dealt with, eg HMRC, Health and Safety, DWP, which director is responsible for these contacts, and what are the timetables for doing so?

CHAPTER 3

THE DUTIES OF DIRECTORS

3.1 INTRODUCTION

Before delving further into the roles of the board and directors in corporate governance, it is necessary to consider the duties of directors from a company law standpoint. The purpose is to provide directors, and potential directors, with an understanding of their legal obligations so that they are able to undertake the roles entrusted to them in the full knowledge of what is expected of them from the law regulating companies, and to be conscious of their legal liabilities. To that end this chapter on directors' duties is written from the perspective of the practising director rather than the expert in company law. Directors may always seek help from the company secretary, or access specialist legal advice, when necessary, and indeed are encouraged to do so when circumstances warrant this course of action.

3.2 THE COMPANIES ACTS 1985 AND 2006

Company law contained in the Companies Act 1985 ('the 1985 Act'), which prevailed until the Act of 2006, stated that directors must act in a way that they believe to be in the interests of the company and its shareholders, both current and future, as a whole. This duty is owed to the company itself and not to individual shareholders. The 1985 Act also stated that directors are to have regard to the interests of the company's employees in general, as well as the interests of shareholders, but this duty is not owed directly to employees. The essence of the new Companies Act 2006 ('the Act') was to codify directors' duties for the first time, ie put them on a statutory basis in law, as well as to introduce the concept of 'enlightened shareholder value'. Both have the effect of making directors duties to the company clearer.

Although this chapter is largely relevant for the directors of smaller quoted and AIM companies, much of it also applies to directors of private companies. It provides directors with guidance on their new general duties resulting from the Act, in comparison with the previous common law duties, and how these duties affect their role. Generally speaking, the relevant sections of the Act are a codification of existing common law rules and equitable principles, save for the regulation of conflicts of interest and in the duty to promote the success of the company, which includes a new requirement for directors to have regard to certain additional factors in their decision making.

These codified general duties continue to be owed to the company not to the shareholders. There are civil consequences if they are breached. Under Part 11 of the Act it is also now easier for members to bring a derivative claim against an individual director on behalf of the company.

The general duties are also owed by a shadow director in the same way, and to the same extent that they are owed by a properly appointed director. Finally, certain aspects continue to apply even when a person ceases to be a director.

3.3   GOVERNMENT STATEMENT ON DIRECTORS' NEW STATUTORY DUTIES (JUNE 2007)

The then Secretary of State at the Department of Trade and Industry, in her statement introducing the new duties for directors, was at pains to allay any concerns over their implications in practice.

> 'The simple high-level guidance for directors (set out below) illustrates the way in which the codification maintains continuity with the existing law: this guidance on how a director has to live up to his position of trust is applicable to the pre-existing common law as well as to the new codification. For most directors, who are working hard and put the interests of their company before their own, there will be no need to change their behaviour.
>
> But compared with most text-book definitions of the common law duties of directors, the new statutory statement captures a cultural change in the way in which companies conduct their business. There was a time when business success in the interests of shareholders was thought to be in conflict with society's aspirations for people who work in the company or in supply chain companies, for the long-term well-being of the community and for the protection of the environment. The law is now based on a new approach. Pursuing the interests of shareholders and embracing wider responsibilities are complementary purposes, not contradictory ones.
>
> I strongly believe that businesses perform better, and are more sustainable in the long term, when they have regard to a wider group of issues in pursuing success. That is a common-sense approach that reflects a modern view of the way in which businesses operate in their community: they interact with customers and suppliers; they make sure that employees are motivated and properly rewarded; and they think about their impact on communities and the environment. They do so at least partly because it makes good business sense.'

The statement above captures the essence of the enlightened shareholder value approach for directors. Their duties may be summarised as in the following simplified and practical guidance:

- To act in the company's best interests, taking everything you think relevant into account.

- To obey the company's constitution and decisions taken under it.

- To be honest, and remember that the company's property belongs to it and not to you or to its shareholders.

- To be diligent, careful and well informed about the company's affairs. If you have any special skills or experience, use them.

- To make sure the company keeps records of your decisions.

- To remember that you remain responsible for the work you give to others.

The duties of a director can be put down to common sense applied with integrity, thoughtfulness and an acute sense of responsibility

3.4 GENERAL DUTIES OF DIRECTORS

The duties of directors, set out in Part 10 of the Act, are as listed below. These duties and supplementary provisions are reproduced in full in Appendix 8.

Introductory:

Section 170	Scope and nature of general duties

The general duties:

Section 171	Duty to act within powers
Section 172	Duty to promote the success of the company
Section 173	Duty to exercise independent judgment
Section 174	Duty to exercise reasonable care, skill and diligence
Section 175	Duty to avoid conflicts of interest
Section 176	Duty not to accept benefits from third parties

Section 177   Duty to declare interest in
                                     proposed transaction or
                                     arrangement

Duties 171–174 inclusive were effective from 1 October 2007. Duties
175–177 inclusive came into effect from 1 October 2008. Each of the
duties are explained and guidance on their application in practice is
covered in **3.4.4–3.4.11**.

3.4.1   The meaning of 'director' and 'shadow director'

In the introduction to the Act it was pointed out that the statutory duties
apply both to directors and shadow directors. In the Act, 'director'
includes any person occupying the position of director, by whatever name
called (s 250). A 'shadow director', on the other hand, means a person in
accordance with whose directions or instructions the directors of the
company are accustomed to act, but a person is not to be regarded as a
shadow director by reason only that the directors act on advice given by
him or her in a professional capacity (s 251).

So far as general duties of directors are concerned, a corporate body is
not to be regarded as a shadow director of any of the subsidiary
companies by reason only that the directors of the subsidiary are
accustomed to act in accordance with its directions or instructions.

3.4.2   Derivative claims

The Act has also made it easier for members to bring a 'derivative claim'
against an individual director on behalf of the company. A derivative
claim may be brought only in respect of a cause of action arising from an
actual or proposed act or omission involving negligence, default, breach
of duty or breach of trust by a director of the company. It is immaterial
whether the cause of action arose before or after the person seeking to
bring or continue the derivative claim became a member of the company.
Further, references to a member of a company include a person who is
not a member but to whom shares in the company have been transferred
or transmitted by operation of law (s 260).

3.4.3   Ensuring directors are aware of their duties

It is important for companies to ensure that all directors are aware of
their duties under the Act. Any one of the following steps, or combination
of steps, might be taken:

- the existing board is given a thorough briefing on their duties;

- all new directors are provided with a briefing as part of their
  induction (induction of directors is covered in greater detail in **3.6**);

- the terms of appointment and description of the role of any director are to contain specific reference to their duties under the Act; and

- the terms of reference of any board committee might also refer to directors' duties.

3.4.4 The scope and nature of directors' general duties (s 170)

The Act states that:

'(1) The general duties specified in sections 171 to 177 are owed by a director of a company to the company.

(2) A person who ceases to be a director continues to be subject—
(a) to the duty in section 175 (duty to avoid conflicts of interest) as regards the exploitation of any property, information or opportunity of which he became aware at a time when he was a director, and
(b) to the duty in section 176 (duty not to accept benefits from third parties) as regards things done or omitted by him before he ceased to be a director.'

3.4.5 Duty to act within powers (s 171)

This section codifies a director's duty to comply with the company's constitution and only exercise powers for the purposes for which they are conferred.

It is important for directors to appreciate that the liability for not complying with the company's constitution is strict.

Below is guidance for companies and their directors to follow:

- Formal procedures should always be followed when a meeting of the board is held, with a distinction always being made between a meeting of the board or a formally constituted committee of the board and other meetings involving directors, eg a chief executive's senior management committee which assists him in the exercise of his or personal delegated financial and/or other authority from the board. Having a clear and comprehensive schedule of matters reserved for the exclusive decision of the board of the company may help to provide clarity of what may and may not be decided outside board meetings. Matters reserved for the board are covered in detail in Chapter 5, 'Company boards and their committees'.

- Directors should be conscious of their company's Articles and the powers in the constitution. For example, this is relevant when considering the issuing of shares, the situations where the directors should be referring to shareholders, and the rules for establishing a quorum.

- If in doubt, directors should always seek the advice and guidance of the company secretary. This important role is examined in Chapter 5.

3.4.6   Duty to promote the success of the company (s 172)

The duty to promote the success of the company has effect subject to any enactment or rule of law requiring directors, in certain circumstances, to consider or act in the interests of creditors of the company.

This duty is the outcome of the extensive debate on enlightened shareholder value which was explored at length during the Company Law Review, which led to the Companies Act 2006. It replaces the common law duty to act in good faith in the interests of the company. The overriding duty is that a director is required to act in the way he or she considers, in good faith, will be most likely to promote the success of the company for the benefit of its members as a whole. In doing so, he or she must have regard (amongst other matters) to the six factors below. Some examples of decisions where a factor may be relevant are given in each case.

(1)   the likely consequences of any decision in the long term (eg cutting the research and development budget within a pharmaceutical company);

(2)   the interests of the company's employees (eg closing down a plant to outsource abroad, thus leading to redundancies among the existing staff);

(3)   the need to foster the company's business relationships with suppliers, customers and others (eg the finance department proposing a tightening of supplier terms of trade in order to improve cashflow);

(4)   the impact of the company's operations on the community and the environment (eg a manufacturing company may have to give serious consideration to the environmental impact of its operations);

(5)   the desirability of the company maintaining a reputation for high standards of business conduct (eg directors need to consider the reputational risks involved in a proposal for the use of private information on competitor activities); and

(6)   the need to act fairly as between members of the company (eg the directors need to ensure that private shareholders are not disadvantaged by the structure of corporate transactions or share issues, or by lack of information).

At times these six factors, and any others that are being considered, may be in conflict, but the key issue for decision making is that the directors should choose the action that will promote the overall success of the company for the benefit of members as a whole, even if that may sometimes have a negative impact on one or more of the above factors.

This duty may give rise to some concern, but to a large extent it only re-enacts and consolidates existing statutory provisions, the common law and best practice. Some key practical points are as follows:

- the six factors above are matters which directors must 'have regard to', but 'traditional considerations' such as profitability, the financial effects on shareholders, etc are still of critical importance as they are central to the duty to 'promote the success of the company for the benefit of the members as a whole';

- in the decision-making process there is generally no absolute wrong or right approach – the directors must make a judgment in good faith for the success of the company having regard to all the information and having taken advice when appropriate;

- papers written for the board, which are not merely information papers, need to refer to the six factors where they are relevant to the decision being made, but not in circumstances where any of those factors does not arise; and

- a system of checking before any paper is finally included in the board pack should be introduced in order to ensure that all the factors regarding a decision that are relevant to directors' duties have been adequately covered in the paper. This checking process would normally be conducted by the company secretary or by the chairman.

3.4.7   Duty to exercise independent judgment (s 173)

A director of a company must exercise his or her judgment independently of the influence of others. Section 173(2) states:

> 'This duty is not infringed by his acting—
> (a)   in accordance with an agreement duly entered into by the company that restricts the future exercise of discretion by its directors; or
> (b)   in a way authorised by the company's constitution.'

From a practical point of view this means that:

- a director should ensure that he or she does not allow personal interests, eg in a particular contract, to affect his or her independent judgment in the interest of the company. A director should ideally excuse him or herself from any meeting at which a decision is to be taken in respect of his or her own property/interest. This is also relevant when the director is considering conflict of interest duties under ss 175–177;

- importantly, where someone is an executive director, he or she is not there to promote a collective executive line, but is there, as is a non-executive director, in his or her own right and should give the board the benefit of his or her own independent judgment, including his or her appreciation of the risks involved in a particular course of action;

- this duty does not prevent a director from exercising his or her power to delegate but he or she must still exercise his or her own judgment in deciding whether to follow the action suggested by that person(s);

- similarly, a director would not be prevented by this duty from seeking legal or other professional advice but, ultimately, the director's final judgment would need to be independent. A director associated with a major shareholder should set any 'representative' function aside and make final decisions on their own merits; and

- likewise, a director who is a family representative in the business may consult his or her family but be clear that he or she will make the final decision.

3.4.8   Duty to exercise reasonable care, skill and diligence (s 174)

Section 174 states:

> '(1) A director of a company must exercise reasonable care, skill and diligence.
>
> (2) This means the care, skill and diligence that would be exercised by a reasonably diligent person with—
> (a)   the general knowledge, skill and experience that may reasonably be expected of a person carrying out the functions carried out by the director in relation to the company [an objective test], and
> (b)   the general knowledge, skill and experience that the director has [a subjective test].'

The use of both tests means that each director must exercise his duty to a minimum standard, as suggested by the objective test, and then the standard is raised under the subjective test if that director has specific skills or expertise. So if, for example, a non-executive director had an accounting qualification, he or she would be expected to exercise more active scrutiny of the accounts, for instance on such aspects as the appropriateness of accounting policies, than a director without such a qualification.

3.4.9 Duty to avoid conflicts of interest (s 175)

Section 175 states:

> (1) A director of a company must avoid a situation in which he has, or can have, a direct or indirect interest that conflicts, or possibly may conflict, with the interests of the company.
>
> (2) This applies in particular to the exploitation of any property, information or opportunity (and it is immaterial whether the company could take advantage of the property, information or opportunity).
>
> (3) This duty does not apply to a conflict of interest arising in relation to a transaction or arrangement with the company.
>
> (4) This duty is not infringed—
> (a)   if the situation cannot reasonably be regarded as likely to give rise to a conflict of interest; or
> (b)   if the matter has been authorised by the directors.'

Authorisation may be given by directors of *private* companies by directors who are independent of the conflict, unless there is a provision in the company's constitution stating otherwise. In practice it would be rare for there to be such a provision requiring authorisation to be given by the members except perhaps in the situation of a management buy-out.

Authorisation may be given by directors of *public* companies if the company's constitution includes a provision for the directors to authorise. Again, such authorisation must be given by directors who are independent of the conflict.

When giving authorisation directors must consider whether their action is most likely to promote the success of the company. When a director has a potential conflict of interest in a particular activity, authorisation may be given by the directors, but the authorisation is only effective if that director is ignored for the purposes of the quorum and voting on any board resolution to authorise the matter. It is good practice for a conflicted director to leave the meeting when discussions take place on matters in which he or she has some personal interest.

Another practical point to consider is whether a director who has the opportunity to take on a new directorship outside the company has a problem in relation to this duty. Multiple directorships would not necessarily need to have formal authorisation from the board – the question is whether having such directorships is likely to give rise to a conflict of interest.

Furthermore, it is recommended that each director should consider if he or she has a conflict of interest through a connected person. Therefore it is important that the director informs those individuals that would be regarded as connected persons. Connected persons are essentially certain family members, certain companies with which the director is connected, trustees of a trust, certain partners and certain firms with legal personality.

Under this duty a conflict of interest also includes a conflict of duties.

3.4.10   Duty not to accept benefits from third parties (s 176)

This duty has codified the common law rule that a director must not exploit his or her position for personal benefit.

Only those benefits which could reasonably be regarded as likely to give rise to a conflict of interest fall within the scope of this duty.

The Act does not permit the acceptance of benefits which fall within the ambit of the duty to be authorised by the board; it has to be approved by the company's members.

This duty has opened up some interesting debates on how far these 'benefits' may extend. Some benefits are easily identified, such as financial rewards or money's worth such as tickets to prestigious sporting or cultural events. Questions have been raised too as to how far this duty will cover the giving or receipt of corporate hospitality.

It is good practice to set up a register of benefits offered and received above whatever level is decided on by the board. It is suggested that the company secretary should report annually to the audit committee on compliance and issues arising.

3.4.11   Duty to declare interest in proposed transaction or arrangement (s 177)

This duty requires a director to declare to the other directors any interest, whether direct or indirect, in a proposed transaction or arrangement with the company. The extent of the interest must also be declared.

A director does not need to declare an interest if it cannot reasonably be regarded as likely to give rise to a conflict of interest.

A director is not required under this duty to disclose facts of which the other directors should already know or ought reasonably to be presumed to know. If a director becomes aware that some of the information declared is not accurate or complete before the transaction or arrangement has taken place, he or she must ensure that he or she corrects the initial declaration so that it is accurate.

A director must declare his or her interest before the transaction or arrangement is entered into by the company. It is good practice for the board to take decisions on related matters without the director present.

The duty may still apply even if the director is not party to the transaction; if the director's spouse would be entering into the transaction or arrangement the director may need to declare an indirect interest in the transaction.

3.5 INDUCTION OF DIRECTORS

The Code makes clear that all directors should receive induction on joining the board, and furthermore should regularly update and refresh their skills and knowledge (A.5). The objective of induction is to inform the director so that he or she can become as effective as possible in his or her new role as soon as possible. On appointment a new director should be provided with certain key essential information. Other information may be provided subsequently.

The Institute of Chartered Secretaries and Administrators (ICSA) have produced guidance in two parts on the materials to be included in an induction pack.

The first includes the essential material that should be provided immediately and the second includes material that should be provided over the first few weeks following the appointment, as and when deemed most appropriate. The director should, however, be provided immediately with a comprehensive list of the total material being made available, together with an undertaking to provide it earlier if required. Some information may have already been provided during the director's due diligence process prior to appointment, or along with the appointment letter.

The topics contained within this list should be supplied to all newly appointed directors. However, the company secretary will need to gauge the level of previous knowledge and adjust them accordingly, particularly in regard to the appointment of executive directors.

The guidance is written with public companies in mind, but is still relevant, with appropriate qualifications, to private companies.

3.5.1   Induction Guidance (ICSA)

Essential information to be provided immediately

The following information is felt to be essential and needs to be given to the director prior to the first board meeting. Methods of delivery vary, some of the information needs to be sent to the director with his or her appointment letter; but some could be deferred until a meeting after the board papers have been issued, so that the company secretary can review the board pack with the director before the first meeting highlighting any relevant issues.

Directors' duties

- Brief outline of the role of a director and a summary of his or her responsibilities and ongoing obligations under legislation, regulation and best practice.

- Copy of UKLA (the UK Listing Authority, ie the FSA) Model Code, and details of the company's procedure regarding directors' share dealings and the disclosure of price sensitive information.

- The company's guidelines:
  - matters reserved for the board;
  - delegated authorities;
  - the policy for obtaining independent professional advice for directors; and
  - other standing orders, policies and procedures of which the director should be aware.

- 'Fire drill' procedures (ie the procedures in place to deal with situations such as hostile takeover bids).

The company's business

- Current strategic/business plan, market analysis and budgets for the year with revised forecast, and 3/5-year plan.

- Latest annual report and accounts, and interims as appropriate.

- Explanation of key performance indicators.

- List of major domestic and overseas subsidiaries, associated companies and joint ventures, including any parent company(ies).

- Summary details of major group insurance policies including Directors' and Officers' liability insurance.

- Details of any major litigation. either current or potential, being undertaken by the company or against the company.

- Treasury issues:
  - – funding position and arrangements; and
  - – dividend policy.

- The Corporate brochure, mission statement and any other reports issued by the company such as an environmental report, with a summary of the main events (such as mergers, divestments, introductions of new products, diversification into new areas, restructuring, etc) over the last 3 years.

Board issues

- Up-to-date copy of the company's Memorandum and Articles of Association/Constitution, with a summary of the most important provisions.

- Minutes of the last three to six board meetings.

- Schedule of dates of future board meetings and board subcommittees if appropriate.

- Description of board procedures covering details such as when papers are sent out, the normal location of meetings, how long they last and an indication of the routine business transacted.

- Brief biographical and contact details of all directors of the company, the company secretary and other key executives. This should include any executive responsibilities of directors, their dates of appointment and any board committees upon which individual directors sit.

- Details of board subcommittees together with terms of reference and, where the director will be joining a committee, copies of the minutes of meetings of that committee during the previous 12 months.

Additional material to be provided during the first few months

The following information is crucial to assist the director to develop his or her knowledge of the company, its operations and staff, but is not necessary for him or her to commence his or her involvement.

- Copies of the company's main product/service brochures.

- Copies of recent press cuttings, reports and articles concerning the company.

- Details of the company's advisers (lawyers, bankers, auditors, registrars, etc), both internal and external, with the name of the partner dealing with the company's affairs.

- The company's risk management procedures and relevant disaster recovery plans.

- Any outlines of the provisions of the Combined Code as appended to the UK Listing Rules together with details of the company's corporate governance guidelines and any investor's corporate governance guidelines which the company seeks to follow.

- Brief history of the company including when it was incorporated and any significant events during its history.

- Notices of any general meetings held in the last 3 years, and accompanying circulars as appropriate.

- Company organisation chart and management succession plans.

- Copy of all management accounts prepared since the company's last audited accounts.

- The company's investor policy and details of the major shareholders.

- Details of the five largest customers with the level of business done over the last 5 years.

- Details of the five largest suppliers to the company.

- Policies as regards:
    - health and safety;
    - environmental issues;
    - ethics and whistleblowing; and
    - charitable and political donations.

- Internal company telephone directory (including any overseas contact numbers and names).

CHAPTER 4

THE NON-EXECUTIVE DIRECTOR

4.1 INTRODUCTION

As far back as the Cadbury Commission Report of December 1992 the calibre of the non-executive members of the board was recognised as being of special importance in setting and maintaining standards of corporate governance. At the same time, and with the intention of countering a perceived overemphasis of their monitoring role, Cadbury pointed to the primary and positive contribution which non-executives are also expected to make, as equal board members, to the leadership of the company. However, over time, it became apparent that overemphasis of their monitoring role was emerging as an unintended side effect in some cases. Nevertheless, Cadbury had made a valuable contribution in raising the profile of the non-executive director.

The critical issue of balance by non-executive directors between monitoring and contributing to the leadership of the company was addressed in the Hampel Committee Report of January 1998, which continued the work of the Cadbury Committee. Hampel commented that:

> 'Non-executive directors are normally appointed to the board primarily for their contribution to the development of the company's strategy. This is clearly right. We have found general acceptance that non-executive directors should have both a strategic and a monitoring function. In addition, and particularly in smaller companies, non-executive directors may contribute valuable expertise not otherwise available to management; or they may act as mentors to relatively inexperienced executives. What matters in every case is that the non-executive directors should command the respect of the executives and should be able to work with them in a cohesive team to further the company's interests.'

Following the work of Cadbury and Hampel and the first publication of the Combined Code in June 1998, non-executive directors have become widely accepted as the custodians of the governance process in publicly listed companies. The demands of the role have implications for the levels of professionalism and commitment required, and for the process of recruitment and appointment. All this was put under the microscope in the Higgs Review, in January 2003, of the role and effectiveness of non-executive directors, and the conclusions were embodied within the next publication of the Combined Code in July 2003, which was then republished in June 2008 with only minor changes.

The Code, supported by reference to the Higgs Review, is a rich source of guidance on the role of the non-executive director. This guidance is divided into the following sections:

- the unitary board context and the critical contribution the role of chairman makes to the effectiveness of non-executive directors;

- legal responsibility and liability;

- the core elements of the role;

- important personal attributes and behaviours required;

- independence and board balance;

- membership of board committees;

- information for non-executive directors;

- induction, professional development and performance evaluation;

- relationships with shareholders;

- recruitment and appointment.

With the exception of the sections on board committees and relationship with shareholders, the guidance is as valuable to non-executive directors on the boards of private companies as it is to those on the boards of smaller quoted and AIM listed companies. In all cases there is no 'one size fits all' formula and a non-executive director's role needs to be tailored to fit the particular circumstances of each company.

4.2   THE UNITARY BOARD AND CHAIRMAN'S ROLE

4.2.1   The unitary board structure

In the unitary board structure, executive and non-executive directors share responsibility for both direction and control of the company. The role and effectiveness of the non–executive director needs to be considered in the context of the board as a whole and the board is collectively responsible for promoting the success of the company by directing and supervising the company's affairs. All directors must take decisions objectively in the interests of the company. The benefit of the unitary board derives from the combination of executive knowledge within the board with the wider experience that the non-executive directors can bring to board discussion and decision making.

The board's role (Code Supporting Principle to A.1) is to provide entrepreneurial leadership of the company within a framework of prudent and effective controls which enables risk to be assessed and managed. The board should set the company's strategic aims, ensure that the necessary financial and human resources are in place for the company to meet its objectives, and review management performance. The board should also set the company's values and standards and ensure that its obligations to its shareholders and others are understood and met.

4.2.2 The chairman

The chairman is pivotal in creating the conditions for overall board and individual non-executive director effectiveness, both inside and outside the boardroom. This crucial aspect is summed up as follows in Code Supporting Principle to A.2:

> 'The chairman is responsible for leadership of the board, ensuring its effectiveness on all aspects of its role and setting its agenda. The chairman is also responsible for ensuring that the directors receive accurate, timely and clear information. The chairman should ensure effective communication with shareholders. The chairman should also facilitate the effective contribution of non-executive directors in particular and ensure constructive relations between executive and non-executive directors.'

Certain provisions of the Code have key relevance for non-executive directors. The chairman should hold meetings with the non-executive directors without the executives present. Led by the senior independent director, the non-executive directors should meet without the chairman present at least annually to appraise the chairman's performance, or such other occasions as are deemed appropriate (A.1.3) and on resignation.

Further, where directors have concerns which cannot be resolved about the running of the company or a proposed action, they should ensure that their concerns are recorded in the board minutes. On resignation, a non-executive director should provide a written statement to the chairman, for circulation to the board, if they have any such concerns (A.1.4).

4.3 LEGAL RESPONSIBILITIES AND LIABILITY

Although the law does not apply different duties to executive and non-executive directors, it has been recognised that the knowledge, skill and experience expected will vary between directors with different roles and responsibilities. This applies both to executive and non-executive directors. However, an important problem faced by directors, and in particular non-executive directors, has been that of knowing with certainty the extent of their duties. The statement of directors' general duties in the new Companies Act 2006, and explained in Chapter 2 on the duties of directors, has considerably reduced this uncertainty.

In addition, the Code includes very helpful guidance on liability of non-executive directors. This guidance builds on directors' duties in relation to care, skill and diligence by making clear that, although non-executive directors and executive directors have the same legal duties and objectives as board members, their involvement is likely to be different. In particular a non-executive director is likely to be able to devote significantly less time to, and in most cases have less detailed knowledge and experience of, the company's affairs.

In this context the following elements of the Code may also be particularly relevant:

(a) in order to enable directors to fulfil their duties, the Code states that:
  (i)   the letter of appointment of the director should set out the expected time commitment (A.4.4); and
  (ii) the board should be supplied in a timely manner with information in a form and of a quality appropriate to enable it to discharge its duties. The chairman is responsible for ensuring that the directors are provided by management with accurate, timely and clear information (A.4.5);

(b) non-executive directors should themselves:
  (i)   undertake appropriate induction and regularly update and refresh their skills, knowledge and familiarity with the company (A.5 and A.5.1);
  (ii) seek appropriate clarification or amplification of information and, where necessary, take and follow appropriate professional advice (A.5 and A.5.2);
  (iii) where they have concerns about the running of the company or a proposed action, ensure that these are addressed by the board and, to the extent that they are not resolved, ensure that they are recorded in the board minutes (A.1.4); and
  (iv) give a statement to the board if they have such unresolved concerns on resignation (A.1.4).

It is up to each non-executive director to reach a view as to what is necessary in particular circumstances to comply with the duty of care, skill and diligence they owe as a director to the company. In considering whether or not a person is in breach of that duty, a court would take into account all relevant circumstances. These may include having regard to the above where relevant to the issue of liability of a non-executive director.

4.4 CORE ELEMENTS OF THE ROLE OF THE NON-EXECUTIVE DIRECTOR

The core elements (Code Supporting Principle to A.1), taking into account that no two boards or sets of business circumstances are ever likely to be the same, are:

Strategy	Non-executive directors should constructively challenge and contribute to the development of strategy.
Performance	Non-executive directors should scrutinise the performance of management in meeting agreed goals and objectives and monitor the reporting of performance.
Risk	Non-executive directors should satisfy themselves that financial information is accurate and that financial controls and systems of risk management are robust and defensible.
People	Non-executive directors are responsible for determining appropriate levels of remuneration of executive directors and have a prime role in appointing, and where necessary removing, senior management and in succession planning.

4.4.1 Two principal components

The two principal components of the role of the non-executive director become clear, namely:

(a) monitoring executive activity; and

(b) contributing to the development of strategy and prosperity of the enterprise.

An overemphasis on (a), monitoring and control, risks non-executive directors seeing themselves, and being seen, as an alien policing influence detached from the rest of the board. An overemphasis on (b), strategy, risks non-executive directors becoming too close to executive management, undermining shareholder confidence in the effectiveness of board governance.

Achieving a proper balance between these two components is the challenge for the non-executive director which calls for particular personal qualities.

4.4.2   The key to non-executive director effectiveness

The key, therefore, to non-executive director effectiveness lies as much in behaviours and relationships as in structures and processes. It is crucial that non-executives establish a spirit of partnership and mutual respect on the unitary board. This requires them to build recognition by executives of their contribution in order to promote openness and trust. Only then can non-executive directors contribute effectively.

The following real company case study is illuminating on these points as well as providing practical insights from the experience of a private company appointing non-executive directors in preparation for flotation on the main list. The company, a sector leader in the international plastics market and bought out by management from its parent company, was successfully floated on the main market and joined the FTSE small cap index after 3 years as a private company. In the run up to the flotation the company appointed two non-executive directors to its board, which up to that point comprised only executive directors including the chairman. With no previous experience of either recruiting or working with non-executive directors on a board, the chairman made the following comments on their appointment:

> 'The Board needs to be on board! What I mean by that is that all members of the board need to have a common understanding of the need for and the role of the non-executive director. In retrospect, it would have been better if I had spent more time on this and relied less on people coming around to the idea and the need. Some of our board took quite a while to go from viewing non-executive directors as an "imposition" to viewing them as a very positive development offering immediate benefits.

> On their role the emphasis should be on contribution to the development of the business rather than acting as a "policeman". Focus on the development of the business will always pay dividends providing the executives use the non-executives correctly – our own experience is that our non-executive directors hit the ground running hard (in part because the executives involved them immediately) and have already made a significant mark. Our board is distinctly improved by the presence of the non-executive directors.

> The presence of non-executives has been very helpful indeed in sorting out roles, contributions, and so on.

> A factor I feel is very important indeed is choosing suitable non-executives for their ability to live up to their title – i.e. be non-executive. The power of non-executive directors depends on their ability to listen, influence and persuade, not to give instructions.

> In our own experience we found that this was likely to be the single area of most concern. The majority of managers spend their lives in executive

positions – the best (almost by definition) will be powerful, strong willed individuals who may find the switch to non-executive director very hard to handle.

This is potentially a very problematic area. I could see boards blinded to the problem by the glittering career of an autocrat, or alternatively avoiding the problem by going for yes-men. In either case the board is not likely to get the optimum contribution from their non-executives.

Another factor, which the board should take into account in taking on non-executives is their ability to act as a counterweight to vested interests elsewhere on the board (whether executive or not). As well may be true with a lot of management buy-outs, there may be short-term pressure from venture capitalists which skews the approach to board discussion. There is no doubt that our board is much better balanced with our independent non-executive directors in place.'

As the non-executive directors do not report to the chief executive and are not involved in the day-to-day running of the business, they can bring fresh perspective and contribute more objectively in supporting, as well as constructively challenging and monitoring, the management team.

They must constantly seek to establish and maintain their own confidence in the conduct of the company, in the performance of the management team, the development of strategy, the adequacy of financial controls and risk management, the appropriateness of remuneration and the appointment and replacement of key personnel and plans for management development and succession. The role of the non-executive director is therefore both to support executives in their leadership of the business and to monitor and supervise their conduct.

In practice, non-executive directors will pursue some of their activities through their role on board committees, but in smaller companies they may particularly provide specific expertise or experience to complement that of the executive team.

4.5 BEHAVIOURS AND PERSONAL ATTRIBUTES OF THE EFFECTIVE NON-EXECUTIVE DIRECTOR

The non-executive director role is complex and demanding and requires skills, experience, integrity and particular behaviours and personal attributes.

Non-executive directors need to be:

- sound in judgment; and

- have an inquiring mind.

They should:

- question intelligently;

- debate constructively;

- challenge rigorously; and

- decide dispassionately.

And they should listen sensitively to the views of others, inside and outside the boardroom.

In order to fulfil their role, non-executive directors must acquire the expertise and knowledge necessary to properly discharge their responsibilities. They must be well informed about the business, the environment in which it operates and the issues it faces. This requires a knowledge of the markets in which the company operates as well as a full understanding of the company itself. Understanding the company is essential to gain credibility and reduce the inevitable disparity in knowledge between executive and non-executive directors. Developing such knowledge cannot be done within the confines of the boardroom alone. Less formal meetings, including with senior and middle management as well as company site visits from time to time, are an essential ingredient to gaining and keeping on top of a full understanding of the company and the issues it faces.

The personal attributes required of the effective non-executive director are founded on:

(1) integrity and high ethical standards – these are a prerequisite for all directors;

(2) sound judgment – this is central to the non-executive director's role and is essential for each of the core elements of the role;

(3) the ability and willingness to challenge and probe – all non-executive directors must have this ability. They should have sufficient strength of character to seek and obtain full and satisfactory answers within the collegiate environment of the board; and

(4) strong interpersonal skills to develop constructive relationships with colleagues.

4.6 INDEPENDENT NON-EXECUTIVE DIRECTORS AND BOARD BALANCE

Whilst all non-executive directors (and of course executive directors) need to be independent of mind, a proportion also needs to be independent in a stricter sense. There is a natural potential for conflict between the interests of executive management and shareholders in a range of instances (eg director remuneration). Although there is a legal duty on all directors to act in the best interests of the company, it has long been recognised that in itself this is insufficient to give full assurance that these potential conflicts will not impair objective board decision making. Much evidence has been accumulated to indicate that a board is strengthened significantly by having a strong group of non-executive directors with *no other connection* with the company. The Code addresses this in two ways:

(1) by including a determination of independence (in the stricter sense) (A.3.1); and

(2) by calling for at least half the board, except in smaller companies (below the FTSE 350), and excluding the chairman, to be made up of non-executive directors determined by the board to be independent. A smaller company should have at least two independent non-executive directors (A.3.2).

The board should identify in the annual report each non-executive director it considers to be independent. The board should determine whether the director is independent in character and judgment and whether there are relationships or circumstances which are likely to affect, or could appear to affect, the director's judgment. The board should state its reasons if it determines that a director is independent notwithstanding the existence of relationships or circumstances which may appear relevant to its determination, including if the director:

(a) has been an employee of the company or group within the last 5 years;

(b) has, or has had within the last 3 years, a material business relationship with the company either directly, or as a partner, shareholder, director or senior employee of a body that has such a relationship with the company;

(c) has received or receives additional remuneration from the company apart from a director's fee, participates in the company's share option or a performance-related pay scheme, or is a member of the company's pension scheme;

(d) has close family ties with any of the company's advisers, directors or senior employees;

(e)   holds cross-directorships or has significant links with other directors through involvement in other companies or bodies;

(f)   represents a significant shareholder;

(g)   has served on the board for more than 9 years from the date of his first election (A.3.1).

Notwithstanding the requirement for independent non-executive directors on a board, non-executive directors who, in addition, are deemed not to be independent (in the stricter sense) may still fill a much valued role on a board.

The role of the senior independent non-executive director (senior independent director) is also acknowledged in the Code (A.3.3).

4.7   MEMBERSHIP OF BOARD COMMITTEES

Much of the contribution from non-executive directors arises from their active membership of board committees, namely the audit, remuneration and nomination committees, and the Code emphasises the need for independence and commitment in the membership of these committees. The value of ensuring that committee membership is refreshed and that undue reliance is not placed on particular individuals should also be taken into account in deciding chairmanship and membership of committees. No one other than the committee chairman and members is entitled to be present at any of the committee meetings, but others may attend at the invitation of the committee (Code Supporting Principles to A.3). The annual report should identify the chairman and members of all three committees, and also set out the number of meetings per annum of the committees and individual attendance by directors (A.1.2). At the AGM the chairman is required to arrange for the chairmen of each of the three committees to be available to answer questions and for all directors to attend (D.2.3).

Composition criteria for committee membership is as follows:

(a)   *audit* – in the case of smaller quoted companies this committee should comprise at least two members who should be independent non-executive directors, and the board should satisfy itself that at least one member of the audit committee has recent and relevant financial experience (C.3.1);

(b)   *remuneration* – again, in the case of smaller quoted companies this committee should also comprise at least two members, who should be independent non-executive directors (B.2.1); and

(c) *nomination* – this committee should comprise a majority of members who are independent non-executive directors. The chairman or an independent non-executive director should chair the committee, but not the chairman when the committee is dealing with the appointment of a successor to the chairmanship (A.4.1).

4.8 INFORMATION FOR NON-EXECUTIVE DIRECTORS

Adequate relevant, significant and clear information is vital for a non-executive director to be effective and it must be provided sufficiently in advance of meetings to enable non-executive directors to give issues thorough consideration. The chairman, supported by the company secretary, should assess what information is required. At the same time non-executive directors should continually satisfy themselves that they have the appropriate information of sufficient quality to make sound judgments. They should not hesitate to seek clarification or amplification where necessary, calling on the services of the company secretary if required.

4.9 INDUCTION, PROFESSIONAL DEVELOPMENT AND PERFORMANCE EVALUATION

Induction and professional development (together) and performance evaluation were two new Main Principles included in the Combined Code of 2003 following the Higgs Review. This was timely. Both are important to the effectiveness of non-executive directors.

4.9.1 Induction

All directors should receive induction on joining the board and should regularly update and refresh their skills and knowledge (A.5). Newly appointed non-executive directors quickly need to build their knowledge of the host organisation to the point where they can use their skills and experience gained elsewhere for the benefit of the company. Therefore, with the assistance of the company secretary, the chairman should ensure that new non-executive directors receive a full, formal and tailored induction on joining the board.

4.9.1.1 *Higgs Review Guidance*

The Higgs Review included the following guidance for companies on the induction of non-executive directors:

As a general rule, a combination of selected written information together with presentations and activities such as meetings and site visits will help to give a new appointee a balanced and real-life overview of the company. Care should be taken not to overload the new director with too much information. The new director should be provided with a list of all the induction information that is being made available to them so that they may call up items if required before otherwise provided.

The induction process should:

1. Build an understanding of the nature of the company, its business and the markets in which it operates. For example, induction should cover:
    *   the company's products or services;
    *   group structure, subsidiaries and joint ventures;
    *   the company's constitutions, board procedures and matters reserved for the board;
    *   summary details of the company's principal assets, liabilities, significant contracts and major competitors;
    *   the company's major risks and risk management strategy;
    *   key performance indicators; and
    *   regulatory constraints.

2. Build a link with the company's people including:
    *   meetings with senior management;
    *   visits to company sites other than the headquarters, to learn about production or services and meet employees in an informal setting. It is important, not only for the board to get to know the new non-executive director, but also for the non-executive director to build a profile with employees below board level; and
    *   participating in board strategy development. "Awaydays" enable a new non-executive director to begin to build working relationships away from the formal setting of the boardroom.

3. Build an understanding of the company's main relationships, including meeting with the auditors and developing a knowledge of in particular:
    *   who are the major customers;
    *   who are the major suppliers; and
    *   who are the major shareholders and what is the shareholder relations policy – participation in meetings with shareholders can help give a first hand feel as well as letting shareholders know who the non-executive directors are.

4.9.2 Professional development

A non-executive director's credibility and effectiveness in the boardroom, however, will depend not just on their existing capability but on their ability to *extend* their knowledge and skills. To meet the exacting standards of professionalism now required in this complex and demanding role, continuing professional development for the non-executive director becomes a necessity. Provision should be properly structured to meet individual needs ranging from what is required by potential non-executives to the requirements of existing non-executive directors. The chairman, with the assistance of the company secretary, should ensure the non-executive directors continually update their skills, knowledge and capabilities, and provide the necessary resources for this (Code Supporting Principle to A.5).

4.9.3 Performance evaluation

The chairman has a key role in arranging the evaluation process for individual non-executive directors. Higgs suggested a list of questions to be considered by the chairman and by the non-executives themselves which provide a sensible basis for review:

(1) How well prepared and informed are they for board meetings and is their meeting attendance satisfactory?

(2) Do they demonstrate a willingness to devote time and effort to understand the company and its business and a readiness to participate in events outside the boardroom such as site visits?

(3) What has been the quality and value of their contributions at board meetings?

(4) What has been their contribution to development of strategy and risk management?

(5) How successfully have they brought their knowledge and experience to bear in the consideration of strategy?

(6) How effectively have they probed to test information and assumptions? Where necessary, how resolute are they in maintaining their own views and resisting pressure from others?

(7) How effectively and proactively have they followed up their areas of concern?

(8)   How effective and successful are their relationships with fellow board members, the company secretary and senior management? Does their performance and behaviour engender mutual trust and respect within the board?

(9)   How actively and successfully do they refresh their knowledge and skills and are they up to date with:
  (a)   the latest developments in areas such as corporate governance framework and financial reporting; and
  (b)   the industry and market conditions?

(10) How well do they communicate with fellow board members, senior management and others, for example shareholders? Are they able to present their views convincingly yet diplomatically and do they listen and take on board the views of others?

4.10   RELATIONSHIP WITH SHAREHOLDERS

As far as non-executive directors are concerned relationships with shareholders is a sensitive area and will be included in Chapter 6, 'Shareholders and Corporate Governance'.

However, the Code states that a company should offer major shareholders the opportunity to meet new non-executive directors (A.5.1).

In addition, non-executive directors should be offered the opportunity to attend meetings with major shareholders and should expect to attend them if requested by major shareholders.

The senior independent director should attend sufficient meetings with a range of major shareholders and listen to their views in order to develop a balanced understanding of the issues and concerns of major shareholders (D.1.1).

In addition, the senior independent director should be available to shareholders if they have concerns which contact through the normal channels of chairman, chief executive or finance director has failed to resolve or for which such contact is inappropriate (A.3.3).

4.11   RECRUITMENT AND APPOINTMENT OF NON-EXECUTIVE DIRECTORS

The nomination and appointments process is crucial to the securing of the best candidates so that the board has an appropriate mix of skills and experience and the personal characteristics of the individuals complement one another as far as is possible. The whole should constitute an effective decision-making body and board team (the unitary board). To that end a vigorous, fair and open recruitment process with appointments based on merit is essential.

To date this has been far from the case for non-executive directors, where a high level of informality has surrounded the process of appointment, with personal contacts or friendships playing a large part. The 'pool' from which non-executives have been selected has also been too narrow with little to no representation of candidates from, for instance, amongst women and those with careers which do not include prior experience on a listed company board. Diversity amongst board members, including amongst the non-executive directors themselves, is recognised as adding strength to board discussion and decision making.

Hampel reported as follows:

> 'Most non-executive directors are executives or former executives of other companies. This experience qualifies them both in constructive policy making and in the monitoring role. Non-executive directors from other backgrounds are often appointed for their technical knowledge, their knowledge of overseas markets or their political contacts. It was put to us that companies should recruit directors from a greater diversity of back-grounds. We do not favour diversity for its own sake, to give a politically correct appearance to the list of board members or to represent stakeholders. But we believe, given the diversity of business and size of listed companies, that there are people from other fields who can make a real contribution on the board.'

The case for diversity needs to be tempered for smaller companies given the scale of their operations and the need, which often arises, for particular expertise and experience to fill any gaps at board level. Nevertheless there is a place for lateral thinking when considering the appointment of non-executive directors.

4.11.1 Due diligence for non-executive directors

At the heart of the process for appointing non-executive directors is the nomination committee, but prior to accepting an appointment non-executive directors should exercise due diligence to satisfy themselves that the host company is an organisation in which they can have faith and in which they will be suited to working.

4.11.1.1 Due Dilligence checklist (ICSA)

Following Higgs, ICSA have produced a checklist of questions (also repeated as an attachment to the 2003 Code) which are given below.

These are not intended to be exhaustive, but are intended to be a helpful basis for the pre-appointment due diligence process that all non-executive directors should undertake. By making the right enquiries, asking the right questions and taking care to understand the replies, a prospective director can reduce the risk of nasty surprises and dramatically increase the likelihood of success.

Questions to ask

The business

- What is the company's current financial position and what has its financial track record been over the last three years?

- What are the exact nature and extent of the company's business activities?

- What is the company's competitive position and market share in its main business areas?

- What are the key dependencies (e.g. regulatory approvals, key licenses)?

Governance and investor relations

- What record does the company have on corporate governance issues?

- Does the company have sound and effective systems of internal controls?

- Who are the current executive and non-executive directors, what is their background and record and how long have they served on the board?

- What is the size and structure of the board and board committees and what are the relationships between the Chairman and the board, the Chief Executive and the management team?

- Who owns the company i.e. who are the company's main shareholders and how has the profile changed over recent years?

- What is the company's attitude towards, and relationship with, its shareholders?

The role of the non-executive director

- Is the company clear and specific about the qualities, knowledge, skills and experience that it needs to complement the existing board?

- If the company is not performing particularly well is there potential to turn it round and do I have the time, desire and capability to make a positive impact?

- Am I satisfied that the size, structure and make-up of the board will enable me to make an effective contribution?

- Would accepting the non-executive directorship put me in a position of having a conflict of interest?

- Do I have the necessary knowledge, skills, experience and time to make a positive contribution to the board of this company?

- How closely do I match the job specification and how well will I fulfill the board's expectations?

Risk management

- Is there anything about the nature and extent of the company's business activities that would cause me concern both in terms of risk and any personal ethical considerations?

- Is any material litigation presently being undertaken or threatened, either by the company or against it?

- Am I satisfied that the internal regulation of the company is sound and that I can operate effectively within its stated corporate governance framework?

- What insurance cover is available to directors and what is the company's policy on indemnifying directors?

Sources of information

- Company report and accounts, and/or any listing prospectus, for the recent years.

- Analysts' reports.

- Press reports.

- Company website.

- Any Corporate Social Responsibility or Environmental Report issued by the company.

- Rating agency reports.

- Voting services reports.

Published material is unlikely to reveal wrongdoing, however a lack of transparency may be a reason to proceed with caution.

Further information may be obtained from discussions with existing directors, senior management, employees, suppliers and customers although care should be taken to preserve confidentiality especially considering that, in itself, the fact that an approach has been made will undoubtedly be deemed to be price sensitive information.

4.11.2　Letter of non-executive director appointment

A sample letter of a non-executive director appointment, taken from the Higgs Review, is included at Appendix 9.

The terms incorporate the Code provisions which make clear that non-executive directors should undertake that they will have sufficient time to meet what is expected of them (A.4.4). The names of non-executive directors submitted for election or re-election should be accompanied by sufficient biographical detail and any other relevant information to enable shareholders to take an informed decision on their election (A.7.1). The chairman should confirm to shareholders when proposing re-election of a non-executive director that, following formal performance evaluation, the individual's performance continues to be effective and demonstrates commitment to the role. Non-executive directors may serve longer than 9 years (eg three 3-year terms) subject to annual re-election (A.7.2).

So far as the remuneration of non-executive directors is concerned, there remains some disagreement on whether non-executives should in addition to their fees participate in share option schemes, with some companies in favour and some preferring a direct grant of shares. Some institutional shareholders are firmly against the granting of share options to non-executive directors. The case against share options for non-executives was made by Cadbury based on preserving their independence:

> 'In order to safeguard their independent position, we regard it as good practice for non-executive directors not to participate in share option schemes and for their service as non-executive directors not to be pensionable by the company.'

For cash-strapped smaller companies the granting of share options to non-executives may be unavoidable if the best candidate for the role is to be attracted to the position.

CHAPTER 5

COMPANY BOARDS AND THEIR COMMITTEES

5.1   INTRODUCTION

The focus of corporate governance of smaller companies is more often than not the composition and effectiveness of the board, which in the UK follows the unitary model of all directors, both executive and non-executive, being together on the one board. This is in contrast to the two-tier model applying in other European countries, in which the board is separated into a supervisory board (the top tier) and a management board. The benefit of the unitary board over the two-tier board derives from the combination of executive knowledge within the board and the wider experience that the non-executive directors can bring to board discussion and decision making. As has been noted previously, this wider experience is of particular value to smaller companies, justifying the thoughtful appointment of suitable non-executive directors.

5.2   THE UNITARY BOARD

In the unitary board structure the executive and non-executive directors share responsibility for both direction and control of the company. The board is accountable to the shareholders, but in law owing its duty to the company, and is *collectively* responsible for promoting the success of the company by directing and supervising the company's affairs.

The Code defines the board's role as

> '. . . to provide entrepreneurial leadership of the company within a framework of prudent and effective controls which enables risk to be assessed and managed. The board should set the company's strategic aims, ensure that the necessary financial and human resources are in place for the company to meet its objectives, and review management performance. The board should set the company's values and standards and ensure that its obligations to its shareholders and others are understood and met.'

All directors must take decisions objectively in the interests of the company. For smaller companies it is worth noting that the definition of the board's role begins with the words 'to provide entrepreneurial leadership'.

The leadership of the board is the chairman's responsibility. The chief executive on the other hand is responsible for the running of the business, ie the leadership of the executive team. The Code is clear on this division of responsibility but, as has been pointed out elsewhere, this separation is often inappropriate for smaller companies where, in extreme cases, the chairman and chief executive are one and the same person. This notwithstanding, what needs to be constantly borne in mind is that the roles of chairman and chief executive are different. In some smaller companies this goes unrecognised and the effectiveness of the board suffers, with consequences for the company and frustration for board members.

Chairmanship of the board is a distinct activity requiring a particular set of skills. Guidance on the role is given at **5.3.1**.

5.3   THE CHAIRMAN'S ROLE IN CORPORATE GOVERNANCE

The board of directors is the focus of corporate governance and responsibilities for the functioning and effectiveness of any board belong to the chairman. It follows, therefore, that the way in which corporate governance principles are put into practice is primarily a matter for board chairmen. This point deserves emphasis – the chairman should take the lead on the application of corporate governance principles. To that end he or she has the support of the company secretary to call upon. The role of the company secretary is considered in **5.5**.

The Code is the framework for corporate governance to which the chairman can turn for guidance. So far as the board and directors are concerned this framework is contained in 'A – Directors' in Section 1 of the Code. This was considered in some detail from the perspective of the smaller company in Chapter 1, 'Corporate Governance and the Combined Code'. The Code's Main Principles which form the basis of this framework and corporate governance guidance for the chairman are encapsulated in the template below:

- every company should be headed by an effective board, which is collectively responsible for the success of the company;

- there should be a clear division of responsibility at the head of the company between the running of the board and the executive responsibility for the running of the company's business. No one individual should have unfettered powers of decision;

- the board should include a balance of executive and non-executive directors (and in particular independent non-executive directors) such that no individual or small group of individuals can dominate the board's decision making;

- there should be a formal, rigorous and transparent procedure for the appointment of new directors to the board;

- the board should be supplied in a timely manner with information in a form and of a quality appropriate to enable it to discharge its duties. All directors should receive induction on joining the board and should regularly update and refresh their skills and knowledge;

- the board should undertake a formal and rigorous annual evaluation of its own performance and that of its committees and individual directors; and

- all directors should be submitted for re-election at regular intervals, subject to continued satisfactory performance. The board should ensure planned and progressive refreshing of the board.

As far as the chairmen of smaller quoted and AIM companies are concerned, these principles should apply universally. Also, they are just as relevant for chairmen of private companies, certainly so far as the thrust of each principle is concerned. Any qualification in their application should be decided on the basis of the private company's particular circumstances.

5.3.1 Guidance for the chairman

The chairman is pivotal in creating the conditions for overall board and individual director effectiveness. The Higgs Review contained useful guidance for chairmen encapsulating their overall role and putting down markers to measure their effectiveness. It is produced below:

Specifically, it is the responsibility of the chairman to:

- run the board and set its agenda. The agenda should take full account of the issues and the concerns of all board members. Agendas should be forward looking and concentrate on strategic matters rather than formulaic approvals of proposals which can be the subject of appropriate delegated powers to management;

- ensure that the members of the board receive accurate, timely and clear information, in particular about the company's performance, to enable the board to take sound decisions, monitor effectively and provide advice to promote the success of the company;

- ensure effective communication with shareholders and ensure that the members of the board develop an understanding of the views of major investors;

- manage the board to ensure that sufficient time is allowed for discussion of complex or contentious issues, where appropriate arranging for informal meetings beforehand to enable thorough preparation for the board discussion. It is particularly important that non-executive directors have sufficient time to consider critical issues and are not faced with unrealistic deadlines for decision-making;

- take the lead in providing a properly constructed induction programme for new directors that is comprehensive, formal and tailored, facilitated by the company secretary;

- take the lead in identifying and meeting the development needs of individual directors, with the company secretary having a key role in facilitating provision. It is the responsibility of the chairman to address the development needs of the board as a whole with a view to enhancing the overall effectiveness as a team;

- ensure that the performance of individuals and of the board as a whole and its committees is evaluated at least once a year; and

- encourage active engagement by all the members of the board.

The effective chairman:

- upholds the highest standards of integrity and probity;

- sets the agenda, style and tone of board discussions to promote effective decision-making and constructive debate;

- promotes effective relationships and open communication, both inside and outside the boardroom, between non-executive directors and the executive team;

- builds an effective and complementary board, initiating change and planning succession in board appointments, subject to board and shareholders' approval;

- promotes the highest standards of corporate governance and seeks compliance with the provisions of the Code wherever possible;

- ensures a clear structure for and the effective running of board committees;

- ensures effective implementation of board decisions;

- establishes a close relationship of trust with the chief executive, providing support and advice while respecting executive responsibility; and

- provides coherent leadership of the company, including representing the company and understanding the views of shareholders.

5.3.2 The chairman's status

A chairman has no legal status under the Companies Act and the only recognition in statute is in relation to the conduct of meetings of the board and shareholders.

The chairman of the board is appointed by the boards and it is for the board to remove him or her from office as chairman. The Articles of Association of public and private companies contain numerous references to the role of chairman, but again only in the content of meetings and board meetings.

Thus:

- the Articles give chairmen wide powers at shareholder and board meetings and usually the casting vote;

- there is no statutory requirement for the chairman to be a director, but the Articles usually prescribe it; and

- appointments in contravention of the Articles are invalid, and a casting vote is ineffective.

As chairman of the company he or she:

- presides at shareholders meetings;

- has a common law duty:
    - to act in good faith in the interests of the company;
    - to preserve order;

-     to ensure business is transacted effectively and in accordance
      with the Articles;
-     to call on members to speak and then to ascertain the will of
      the meeting;
-     to be mindful of minority rights;
-     to ensure the venue for meetings is suitable;
-     to deal with points of order immediately; and
-     to use his or her discretion as to whether a person should be
      ejected.

A chairman's ruling on a point of order is final, but may be challenged in
the courts if it is in breach of the Articles or is unreasonable.

A chairman may adjourn a meeting without consent in order to preserve
order. However, the adjournment must not last longer than is reasonably
necessary to restore order; otherwise consent is needed.

5.4 THE BOARD'S ROLE

The board's role as set out in the Code was described at **5.2**.

Sir Adrian Cadbury, in his book *The Company Chairman*[1] summarised
the responsibilities of chairmen to their boards as follows:

> 'The chairman has the responsibilities to ensure that the board—
> • provides leadership and vision
> • has the appropriate balance of membership
> • performs effectively.'

He pointed out that 'the heart of the job of chairman is to get the best out
of their boards', at the same time being careful not to underestimate the
challenge which this presents to chairmen. Meeting this challenge
demands the highest levels of competence and skill on their part.

It is the board leadership of the company that drives growth and the
increase in value for shareholders. Sir John Harvey-Jones, in his book
Making it Happen,[2] summed up a board's responsibility for leadership of
the company as follows:

> 'The business that is not being purposefully led in a clear direction which is
> understood by its people is not going to survive (and all of history shows
> this is the case).'

---

[1]   Sir Adrian Cadbury *Corporate Governance and Chairmanship* (Oxford University Press,
      2002).
[2]   John Harvey-Jones *Making it Happen* (Collins, 1988).

Sir Adrian Cadbury in *Corporate Governance and Chairmanship*[3] summarised the main functions of the board as follows:

- to define the company's purpose;

- to agree strategies and plans for achieving that purpose;

- to establish the company's policies;

- to appoint the chief executive;

- to monitor and assess the performance of the executive team; and

- to assess the board's own performance.

That these functions are carried out successfully is ultimately the responsibility of the chairman.

The chairman's task to run board meetings in an effective manner is a challenge in itself and not the subject of this book. Cadbury's 'Corporate Governance and Chairmanship' is an excellent source of help, and, for private company boards particularly, Patrick Dunne's *Running Board Meetings*[4] is a valuable resource.

5.4.1 Matters reserved for the board

A list of matters which should be presented to the board, taken from the QCA Guidance for smaller quoted companies, is produced at Appendix 10. This list also applies to AIM companies. A shorter one for private companies was provided at **2.6.2** of Chapter 2, 'The Governance of AIM listed and Private Companies'.

Matters reserved for the board are grouped under four main headings:

- **Management structure and appointments**
  This mainly includes people-related issues at board and senior management levels, delegation of the board's powers, and matters to be referred to the board for decision.

- **Policy and strategy**
  Business strategy risk management and internal controls form the core of matters for the board under this heading.

- **Transactions**
  This mainly covers substantial transactions which have significant implication for the company, e g a major acquisition or disposal.

---

[3]   Ibid.
[4]   Patrick Dunne *Running Board Meetings* (Kogan Page, 2nd edn, 1999).

- **Finance**
  Finance covers all funding and treasury matters, financial reporting including the appointment of auditors, dividend policy and operating budgets.

5.5 THE COMPANY SECRETARY

It is sometimes said that the most underestimated people in business are the company secretaries. This statement contains more than a grain of truth. Company secretaries play an important role, making a significant contribution to the proper functioning of the board and are a source of information and other support to individual directors. In particular, the company secretary is an invaluable support to the chairman.

The Companies Act 2006 states that a private company is not required to have a secretary (s 270), but that a public company must have a secretary (s 271). This appointment is the responsibility of the board of directors, yet despite this legal requirement the law does not state explicitly what the company secretary should do once appointed.

The company secretary's role, nevertheless, is generally accepted as concerning three main areas:

- the board;

- the company; and

- the shareholders.

Within each the role can be very diverse and in smaller companies the company secretary is more likely to be involved in a wider range of administrative duties than his or her counterpart in larger companies. Also in smaller quoted and AIM companies it is not uncommon for the finance director to also be the company secretary. In any event the company secretary is deemed in law to be an officer of the company.

The ICSA list the core duties of the company secretary as falling into the following categories, ie dealing with:

- board meetings;

- general meetings;

- Memorandum and Articles of Association;

- stock exchange requirements;

- statutory registers;

- statutory returns;

- reports and accounts;

- share registration;

- shareholder monitoring;

- share and capital issues;

- acquisitions, disposals and mergers;

- company seal; and

- registered office.

In addition to playing a central role in the administration of a company's affairs implied by this list of core duties the company secretary also plays a central role in corporate governance.

5.5.1   The company secretary's role in corporate governance

The company secretary's role in corporate governance comes very much to the fore in the application of the Code's Main Principle A.5, 'Information and Professional Development':

> 'The board should be supplied in a timely manner with information in a form and of a quality appropriate to enable it to discharge its duties. All directors should receive induction on joining the board and should regularly update and refresh their skills and knowledge.'

Whilst the primary responsibility for corporate governance and application of the Code rests with the board, and particularly with the chairman, in practice it is the company secretary who shoulders the administrative responsibility.

To that end Supporting Principle to A.5 states that:

> 'The company secretary should be responsible for advising the board through the chairman on all governance matters.'

The effectiveness of the company secretary in corporate governance will therefore hinge to a large extent on the quality of his or her working relationship with the chairman. Further, though there may be certain matters on which the company secretary reports to the chief executive, this should not in any way undermine his or her responsibility to the board on all matters of corporate governance.

The Supporting Principles to A.5 crystallise the role of the company secretary in corporate governance as follows:

> 'Under the direction of the chairman, the company secretary's responsibilities include ensuring that good information flows within the board and its committees, and between senior management and non-executive directors, as well as facilitating induction and assisting with professional development as required.'

Professional development of directors, executive and non-executive, is probably an area to which smaller quoted, AIM and private companies pay least attention. In light of a director's responsibilities and legal obligations this is somewhat foolhardy. The director's role performed effectively demands a high level of skills and knowledge which need to be refreshed and honed from time to time.

All directors should have access to the advice and services of the company secretary (A.5.3). Through ensuring the flow of good information and being a source of independent advice and guidance on regulatory and legal matters, for example, the company secretary is able to support and enhance the effectiveness of the non-executive directors. Given the important role non-executives play in corporate governance, this places the company secretary in a pivotal position.

It was pointed out earlier that, in smaller companies, the roles of company secretary and finance director are sometimes combined. Higgs pointed out the dangers in their combination and how to deal with them:

> 'Around 40% of companies outside the FTSE-350 combine the roles [of company secretary and finance director]. There are obvious tensions in this in the context of impartiality and information provision. It is therefore desirable for [larger] companies, who are able, to separate the roles, and for smaller companies with limited resources to recognise the potential for conflict of interest and to build "Chinese walls" between the roles by ensuring that information received in one capacity is not used for other purposes.'

It is therefore critical to safeguard the integrity of the position of company secretary so that objectivity is not compromised in any way.

The company secretary fills a key role in corporate governance. The Companies Act places a legal obligation on the directors of smaller quoted and AIM companies to appoint a company secretary. The Code makes this explicit in A.5.3:

> 'Both the appointment and removal of the company secretary should be a matter for the board as a whole.'

5.5.2 Board minutes

It is standard practice for the company secretary to administer and attend board meetings (if they do not do so by right in their capacity as a director, eg finance director), and also to prepare minutes of board meetings. Well conducted board meetings, central to good corporate governance, are primarily the responsibility of the chairman who must also ensure that board decisions are properly minuted.

The 2006 Act in s 248 states that every company must cause minutes of all proceedings at meetings of its directors to be recorded. Further, that records must be kept for at least 10 years from the date of the meeting. If a company fails to comply with this section, an offence is committed and every officer of the company is in default.

In respect of minutes as evidence, s 249 states that minutes recorded in accordance with the above section, if purporting to be authenticated by the chairman of the meeting or by the chairman of the next directors' meeting, are evidence of the proceedings at the meeting. The meeting is deemed to have duly taken place, and all appointments at the meeting deemed valid.

The minimum requirements for board minutes should only be that they clearly state the decision reached and actions to be taken. This should be the benchmark. Of necessity, board minutes are a summary and can never in practice emulate the thoroughness with which important board papers should be prepared. Cadbury in *Corporate Governance and Chairmanship* advises that:

> 'In drafting the board minutes company secretaries need to ensure they record the board decisions but offer no hostages to fortune should they be called in evidence by any of the regulatory authorities.'

There is also the issue of inadvertently revealing commercially confidential information to be considered.

The Code's reference to the minutes arises where a director has concerns which cannot be resolved to his or her satisfaction:

> 'Where directors have concerns which cannot be resolved about the running of the company or a proposed action, they should ensure that their concerns are recorded in the board minutes. On resignation, a non-executive director should provide a written statement to the chairman, for circulation to the board, if they have any such concerns.' (A.1.4)

5.6   BOARD EFFECTIVENESS

In **5.4**, on the board's role, it was pointed out that one of the three key responsibilities of chairmen to their boards is to ensure that the board performs effectively. This is crucial to good governance. Although not specifically aimed at smaller companies, the following checklist has stood the test of time as a prompt for chairmen in thinking about how their boards are performing.

The late Hugh Parker of McKinsey had this to say about measuring board effectiveness in his 'Letters to a New Chairman' (Director Publications, 1990):

> 'I have developed a check-list of six questions that I believe can be used by a chairman to test the effectiveness of his own board – and from that, as a starting-point, to decide what can be done to improve it.
>
> 1.   Has the board recently (or indeed ever) devoted significant time and serious thought to the company's longer-term objectives, and to the strategic options open to it for achieving them? If so, have these deliberations resulted in a board consensus or decision on its future objectives and strategies, and have these been put in writing?
>
> 2.   Has the board consciously thought about and reached formal conclusions on what is sometimes referred to as its basic "corporate philosophy" – i.e. its value system, its ethical and social responsibilities, its desired "image" and so forth? If so have these conclusions been codified or embodied in explicit statements of policy – for example, in respect of terms of employment, etc.? Does the company have formal procedures for recording and promulgating major board decisions as policy guidelines for down-the-line managers?
>
> 3.   Does the board periodically review the organisational structure of the company, and consider how this may have to change in future? Does it review and approve all senior appointments as a matter of course? Are adequate "human resource development" programmes in place?
>
> 4.   Does the board routinely receive all the information it needs to ensure that it is in effective control of the company and its management? Have there been any "unpleasant surprises" – for example, unfavourable results or unforeseen crises – that could be attributed to lack of timely or accurate information?
>
> 5.   Does the board routinely require the managing director to present his annual plans and budgets for their review and approval? Does the board regularly monitor the performance of the managing director and his immediate subordinate managers in terms of actual results achieved against agreed plans and budgets?
>
> 6.   When the board is required to take major decisions on questions of future objectives, strategies, policies, major investments, senior appointments etc., does it have adequate time and knowledge to make these decisions soundly – rather than finding itself overtaken by events and, in effect, obliged to rubber-stamp decisions already taken or commitments already made?

If the answers to all these questions are affirmative, it is safe to say that you have an effective board. If the answers are negative – or perhaps not clear – then you already have some indications of what needs to be done to strengthen your board.'

5.6.1   Board size and balance

The Supporting Principle to A.3 of the Code puts the point to be made on board size succinctly:

> 'The board should not be so large as to be unwieldy. The board should be of sufficient size that the balance of skills and experience is appropriate for the requirements of the business.'

However, for smaller quoted companies under the Code (and for AIM companies) the size of the board is influenced by the requirement for at least two independent non-executive directors in addition to the chairman (A.3.2). This minimum number of independent non-executives is also demanded for compliance with the composition of board committees under the Code. Committees of the board are dealt with in **5.7**.

This qualification to the composition of boards could result in a board of undue size for a smaller company, in addition to the extra costs of directors' fees. The guidance to be applied in order to keep such boards to a manageable size is for the chairman to be included as one of the independent non-executive directors. With proper explanation, institutional shareholders accept this position provided there is an intention on the part of the company to rectify the position as the company grows and develops. It is for the company to keep the position under review.

5.6.2   Board performance evaluation

The Code includes as a Main Principle (A.6) the need for the board to undertake a formal and rigorous annual evaluation of its own performance and that of its committees and individual directors, and to state in the company's annual report how this evaluation has been conducted (A.6.1).

Board reviews are the responsibility of the chairman and can sometimes be regarded as a sensitive area to be avoided altogether in some extreme cases. This is inadvisable (in addition to being in contravention of the Code), if for no other reason that the opportunity is lost to identify and correct any weaknesses so that time devoted to board meetings is well spent. For convenience this section includes performance evaluation of committees of the board and individual directors, including the chairman him or herself. Evaluating the performance of individual non-executive directors was included in Chapter 4, 'The Non-executive Director'.

The chairman's responsibility begins with selecting a process of evaluation, and at the outset this boils down to the choice between conducting the review internally or using an external third party. The latter choice has the advantage of bringing objectivity to the process. However, the necessary degree of objectivity to make the process effective is not necessarily lost if the process is conducted without the help of an external party. It is for the chairman to set the right 'tone' to ensure that a review conducted internally is satisfactory. Most smaller companies appear to opt for an internal review and, provided objectivity is preserved, this is acceptable and also understandable.

As to the review process itself, the choice is again between two alternatives, which broadly speaking are either a structured or a less structured approach. Again it is for the chairman, carrying the board with him or her, to decide. The following guidance, taken from the Higgs Review, lists some of the questions that should be considered in a performance evaluation. They are, however, by no means definitive or exhaustive and companies will need to tailor the questions to suit their own needs and circumstances.

The responses to these questions and others should enable boards to assess how they are performing and to identify how certain elements of their performance areas might be improved.

Guidance on board performance evaluation

- How well has the board performed against any performance objectives that have been set?

- What has been the board's contribution to the testing and development of strategy?

- What has been the board's contribution to ensuring robust and effective risk management?

- Is the composition of the board and its committees appropriate, with the right mix of knowledge and skills to maximise performance in the light of future strategy? Are inside and outside the board relationships working effectively?

- How has the board responded to any problems or crises that have emerged and could or should these have been foreseen?

- Are the matters specifically reserved for the board the right ones?

- How well does the board communicate with the management team, company employees and others? How effectively does it use mechanisms such as the AGM and the annual report?

- Is the board as a whole up to date with latest developments in the regulatory environment and the market?

- How effective are the board's committees? (Specific questions on the performance of each committee should be included such as, for example, their role, their composition and their interaction with the board.)

The processes that help underpin the board's effectiveness should also be evaluated, e.g.:

- Is appropriate, timely information of the right length and quality provided to the board and is management responsive to requests for clarification or amplification? Does the board provide helpful feedback to management on its requirements?

- Are sufficient board and committee meetings of appropriate length held to enable proper consideration of issues? Is time used effectively?

- Are board procedures conducive to effective performance and flexible enough to deal with all eventualities?

In addition, there are some specific issues relating to the chairman which should be included as part of an evaluation of the board's performance, e.g.:

- Is the chairman demonstrating effective leadership of the board?

- Are relationships and communications with shareholders well managed?

- Are relationships and communications within the board constructive?

- Are the processes for setting the agenda working? Do they enable board members to raise issues and concerns?

- Is the company secretary being used appropriately and to maximum value?

The results of board evaluation should be shared with the board as a whole, while the results of individual assessments should remain confidential between the chairman and director concerned.

The Supporting Principle to A.6 points out that:

> 'Individual evaluation should aim to show whether each director continues to contribute effectively and to demonstrate commitment to the role (including commitment of time for board and committee meetings and any other duties). The chairman should act on the results of the performance evaluation by recognising the strengths and addressing the weakness of the board and, where appropriate, proposing new members to be appointed to the board or seeking the resignation of directors.'

5.7 BOARD COMMITTEES

From a practical point of view there is one good reason for forming committees of the board: they can make the board's task more manageable. This reason lies alongside the Code requirements for board committees, namely the audit, remuneration and nomination committees.

The status of board committees was succinctly described by Cadbury in *Corporate Governance and Chairmanship*. His description stands as a guiding principle for smaller (as well as larger) companies:

> 'They [board committees] are established by the board. Their terms of reference and membership are set by the board. They report their recommendations to the board, which is responsible for deciding on their implementation. Board committees have no powers of their own, except where the board has delegated powers to them. Authority, therefore, remains with the board, which is responsible for ensuring that the terms of reference of their committees are clear and that they are reviewed annually. It is up to the chairmen of board committees to keep their committees within their bounds.'

The Code requires two of the three corporate governance committees, namely the audit and remuneration committees, to be wholly comprised of independent non-executive directors, and for independent non-executive directors to be in the majority on the nomination committee. It is through membership of these committees that independent non-executive directors are able to make a particular and valuable contribution to the governance of the company. For smaller companies, especially, this should not be at the expense of the value they can also bring, working with the executive on the development of strategy and growth of the company.

The Code requirements for and the functioning of the audit, remuneration and nomination committees under the Code were considered in Chapter 1, 'Corporate Governance and the Combined

Code'. Below is a summary of composition criteria for each of the committees as it applies to smaller quoted (and AIM) companies:

- **audit** – a minimum of two members who should all be independent non-executive directors. The board should also satisfy itself that at least one member of the audit committee has recent and relevant finance experience;

- **remuneration** – a minimum of two members who should all be independent non-executive directors; and

- **nomination** – a majority of the members should be independent non-executive directors.

Without prejudicing the integrity of good corporate governance, the circumstances of smaller companies, particularly those with small boards, need to be taken into account when applying the Code's requirements on board committees. The following points serve to introduce flexibility to governance arrangements so far as board committees are concerned, so that they are workable for smaller companies:

- the chairman may be considered one of the independent non-executive directors so that the requirement for a minimum of two members is satisfied;

- however, except in the case of the nomination committee, the chairman should not be chairman of any committee;

- it is reasonable for the chairman to be appointed chairman of the nomination committee given his or her responsibility for the board as a whole;

- the chairman should not, however, be chairman of the nomination committee when the committee is dealing with the appointment of his or her successor;

- provided the criteria for the nomination committee above are respected, it is not unreasonable for the whole board to be the nomination committee;

- given the limitation of a small board, it is likely that the same two persons (in the case of a very small board) will comprise all three committees.

Detailed guidance on the three committees has been drawn up by the ICSA and is reproduced in full in Appendix 11 (Remuneration Committee), Appendix 12 (Audit Committee) and Appendix 13 (Nomination Committee). This guidance contains the relevant links to the

Code and Model Terms of Reference for each of the Committees. The guidance is comprehensive in each case and smaller companies are advised to tailor the guidance to their particular circumstances, whilst adhering to the basic principles.

Practical examples of board committees and their operation are illustrated at **6.2** – 'Corporate Governance Reporting'.

CHAPTER 6

SHAREHOLDERS AND CORPORATE GOVERNANCE

6.1 INTRODUCTION

The chapters so far have dealt with the principles of corporate governance and applied them to the running of a smaller company. At the core has been a focus on the board and its directors, who have the ultimate responsibility for the direction and control of the business and are accountable to the shareholders as the company's owners.

Corporate governance is a model of two parts – the company and its shareholders, and, as pointed out in Chapter 1, it is for shareholders to evaluate the company's corporate governance arrangements. To that extent the viability of the Code's 'comply or explain' regime, which underpins the principles-based approach to corporate governance and keeps regulation at bay, is in the hands of the shareholder. Therefore the nub of principles-based corporate governance is communication between company boards and shareholders.

For smaller companies in particular (and for companies generally) it is crucial that this basis for governance prevails, more or too much regulation can lead to the unintended consequence of stifling innovation and entrepreneurship, sounding the death knell for the smaller company. But there is a further important reason why corporate governance and its relationship with shareholders matters, and this lies with raising capital to finance the company's operations.

Although the link between corporate governance and raising capital is difficult to establish scientifically, scrutiny of the behaviour of institutional shareholders shows that a company's corporate governance is important to their decision to invest. It is a condition of listing on the main market by smaller quoted companies that they adopt the Code and apply the corporate governance principles if capital is to be raised from institutional shareholders by this means. The same has been pointed out for AIM companies. This apart, what in particular do institutional shareholders focus on when reviewing a smaller company's corporate governance arrangements before making the decision to invest? This is discussed later in this chapter.

The first part of this chapter considers communication on corporate governance between institutional shareholders and smaller company boards. It is divided into:

- reporting on corporate governance arrangements by companies in their annual reports; and

- engagement between company boards and institutional shareholders, which requires dialogue between the two parties.

6.2 CORPORATE GOVERNANCE REPORTING[1]

6.2.1 Smaller quoted companies

For smaller quoted companies under the Code, corporate governance disclosure requirements are set out in three places:

- the Financial Services Authority (FSA) Listing Rule 9.8.6, which also includes the 'comply or explain' requirement. This Listing Rule was described in **1.5.1** of Chapter 1;

- the FSA Disclosure and Transparency Rules, Section 7.1 and 7.2, which set out certain mandatory disclosures; and

- the Code. In addition to providing an explanation where they choose not to comply with a Provision, companies must disclose specified information in order to comply with certain provisions.

The Disclosure and Transparency Rules and the Code requirements in Schedule C: Disclosure of Corporate Governance Arrangements of the Combined Code, are reproduced at Appendix 14. There is some overlap between the mandatory disclosures required under the Disclosure and Transparency Rules and those expected under the Combined Code. Areas of overlap are summarised in the Appendix to this Schedule. In respect of disclosures relating to the audit committee and the composition and operation of the board and its committees, compliance with the relevant provisions of the Code will result in compliance with the relevant Rules.

Listing Rule 9.8.6 R states that in the case of a listed company incorporated in the UK, the following items must be included in its annual report and accounts:

---

[1] New provisions on company communications to shareholders and others in the Companies Act 2006, which include provisions facilitating communications in electronic form and by means of a website, came into effect on 20 January 2007. ICSA's 'Guidance on Electronic Communications with Shareholders 2007' may be obtained from the ICSA website (see Useful Websites).

(1) a statement of how the listed company has applied the Main Principles set out in Section 1 of the Combined Code, in a manner that would enable shareholders to evaluate how the principles have been applied;

(2) a statement as to whether the listed company has:
   (a) complied throughout the accounting period with all relevant provisions set out in Section 1 of the Combined Code; or
   (b) not complied throughout the accounting period with all relevant provisions set out in Section 1 of the Combined Code and if so, setting out:
       (i)   those provisions, if any, it has not complied with;
       (ii) in the case of provisions whose requirements are of a continuing nature, the period within which, if any, it did not comply with some or all of those provisions; and
       (iii) the company's reasons for now non-compliance.

Following the requirements of Listing Rule 9.8.6 R above is intended to provide shareholders with a clear and comprehensive picture of a company's governance arrangements. The Financial Reporting Council's Preamble to the Code (June 2008) contains the following useful guidance on application of the Listing Rule and the response from shareholders:

'Main Principles

In relation to the requirement to state how it has applied the Code's main principles, where a company has done so by complying with the associated provisions it should be sufficient simply to report that this is the case; copying out the principles in the annual report adds to its length without adding to its value. But where a company has taken additional actions to apply the principles or otherwise improve its governance, it would be helpful to shareholders to describe these in the annual report.

[Note – There is no prescribed format for describing how a company has applied corporate governance principles.]

Provisions

If a company chooses not to comply with one or more provisions of the Code, it must give shareholders a careful and clear explanation which shareholders should evaluate on its merits. In providing an explanation, the company should aim to illustrate how its actual practices are consistent with the principle to which the particular provision relates and contribute to good governance.

Smaller listed companies, in particular those new to listing, may judge that some of the provisions are disproportionate or less relevant in their case. Some of the provisions do not apply to companies below the FTSE 350. Such companies may nonetheless consider that it would be appropriate to adopt this approach in the Code and they are encouraged to do so.

Shareholders

Shareholders should pay due regard to a companyies' individual circumstances and bear in mind in particular the size and complexity of the company and the nature of the risks and challenges it faces. Whilst shareholders have every right to challenge a company's explanations if they are unconvincing, they should not be evaluated in a mechanistic way and departures from the Code should not be automatically treated as breaches. Institutional shareholders should be careful to respond to the statements from companies in a manner that support the "comply or explain" principle and bear in mind the purpose of good corporate governance. They should put their views to the company and be prepared to enter a dialogue if they do not accept the company's position. Institutional shareholders should be prepared to put such views in writing where appropriate.'

The June 2008 edition of the Code (see Appendix 1) took effect at the same time as new FSA Corporate Governance Rules implementing European requirements relating to audit committees and corporate governance statements. The relevant sections of these Rules are summarised in Appendix 14. There is some overlap between the content of the Code and the Rules. However, where a company chooses to explain rather than comply with the Code, it will need to demonstrate that it nonetheless meets the minimum requirements set out in the Rules.

A checklist for corporate governance reporting is provided at Appendix 15. The Main Principles and the Code provisions are collected in one document to assist with the corporate governance narrative on application of the principles and the statement on compliance or non-compliance with the provisions. Further assistance with explaining application of the principles may be sought by reference to the Supporting Principles in Section 1 of the Code at Appendix 1.

Guidance on reporting requirements on remuneration in accordance with 'The Directors' Remuneration Report Regulations 2002' is provided by the ICSA 'Guidance on Listed Company Reporting Requirements for Directors' Remuneration' which is reproduced at Appendix 16.

6.2.1.1   *Auditor's report on corporate governance*

The FSA Listing Rules require that the auditors of a smaller quoted company review compliance with nine provisions of the Code and report on any non-compliance. The review relates to Code Provisions:

(a)   C.1.1;

(b)   C.2.1; and

(c)   C.3.1 to C.3.7.

These provisions may be found in Section 1 of The Combined Code on Corporate Governance (June 2008) at Appendix 1.

6.2.1.2   Corporate governance reporting in practice

Alexandra plc

An example of corporate governance reporting in practice is taken from the 31 January 2008 Annual Report of Alexandra plc, a 'fledgling' FTSE small cap company. Alexandra is an international supplier of workplace clothing with revenue of £78m.

The corporate governance statement is presented under the following headings:

- Directors;

- Board committees;

- Remuneration committee;

- Relations with shareholders;

- Accountability and audit; and

- Audit committee.

Alexandra is also an example of a company with a small board of two executive and two non-executive directors. Both of the non-executive directors, which includes the chairman, are considered independent and both comprise the remuneration and audit committees. Due to the company's size the board does not consider a permanent nomination committee to be appropriate. Instead, such a committee is formed as required.

The Company's corporate governance statement is presented below.

'CORPORATE GOVERNANCE

The Group manages its affairs in accordance with the principles of corporate governance contained in the Combined Code on Corporate Governance ("Combined Code") issued by the Financial Services Authority in July 2003 and updated in June 2006.

This statement describes how the principles of Good Governance have been applied to the Group, including both the main Principles and the Supporting Principles as described in section 1 of the Combined Code. This should be read in conjunction with the Report on the Directors' Remuneration, which covers the Principles on Directors' Remuneration.

The Group has complied with the provisions set out in Section 1 of the Combined Code throughout the year except where indicated below.

DIRECTORS

The Board currently comprises two Executive and two Non-Executive Directors. Their details including information on their backgrounds are set out on page 17. The Board has a wide range of experience and in the case of the Non-Executive Directors independence which is invaluable in the Board's deliberations. During the year Mr C A Marsh was appointed as Non-Executive Director of Structured Investment Products plc and CVS Group plc. These changes will not have any significant impact on his commitment to the Group. The Directors consider that the current size of the Board is appropriate for the requirements of the business.

Ms E New was appointed on 19 April 2006 and the Board has concluded that she is independent on the basis of the criteria specified in paragraph A.3.1 of the Combined Code and generally. Ms E New is the Senior Independent Director.

There is a clear delineation of responsibility between the Chairman, Chief Executive and the other Directors. The Chairman is responsible for the effective running of the Board whilst the Chief Executive is responsible for operating the business and implementing the Board's strategies and policies.

Directors have the right to seek independent professional advice in the furtherance of their duties at the Company's expense. In addition, all the Directors have access to the advice and services of the Company Secretary who is responsible to the Board for ensuring agreed procedures, rules and regulations are followed.

The business of the Group is managed by the Board of Directors, which met formally ten times during the year. All Directors attended all meetings with the exception of Ms E New who did not attend two meetings in July 2007 and December 2007. The meetings follow a formal agenda covering matters specifically reserved for decision by the Board. These include key areas of the Group's affairs such as overall strategy, organisational and compliance issues, acquisition policy, approval of annual and interim results and budgets, major capital expenditure programmes and financing issues. The Board also reviews trading performance and receives regular reports and presentations on all aspects of the business. To enable the Board to discharge its duties, all Directors receive appropriate and timely information. Briefing papers are distributed by the Company Secretary to all Directors in advance of the Board meetings. In addition, there is frequent contact between meetings to progress the Group's business.

The Executive management team have the responsibility of implementing the strategies and policies determined by the Board and monitoring the operational and financial performance of the business against budgets and forecasts.

During the year there were no formal performance evaluations of the Board and its Committees. However, the contribution by the Directors to the Board and its Committees was reviewed informally. The Board intends to formalise a programme of performance evaluation during the current year.

In accordance with the Company's Articles of Association, one third of the Directors submit themselves for re-election each year at the Annual General Meeting so that each Director seeks re-election at least triennially. New Directors appointed during the year, and Non-Executive Directors who are not independent, seek re-appointment at the next Annual General Meeting.

BOARD COMMITTEES

The Board has appointed two formal committees: the Audit Committee and the Remuneration Committee, each of which operate within clearly defined terms of reference.

Due to its size, the Board does not consider a permanent Nomination Committee to be appropriate. Instead such a Committee is formed as required to assess candidates for appointment as a Director. No such Committee met during the year.

REMUNERATION COMMITTEE

The Remuneration Committee comprises the Non-Executive Directors and met four times last year. All members attended every meeting. The Code requires that the Committee is chaired by an Independent Non-Executive Director and comprises two independent Non-Executive Directors in addition to the Company Chairman. During the year and the current year to date there were only two members of the Committee, including the Chairman. Ms E New chaired the Committee. The Committee determines the contract terms, remuneration and other benefits of each of the Executive Directors. The Chief Executive normally participates in the discussions of the Remuneration Committee except when his own performance or remuneration is under review. Where appropriate, the Committee takes advice from external remuneration consultants. The Executive Directors determine the remuneration of the Non-Executive Directors. The Report on the Directors' Remuneration is set out on pages 59 to 62.

RELATIONS WITH SHAREHOLDERS

The Group encourages communication with both its institutional and private shareholders. The Chairman, Chief Executive and Finance Director undertake a formal programme of presentations to both shareholders and prospective shareholders in the periods following the: announcement of its full year and interim results and other appropriate times during the year. The Board is of the opinion that additional routine meetings with the Senior Independent Director would not assist further in the dialogue with shareholders. However, the Senior Independent Director is available to meet with shareholders at their request.

In addition to the circulation of external brokers' reports to the Board, feedback is provided to the Board and in particular the Senior Independent Director, on any issues raised by the Shareholders at these meetings.

All Directors are normally present to answer questions at the Annual General Meeting.

ACCOUNTABILITY AND AUDIT

The Board seeks to ensure that its Annual Report and other public financial statements provide a clear assessment of the Group's position. On the basis of the current financial projections and facilities available, the Directors have formed a judgement that there is a reasonable expectation that the Group has adequate resources to continue in operational existence for the foreseeable future and, accordingly, consider it is appropriate to adopt the going concern basis in preparing the financial statements.

The Directors have responsibility for the Group's systems of internal control and for regularly reviewing its effectiveness. It is recognised that such a system is designed to manage rather than eliminate the risk of business objectives not being achieved, and can only provide reasonable and not absolute assurance against material misstatement or loss.

An ongoing process for identifying, evaluating and managing the significant risks faced by the Group has been established and was operational throughout the year to 31 January 2008. The process is regularly reviewed by the Board and accords with 'Internal Control – Guidance for Directors on the Combined Code' produced by the Turnbull working party. Corrective action has been taken to rectify an issue concerning stock valuation within the Group's internal management accounts during the year. This does not affect the contents of the Annual Report and Accounts.

The management of all forms of business risk is an important part of ensuring the Group creates and protects value for its shareholders. The process involves the identification of specific risks in many different areas, the assessment of those risks in terms of their potential impact, the likelihood of them materialising and then making decisions as to the most appropriate method of managing them. The latter may include regular monitoring, investment in additional resources, transfer of risk to third parties via insurance or hedging agreements and contingency planning.

The Board has reviewed the need for an internal audit function and has concluded that sufficient internal controls exist within the Group and that the operation is not large enough to warrant a dedicated internal audit function. However, the Group did undertake a number of specific audit procedures during the course of the year.

AUDIT COMMITTEE

The Audit Committee, which is chaired by Mr C A Marsh and comprises the Non-Executive Directors, met twice during the year. All members attending every meeting. Other Board members attended the Committee meetings at the invitation of the Committee Chairman. Mr C A Marsh is considered to have the most recent and relevant financial experience required for this role.

The Committee is responsible for reviewing a wide range of matters including the half year and annual financial statements before submission to the Board, corporate public announcements prior to their release and for monitoring the Internal financial controls which are in place to ensure the integrity of information reported to the shareholders. The Audit Committee advises the Board on the appointment and remuneration of the external auditors and discusses the nature, scope and results of the audit with the external auditors. In addition, the Committee reviews the performance of the Company's external auditors, Nexia Smith & Williamson LLP, and the effectiveness of their audit process.

The Committee regularly monitors the non-audit services being provided by the external auditors to ensure their objectivity and independence is not compromised. During the year the non-audit work carried out included tax compliance.

The Committee is of the opinion that the nature of this work does not prejudice the auditors' independence and objectivity, and accordingly a resolution to re-appoint Nexia Smith & Williamson LLP will be proposed at the Annual General Meeting.'

Ricardo plc

A further example of corporate governance reporting in practice by a much larger and more established FTSE small cap company is taken from the 30 June 2007 Annual Report of Ricardo plc. Ricardo, with revenue of £172m, is a leading provider of product innovation, technology, engineering and strategic consulting to the world's leading automakers, vehicle component and system manufacturers, government agencies and industry regulatory bodies.

Ricardo's corporate governance statement, 'Corporate Governance in Practice', is particularly embracing and divided into the following sections:

- Combined Code on Corporate Governance;

- board of directors;

- audit committee;

- remuneration committee;

- nomination committee;

- boards of subsidiary companies;

- shareholder communications;

- going concern;

- internal control and risk management; and

- compliance with the Code.

The Statement is comprehensive and informative. It is a good example of corporate governance reporting by a company nearer the top of the range (by size) of small caps and provides a useful comparison with the much smaller company Alexandra plc. Because of its greater length the Statement is reproduced at Appendix 17.

6.2.2 AIM companies

Whilst AIM companies do not fall under the Code they are encouraged, and for good reasons as explained in Chapter 2, to apply the principles of corporate governance as presented in the Code. Corporate Governance Guidelines for AIM companies based on the Code, and set out by the QCA in Appendix 5, are presented as the source of help for AIM companies. The Guidelines include a list of basic disclosures which are highlighted below:

Basic disclosures for AIM companies

As well as explaining how the company achieves good governance, the annual report should also include the following 'Basic Disclosures':

- a statement of how the board operates, including a high level statement of which types of decisions are to be taken by the board and which are to be delegated to management;

- the identity of the chairman, the deputy chairman (where there is one), the chief executive, the senior independent director and the chairmen and members of the nomination, audit and remuneration committees;

- the identity of those directors the Board considers to be independent and the reasons why it has determined a director to be independent notwithstanding factors which may appear to impair that status;

- the board should describe any performance evaluation procedures it applies;

- the names of directors, accompanied by sufficient biographical details (with any other relevant information) to enable shareholders to take an informed decision on the balance of the Board and the re-election of certain of them;

- the number of meetings of the Board (normally monthly) and of the Committees and individual directors' attendance at them;

- an explanation of the directors' responsibility for preparing the accounts and a statement by the auditors about their reporting responsibilities;

- a statement by the directors that the business is a going concern, with supporting assumptions or qualifications as necessary;

- an explanation to shareholders of how, if the auditor provides significant non-audit services, auditor objectivity and independence is safeguarded.

The QCA recommends that the corporate governance statement setting out how good governance is achieved should be published on the company's website.

Under the London Stock Exchange AIM Rules for Companies, published in February 2007, Rule 26 requires each AIM company, on admission, to maintain a website and lists the information to be made available, which includes, amongst other requirements:

- a description of its business;

- the names of its directors and brief biographical details of each;

- a description of the responsibilities of the members of the board of directors and details of any committees of the board of directors and their responsibilities;

- its country of incorporation and main country of operation; and

- its current constitutional documents (eg its articles of association).

The complete list of information requirements under Rule 26 may be obtained from the Exchange (see Useful Websites).

6.3   ENGAGEMENT BETWEEN COMPANY BOARDS AND INSTITUTIONAL SHAREHOLDERS

Corporate governance reporting of a high quality by companies and effective engagement between companies and their institutional share-holders are both essential to the sustainability of the 'comply or explain' basis for the Combined Code (as discussed at **6.1**). However, whilst both are communication, engagement requires dialogue and contact between the two parties.

There are two aspects to engagement on corporate governance. One, already established, is in connection with compliance or non-compliance with the Code. The other is with seeking improvements to preserve and increase shareholder value. The first aspect could be described as embodying the 'internal' or 'structural' perspective on corporate governance, and the second the 'external' or 'strategic' perspective. The second is referred to as active engagement and embodies a wider purpose, namely the enhancement of shareholder value. Both aspects are components of 'responsible' ownership by institutional shareholders.

Engagement between companies and shareholders plays a crucial part in making corporate governance work and be effective. However, so far as smaller quoted companies and AIM companies are concerned good engagement practice is not universally understood or put into effect. There is scope for much improvement, but first some key issues need to be resolved.

This section on engagement identifies the key issues and provides practical recommendations and guidelines on engagement for companies and institutional shareholders. It is based on an explanation of engagement's current status and impediments to engagement, whilst taking other perspectives on engagement into account.

The Code context for engagement is embodied in two Main Principles, one for companies and the other for institutional shareholders.

The Main Principle applying to companies states that:

> 'There should be a dialogue with shareholders based on the mutual understanding of objectives. The board as a whole has responsibility for ensuring that a satisfactory dialogue with shareholders takes place.' (D.1)

Its counterpart applying to institutional shareholders states that:

> 'Institutional shareholders should enter into a dialogue with companies based on the mutual understanding of objectives.' (E.1)

6.3.1 The current status of engagement

6.3.1.1 Overview

The code of conduct which applies to institutional shareholders, namely the Institutional Shareholders Committee's 'Responsibilities of institutional shareholders and agents – statement of principles' (which was updated in June 2007 and is produced in full in Appendix 18), includes guidelines on engagement with company boards. Institutional shareholders are required to adopt this statement of principles, and recent surveys by the Investment Management Association (IMA) and NAPF (see below) indicate that engagement activity and resources devoted to it are on the increase. However, these surveys are dealing mainly with engagement with boards of the FTSE 350 and can cover ethical, environmental and social issues as well as engagement on governance issues, ie board structure, composition and remuneration. Scanning a number of institutional shareholders' engagement policies reveals different degrees of activity and reporting, as well as, in some cases, a particular focus on social and ethical issues. It is clear from this that engagement with the boards of smaller companies, whose businesses are on a different scale to that of larger companies, needs to be given more careful consideration.

6.3.1.2 Conclusions from evidence-based research on engagement

The Foundation for Governance Research and Education (FGRE), in 2005/06, conducted preliminary research based on discussions at senior level with companies drawn from the FTSE small cap index and with governance specialists, fund managers and analysts amongst institutional shareholders.

The discussions covered questions on engagement such as:

(a) What are the points of contact between companies and shareholders?

(b) Which elements of the Code take priority alongside other key issues for engagement, such as strategy, risk management, capital structure, dividend policy?

(c) What bearing might a company's market capitalisation have on engagement activity?

The response from smaller quoted companies was that engagement is variable, ranging from good with significant shareholders to merely routine at results time and nothing more. Typically the contact is with the chief executive and finance director (when governance is rarely discussed), with little or no contact with other board members. The overall conclusion was that engagement with institutional shareholders is less than satisfactory.

Discussions with institutional shareholders showed that engagement is, in the main, by fund managers and is best described as 'varied', meaning without any pattern save for two noticeable features:

(a)   the focus on engagement with the chief executive and finance director; and

(b)   no engagement at all, apart from at results time, unless company performance deteriorates, at which point contact is stepped up significantly.

Engagement is taken more seriously at the time of the initial investment and lapses thereafter. It is also relevant to note that, for the FTSE small caps, contact with the chairman and non-executives rarely takes place outside AGMs.

In general, as far as the Code goes, institutional shareholders are mostly concerned with company board structure, composition, effectiveness and succession.

Research on AIM companies in 2007/08, sponsored by ICAS[2] and on a small sample, revealed that the majority scheduled meetings with institutional shareholders, albeit the frequency of meetings was variable. At the same time institutional investors in these AIM companies considered corporate governance to be important.

Further research by FGRE in 2007 included exploring the role company *advisers and brokers* play in the engagement process. In the view of one major company adviser:

> 'Companies need to know and engage with their more important shareholders, typically around six in number. Advisers to companies, particularly those new or relatively new to the capital markets, are in a strong position to play a key role in facilitating this engagement.'

Company advisers and brokers would seem to be in a strong position to play a key role in facilitating the engagement between boards and shareholders on governance issues. The very nature of broking has, as the primary objective, the generation of fees by encouraging and facilitating the sale and trading of shares in the client company, and all aspects of the service must, of necessity, revolve around this. At the same time, whilst putting client companies and their shareholders into contact is clearly a

---

2   C Mallin and K Ow-Yong 'Corporate Governance in Alternative Investment Market (AIM) Companies' (April 2008).

part of the service, the evidence for their encouraging this contact to facilitate engagement for discussion of governance issues is not immediately apparent. This may indicate a missed opportunity.

Anecdotal evidence from discussions with institutional shareholders on the role of company advisers and brokers is mixed. Whilst there is general acceptance that advisers and brokers are in a privileged position to facilitate proper engagement, this evidence indicates that their effectiveness in this regard is patchy.

6.3.1.3   *Financial Reporting Council (FRC) Reviews*

During September and October 2006 the FRC held a series of meetings with over 40 chairmen of FTSE 250 companies and small cap companies to hear their views on the impact of the Combined Code and other corporate governance matters. Views were mixed on how well 'comply or explain' was working, and on the quality and level of engagement between institutional shareholders and company boards. Agreeing with a conclusion of the FGRE evidence-based research, it is interesting to note that most participants also reported that institutional shareholders showed little or no interest in meeting either the chairman or the senior independent director unless there were problems with the company. The later Review of the Combined Code, published by the FRC in November 2007, whilst noting an increase in engagement activity by institutional shareholders, nevertheless revealed engagement to still be a point for concern.

6.3.1.4   *IMA Survey[3]*

In August 2007 the IMA published their fourth survey of fund managers' engagement with companies for the year ended 30 June 2006, which indicated improving levels of engagement by their members (UK asset managers) and of resources devoted to engagement. However, for the purposes of this chapter, there are two important caveats:

- the small sample size of only 33 member firms taking part in the survey, albeit their funds under management represented 32% of the market cap (as measured by the FTSE All Share Index); and

- the investee companies covered are drawn from the FTSE All Share Index and therefore do not provide a sufficiently sharp focus on engagement with FTSE small cap companies.

---

[3] 'Engagement with companies for the year ended 30 June 2006' (IMA, August 2007).

6.3.1.5   NAPF Survey[4]

The NAPF reported on their third survey of pension funds engagement with companies in August 2007. The survey was addressed to large pension funds (more than £1bn under management) and 39 responded. This survey also found increasing levels of engagement and resources devoted to engagement, but the same caveats as for the IMA survey above apply – small sample size and an insufficiently sharp focus on engagement with FTSE small cap companies.

6.3.1.6   Hermes UK Focus Fund research

Further useful insights into the engagement activities of shareholder activists can be gleaned from evidence from a clinical study of the Hermes UK Focus Fund.[5] These engagements involved contact with chairmen, CEOs and CFOs. In more than half the cases, contact was also made with other executives such as divisional managers, heads of investor relations and with non-executive board members. The objective of engagement is to bring about substantial changes to the governance structure of the target companies with a view to enhancing value. Subjects for engagement included restructuring, board changes, financial policies and, under other policies, improved investor relations for example. The study provided substantive evidence of gains from shareholder activism and suggested that well-focused engagements can result in substantial public returns to outside shareholders as well as those actually involved in the engagements.

6.3.2   Impediments to engagement

Effective engagement, particularly amongst FTSE small cap companies, is not widespread. This state of affairs could lead to the undermining of the principles-based approach to corporate governance and with it the 'comply or explain' basis for the Code if it means that a box-ticking approach to the Code is taken instead. Ineffective engagement is also an opportunity missed on the part of shareholders to work with company boards on improvement and development of their investee company's corporate governance to achieve sustainability and increase shareholder value.

However, and this applies especially to the small caps which are large in number, there are cost and resource constraints on both the company and shareholder. The issue of costs and resources (including time) is particularly acute amongst shareholders in small caps, given the size of their portfolios which can run into several hundred investee companies. The incentives to engage do not appear sufficient to encourage a more

---

4   'Pension Funds' Engagement with Companies' (NAPF, August 2007).
5   M Becht, JR Franks, C Mayer and S Rossi 'Returns to Shareholder Activism, Evidence from a Clinical Study of the Hermes UK Focus Fund' (European Corporate Governance Institute, December 2006).

proactive approach. Cost versus benefit analysis is needed to gain a better understanding of this, but FGRE's research also revealed an attitude of indifference to corporate governance amongst some UK institutional shareholders in smaller quoted companies. There is also some evidence to indicate that some fund mangers are not responsive to smaller company's requests for meetings. Further, many fund managers focus on performance relative to the Index rather than on achieving superior absolute returns. This reduces the incentive to engage. It should, however, increase the incentive to take an interest in corporate governance standards of the market as a whole.

Other impediments to engagement exist. To the extent that institutional shareholders outsource their engagement responsibilities to agents acting on their behalf, the efficiency and effectiveness of these agents is called into account. At present this is a little understood area.

Lastly, the increasing ownership of UK shares by foreign investors could result in a further impediment to engagement because of unfamiliarity with UK corporate governance, perhaps exacerbated by the distance geographically between the parties. A recent survey on share ownership by the Office of National Statistics (2006)[6] showed that investors from outside the UK owned 40% of UK shares listed on the UK Stock Exchange at the end of 2006, up from 36% at the end of 2004.

6.3.3   Other perspectives on engagement

The listed company model runs on the agency principle, where management and ownership of the company are separated. For very large companies the agency principle is tested because of the large number of shareholders. For smaller companies with a smaller number of shareholders the interests of shareholders and management should, on the face of it at least, be more easily aligned to their mutual benefit. This suggests that, in seeking more effective engagement between institutional shareholders and the boards of FTSE small cap companies, it is worth taking a look at the private equity model and the activities of hedge funds (in their shareholder activist role) to see if anything useful can be learnt. In both these cases the number of 'active' shareholders is also small.

6.3.3.1   The private equity model

Institutional investors in private equity are limited partners in funds managed by the private equity firm in their capacity of general partner. Engagement in this model is between the general partner and limited partners in contrast to the listed model, where engagement is directly between institutional shareholders and company boards. Another key differentiating feature of private equity is the short chain of

---

[6]   Source: Office for National Statistics 'Share Ownership 2006' (HMSO, 2007).

communication between the general partner and the executives of the investee company, facilitating effective engagement (as well as alignment of interests). Typically the general partner has one or more of its representatives on the investee company board.

An objective of engagement is enhanced company value. To what extent does engagement as practised in the private equity model enhance company value and is this enhancement greater than for the listed company model? The Walker Report on 'Guidelines for disclosure and transparency in private equity', published in November 2007, launched an industry-wide initiative to assess this enhanced value. Whilst the initiative overall is directed principally at promoting understanding of private equity, the resulting analysis will permit the bench-marking of private equity performance alongside that of quoted companies in the UK in comparable industry or business areas. Preliminary indications suggest that the performance of private equity has been fairly consistently stronger in terms of growth, enterprise, earnings and employment, eg a British Venture Capital Association report indicates private equity returns of 20.1% over the period 1997–2007, comfortably beating the corresponding returns for the FTSE small cap index of 6.5%. Further and rigorous analysis will be required to provide evidence to justify this proposition, why this is so, and what regulatory or other impediments might stand in the way of enhanced performance by quoted companies. This debate centres in particular on the very direct alignment of interest achieved by private equity between ownership and management, an alignment that is at least attenuated in the case of quoted companies by the complexity of regulation designed to protect owners and the integrity of the public market.

Relevant to the comparison with the private equity model is the expected hold period for an individual portfolio company. This is normally well below 10 years and most commonly in the range of 3 to 5 years before the general partner exists by means of an Initial Public Offering, sale to another private equity firm or to a strategic buyer. This holding period is not unlike that practised by long-term institutional shareholders but considerably shorter than the investment horizons of short-term investors.

It should be added that the substantive content and frequency of communication between general partner and limited partner is typically much greater than that between a listed company and its shareholders, in large part because limited partners are committed as insiders and there is no public market for trading in the asset which is the share of the fund held by the limited partner. In general, limited partners are much better informed about the position and performance of portfolio funds in which they have invested than most investors in companies which are listed.

The above provides no clear signals for engagement by institutional shareholders with smaller companies, but it may warrant further consideration. For instance, anecdotal evidence suggests that some private equity investors focus particularly on the mix of skills on the board, which might provide a useful benchmark for smaller company governance.

6.3.3.2   The hedge fund model

The striking comparison between (traditional) institutional shareholders and hedge fund activists is that the former typically engage ex-post and the latter ex-ante. Kahan and Rock[7] suggested that:

> 'Mutual fund and public pension fund activism, if it occurs, tends to be incidental and ex post: when fund management notes that portfolio companies are underperforming, or that their governance regime is deficient, they will sometimes become active. In contrast, hedge fund activism is strategic and ex ante: hedge fund managers first determine whether a company would benefit from activism, then take a position and become active.'

Undoubtedly, what we are dealing with here is active engagement by hedge funds seeking to increase shareholder value. The hedge fund engagement agenda can include seeking changes to a company's governance structures or processes, and also:

- influencing board and management decisions about the company's capital structure and its use of capital;

- influencing the company's operational strategies;

- intervening in the market for corporate control (eg calling for a company to put itself up for sale, supporting or opposing a proposed take-over or merger).

Managers of activist hedge funds identify companies that present high value opportunities for engagement. Various researchers have tried to identify the factors that appear to attract engagement by activist hedge funds. Frequently mentioned factors include the following:

- size of company – the smaller the market capitalisation of the company the lower the volume of the investment needed. On the other hand, larger companies are increasingly becoming the subjects of engagement as hedge funds increase the value of their assets under management and therefore have sufficient capital to invest large sums in larger companies;

- cash rich companies;

---

7   M Kahan and EB Rock 'Hedge Funds in Corporate Governance and Corporate Control' (University of Pennsylvania Law School, July 2006).

- companies with low leverage;

- companies with a poor share price performance;

- perceived discrepancies between company asset and market values;

- management/governance weaknesses. Interestingly enough, however, for activist hedge funds, weak management and governance processes and structures are relevant but not sufficient reasons in themselves to select a company for engagement. In addition, there must be short- to medium-term opportunities to realise an increase in long-term value;

- excessive premiums on proposed acquisitions – if market participants conclude that the company is proposing to pay too much for another company or other asset the stock price of the proposed acquirer is likely to fall, thereby attracting activists who now consider the acquired stock to be under valued.

What, therefore, might be learnt for engagement with FTSE small cap companies by institutional shareholders from the hedge fund model? First, the incentive is increased shareholder value, suggesting that engagement brings an economic benefit. Secondly, engagement is more nearly a continuing activity (for as long as the shareholding exists). Thirdly, the focus is on those governance issues which are relevant, in the particular circumstances of the company under consideration, for sustainability and the increase of shareholder value.

6.3.4 A case study on engagement

Wyevale Garden Centres ('Wyevale') is an example of constructive engagement which resulted in increased shareholder value.

Founded in 1961, Wyevale is the UK's leading independent garden chain. The company has been the pioneer in the garden chain sector from its original site in the 1960s and modelled itself on trends from the US. Having grown organically to 14 sites, the company listed in 1987 to fund its growth and made acquisitions in a fragmented industry. Subsequently the company completed a series of acquisitions, culminating in the purchase of major rival Country Gardens in 2000.

The company was delisted in May 2006 upon acquisition by a consortium led by West Coast Capital, the investment vehicle of retail entrepreneur, Tom Hunter. The last full year results as a listed company showed sales of £193m, generating a pre-tax profit of £15m (for the previous year pre-tax profit was £21m on sales of £190m).

Hermes, through its UK small companies focus fund, became an investor in Wyevale in December 2003 buying in at 338.5p per share. In total Hermes now held 5.5% of Wyevale's share capital and cited a number of reasons why, in their view, the shares were at a discount to fair value. These included:

(a)   poor governance;

(b)   over payment for acquisitions;

(c)   investor confidence at a low because of a series of profit warnings;

(d)   losing focus as a specialist retailer;

(e)   outmoded retail skills; and

(f)   weak financial discipline and insufficient focus on shareholder value.

The company had a history of poor investor relations and of limited engagement with their investor base.

The engagement programme initiated by Hermes and promoted to both executive and non-executive members of the board over a long period of time, began with a meeting and presentation of the issues to the chairman in April 2004. It may be summarised as follows:

•   to establish a succession plan at chairman level;

•   to construct a programme for the sale of underperforming stores, many sitting on highly valuable freehold edge-of-town sites to release significant capital for investment in refurbishment of the remaining stores;

•   to examine the capital structure with a view to establishing and articulating a clear capital allocation strategy;

•   to strengthen the executive management team at board level; and

•   to support the future acquisition of large stores where much higher returns could be earned from being in more powerful destinations.

In the event, the then chairman stepped down and a successor was appointed. Also a new chief executive, chief operations officer and marketing director were introduced to drive change.

Continuing support for the board, based on an ongoing dialogue with the new chairman, particularly over the months leading up to the bid by West Coast Capital, ensured a successful outcome. After buying in at 338.5p per share, the consortium led by West Coast Capital acquired Wyevale for 555p per share, representing an increase in shareholder value of some 64%.

6.3.5 The key issues on engagement

Engagement requires more than just contact between the parties. It must include dialogue.

In practice there are different degrees of engagement ranging from dialogue to explain a departure from the Code to more active engagement with the objective of increasing shareholder value. Here the dialogue is usually aimed at seeking a change in behaviour and recognises that people are at the heart of governance issues. The dialogue must be a positive and worthwhile experience for both parties, company and institutional shareholders.

(1) Where does the responsibility for initiating engagement lie – with company boards or institutional shareholders?
  (a) Arguably with company boards in the first instance because they are naturally most familiar with the company's circumstances. Institutional shareholders should nevertheless be prepared to initiate the engagement. Active shareholders will, as likely as not, take the initiative with companies that are considered to be underperforming, ie where there is an opportunity to increase shareholder value or a need to arrest decline in shareholder value.
  (b) However, for company boards to identify those key shareholders for engagement can prove a challenge because of the diversity of types of shareholding arising from today's composition of capital markets and array of investment instruments.
  (c) Engagement should not, on the other hand, be in any sense mandatory. Well-run companies, complying with the Code and providing reports of high quality, should not be requested to spend time, and their institutional shareholders time, on engagement. Consideration should be given to reducing the reporting and regulatory burdens for such companies, releasing more time to be spent on managing and growing the business.

(2) Should the engagement be with the fund manager or governance specialist? There are some important issues underlying this question, amongst which the most fundamental are:
  (a) the need to draw a distinction between fund managers as traders, ie making the buy/sell decision on the stock, and those more akin to the underlying investor, taking an active interest in the performance of the company rather than simply the day-to-day movement of the share price;

(b) the skills required to engage with boards on governance issues are not normally required of fund managers to be effective in their investment role. There are two remedies: either to ensure that fund managers have the necessary skills, or for fund managers to have recourse to governance specialists with the required skills;

(c) in either case, in addition to a proper understanding of the company's circumstances, effective and constructive engagement with company board members requires interpersonal, questioning and other behavioural attributes;

(d) where there are governance specialists with the required skills how are they best integrated into the fund management process? Effective integration is necessary to avoid the mixed signals on governance that some companies experience.

(3) Where does the responsibility for identifying the governance issues that require engagement lie – with company boards or institutional shareholders?

(a) Again, for reasons of familiarity with the company's circumstances, responsibility must lie mainly with the board. But institutional shareholders should also be prepared to raise governance issues of which the company may be unaware.

(b) Once governance issues have been identified by the company, the fund manager must be responsive to requests for meetings by the company. This is not always the case. Responsibility is therefore two way.

(c) The quality of reporting also has a part to play. The better the quality, the easier the identification of governance issues which require engagement for their resolution. Companies need to be more forthcoming in their governance reports, and institutional shareholders need to be more understanding of explanations.

(d) To establish a definitive list of key governance issues for companies and institutional shareholders, so as to provide a basis for initiating engagement, is probably unrealistic in view of the variety of circumstance that apply to such a significantly large number of companies in an investment portfolio. However, generically they will usually fall into one or more of the following categories: board composition, effectiveness and succession; strategy; risk management; capital structure; and remuneration versus performance.

(4) Accepting that in practice there are different degrees of engagement – ranging from engagement to explain Code exceptions to active engagement to increase shareholder value – under what circumstances does active engagement apply? This begs the question of costs versus benefits and may bring into play a threshold for percentage shareholding and/or the value of the shareholding below which active engagement becomes uneconomic.

(a) Active engagement applies where there is clear opportunity to increase shareholder value. This might arise for a number of reasons of which the need to rectify underperformance is but one.

(b) That there is an economic case for active engagement is demonstrated by the presence of shareholder activists in the market, and arguably they are behaving as responsible owners insofar as they are working to increase shareholder value.

(c) On the face of it, therefore, there is a case for active engagement by traditional shareholders investing over the longer term, most probably when their shareholdings are sufficiently material. There is an economic value to such engagement if it is properly targeted. It would appear highly likely that there are particularly appropriate companies for active engagement amongst the small cap quoted sector. Newly listed companies could present especially worthwhile subjects for active engagement for example.

(5) The evidence indicates that active engagement with FTSE small cap companies by fund managers is by no means universal. To the extent that there is an economic value to this engagement, this is to the disadvantage of beneficial owners. This raises the fundamental question: are the incentives for fund managers to actively engage sufficient?

(a) The responsibility for ensuring that the investment mandate agreed with the fund managers provides sufficient incentives to engage rests with the fund's trustees as part of their fiduciary duties.

(b) In considering incentives and fund manager mandates it is important to take into account that there has been a significant shift from relative to absolute return strategies by the fund management industry in recent years.

(c) Beneficial owners of shares might reasonably assume that fund managers are engaged in appropriate cases to preserve and increase the value of their investments, and that this is included in the management fee.

(6) Are there gains for the fund manager from less active forms of engagement?

(a) This is difficult to establish without further evidence but it might be assumed that, at the very least, some form of engagement is a necessary step to preserving shareholder value.

(b) Another course is disengagement, ie selling the shares, which might trigger the board to take action to rectify the underperformance. But is this responsible share ownership when a possible knock-on effect is a shrinkage of the company and what that might mean for levels of employment, etc which could have been avoided?

(7) How do small cap portfolio fund managers cope with a large number of investee companies?

    (a) Part of the answer must lie in focusing only on those governance issues that matter and where responsibility lies for identifying those issues is discussed under (3) above.

    (b) Cost and resource constraints are clearly an important impediment to engagement for small caps, and their institutional shareholders in particular. In some cases the solution for institutions may lie in outsourcing their engagement responsibilities, albeit that there is still a cost involved. Organisations such as Governance for Owners and Hermes Equity Ownership Services (HEOS) provide such a service, but the employment of engagement agents generally appears somewhat limited to date, certainly so far as UK institutions are concerned. HEOS, on the other hand, reports a growing take up of its services by overseas investors such as pension funds.

    (c) The position on outsourcing engagement is in contrast to the more extensive use of voting agencies, by institutional shareholders. When voting recommendations avoid a 'box-ticking' approach, then a basis for more focused and time efficient engagement by institutional shareholders is provided. Unfortunately, anecdotal evidence indicates that some voting agencies are perceived as 'box tickers' by many companies.

    (d) Outsourcing of responsibility for engagement by institutions is not widespread and is not sufficiently tested to provide a resolution, or one of the resolutions, to the institutional shareholders logistical problem.

(8) How important is the involvement of chairmen in the engagement process?

    (a) The chairman sets the tone from the top on relations with institutional shareholders, but his or her involvement in engagement varies – more active engagement conceivably justifies greater chairman involvement.

    (b) There is arguably a case for chairmen to be more visible in the company's relationships generally with institutional shareholders nevertheless, without upsetting current arrangements. Investor relations, professionally and objectively executed, are an important facilitator of developing contact and engagement between institutional shareholders and the boards of smaller quoted companies

(9) Do company advisers and brokers have a role in engagement?
Company advisers and brokers should be in a strong position to play a key role in facilitating the engagement between boards and shareholders on governance issues, but the indications are that not enough is being made of this opportunity.

(10) What is there to learn on engagement from the private equity model?
  (a) There is probably more to learn from the hedge fund model than the private equity model for engagement with FTSE small cap companies.
  (b) Hedge funds, in their activist role, provide evidence for active engagement increasing shareholder value, but typically operate with cost and incentive structures which differ from those of institutional shareholders. This does not rule out lessons to be learned. For example, the skills and experience of successful activists could provide a guide to the level of skills required within institutional shareholders for engagement to be effective.
  (c) However, this is not to completely discard the private equity model as a source of reference. To the extent that private equity investors take corporate governance into account, such evidence as there is indicates that their major concern is with the board, and not least with the mix of skills on the board.

6.3.5.1 *Key issue conclusions*

As evidence accumulates to show that active engagement carefully targeted can lead to an increase in shareholder value, the message needs to be reinforced to encourage the fund management industry to take engagement with the boards of FTSE small caps more seriously. Engagement is to underpin the 'comply or explain' principle in those cases where explaining departure from the Code is also important. This too needs dialogue between company boards and institutional shareholders.

It is in the interests of the beneficial owners of shares in companies that opportunities for increasing shareholder value through active engagement are taken by institutional shareholders. Appropriate incentives will need to be included in fund management mandates for this to happen.

However, for this outcome to be realised the important question of incentives based upon meaningful cost versus benefits analysis must be addressed. There is a need for further attention to be paid to this issue and to some of the other outstanding issues.

6.3.6 Practical recommendations and guidelines on engagement

Notwithstanding the inclusion of dialogue between companies and institutional shareholders in the Code, it is clear that there is a need for impediments to engagement to be addressed and for a set of guidelines on best practice. This section makes practical recommendations and provides guidelines on engagement for smaller companies, whilst at the same time recognising that there will be further developments to engagement practice and refinement to guidelines in due course.

The recommendations and guidelines on engagement applying to smaller quoted (and AIM) companies and their institutional shareholders are set out below.

(1) Company boards should be proactive in identifying those governance issues which are key to the company's sustainability and to increasing shareholder value in the longer term. They should be prepared to include them on the agenda for engagement, and institutional shareholders should be ready to respond. Companies and their institutional shareholders should maintain focus on these key governance issues.

(2) Company boards should initiate the engagement in most instances, but institutional shareholders should be prepared to initiate active engagement with those companies where there is an opportunity to increase shareholder value in the longer term.

(3) Companies should aim to identify and maintain a dialogue with their key institutional shareholders, which typically number around six.

(4) Chairmen should include a report on contact with the company's major shareholders in their Governance Reports.

(5) The more active the engagement is, the more the chairman should be involved but, in general, chairmen should be more visible in the company's relationship with their institutional shareholders without upsetting current arrangements.

(6) When contact with the chairman is inappropriate, or in his or her absence, contact should be with the senior independent director. The non-executive directors should not be the point of contact for institutional shareholders for engagement on governance issues.

(7) Reporting and regulatory burdens should be reduced for well-run companies complying with the Code and providing reports of high quality. This recommendation is aimed at regulators but included here because of its importance to smaller companies.

(8) Engagement should not be mandatory.

(9) Institutional shareholders should ensure that fund managers and/or their governance specialists have the required skills, including interpersonal skills, and level of experience to engage with company board members on governance issues.

(10) Institutional shareholders should ensure that, where engagement on governance issues is the responsibility of governance specialists, they are integrated into the fund management process.

(11) Institutional shareholders should be prepared to raise governance issues of which the company is unaware.

(12) Incentives for institutional shareholders to actively engage with companies to preserve and enhance shareholder value should be incorporated into investment mandates.

(13) The use of company advisers and brokers to facilitate engagement should be enhanced. This recommendation is included because of its implications for smaller companies. Companies should in any event pay particular attention to their investor relations activities and consider the use of specialist investor relations firms for advice and support in this important area.

Further practical research will be needed to progress recommendation (7) and (9). Further research will also be required on incentives (12). This must be based on sound cost versus benefits analysis, with a view to clearly identifying the criteria (eg level and value of shareholding) where active engagement is warranted, and establishing the economic justification for resources devoted to engagement. In addition, work should be initiated to explore the feasibility of institutional shareholders outsourcing their engagement responsibilities as a means of overcoming the logistical problem arising from large portfolios of investee companies.

6.4 CORPORATE GOVERNANCE AND RAISING CAPITAL

A recurring theme in parts of this book has been a connection between corporate governance and raising capital for smaller quoted and AIM companies, ie those listed on a public market. It is by now self-evident that a smaller company seeking to raise capital through a listing on the main market has to 'sign up' to the Code, and that AIM companies are increasingly encouraged to follow its principles of good governance. Empirical evidence from institutional shareholders indicates that, whilst some do take corporate governance arrangements into account in their investment decisions, some claim that at best corporate governance ranks low down their list of investment criteria.

The big question is – Is there a link between corporate governance and the cost of capital? Does good governance lower the cost of capital, as reflected in the 'premium' institutional shareholders are prepared to pay for the shares of a well-governed company?

For smaller quoted (and AIM) companies there is insufficient evidence to provide unequivocal support for this proposition. For larger companies several attempts have been made to establish a link and these suggest that institutional shareholders *are* prepared to pay a share price premium for well-governed companies, thus lowering the cost of capital for these companies.

However, what empirical evidence there is, and more particularly observation of the investment behaviour of institutional shareholders, is sufficient to establish that good corporate governance and successful capital raising go hand in hand. Smaller companies on a public market with a view to raising capital for investment to grow their business ignore this at their peril. The same could equally be said for private companies seeking external capital.

Institutional shareholders in smaller quoted companies, whatever level of importance they claim to give to a company's governance arrangements, invariably consider carefully the composition of the board and its likely effectiveness when deciding to invest. Because the board lies at the heart of corporate governance this only serves to emphasise that shareholders in smaller quoted companies *do* take corporate governance seriously. So far as the board is concerned, their particular focus is, more often than not, on the quality and effectiveness of the chief executive and finance director. They are also concerned to ensure that there is a sufficient degree of independent non-executive director presence on the board.

What has been noted above for smaller quoted companies could well be applied to institutional shareholders in AIM companies. Providers of external capital to private companies are also concerned about the composition and effectiveness of the board.

Good governance is necessary to generate confidence and trust of shareholders in order for them to provide the capital required for investment and growth of the smaller company.

APPENDIX 1

THE COMBINED CODE ON CORPORATE GOVERNANCE (JUNE 2008): CODE OF BEST PRACTICE – SECTIONS 1 AND 2

SECTION 1 COMPANIES

A. DIRECTORS

A.1 The Board

Main Principle

Every company should be headed by an effective board, which is collectively responsible for the success of the company.

Supporting Principles

The board's role is to provide entrepreneurial leadership of the company within a framework of prudent and effective controls which enables risk to be assessed and managed. The board should set the company's strategic aims, ensure that the necessary financial and human resources are in place for the company to meet its objectives and review management performance. The board should set the company's values and standards and ensure that its obligations to its shareholders and others are understood and met.

All directors must take decisions objectively in the interests of the company.

As part of their role as members of a unitary board, non-executive directors should constructively challenge and help develop proposals on strategy. Non-executive directors should scrutinise the performance of management in meeting agreed goals and objectives and monitor the reporting of performance. They should satisfy themselves on the integrity of financial information and that financial controls and systems of risk management are robust and defensible. They are responsible for determining appropriate levels of remuneration of executive directors and have a prime role in appointing, and where necessary removing, executive directors, and in succession planning.

Code Provisions

A.1.1 The board should meet sufficiently regularly to discharge its duties effectively. There should be a formal schedule of matters specifically reserved for its decision. The annual report should include a statement of how the board operates, including a high level statement of which types of decisions are to be taken by the board and which are to be delegated to management.

A.1.2 The annual report should identify the chairman, the deputy chairman (where there is one), the chief executive, the senior independent director and the chairmen and members of the nomination, audit and remuneration committees. It should also set out the number of meetings of the board and those committees and individual attendance by directors.

A.1.3 The chairman should hold meetings wit h the non-executive directors without the executives present. Led by the senior independent director, the non-executive directors should meet without the chairman present at least annually to appraise the chairman's performance (as described in A.6.1) and on such other occasions as are deemed appropriate.

A.1.4 Where directors have concerns which cannot be resolved about the running of the company or a proposed action, they should ensure that their concerns are recorded in the board minutes. On resignation, a non-executive director should provide a written statement to the chairman, for circulation to the board, if they have any such concerns.

A.1.5 The company should arrange appropriate insurance cover in respect of legal action against its directors.

A.2 Chairman and chief executive

Main Principle

There should be a clear division of responsibilities at the head of the company between the running of the board and the executive responsibility for the running of the company's business. No one individual should have unfettered powers of decision.

Supporting Principle

The chairman is responsible for leadership of the board, ensuring its effectiveness on all aspects of its role and setting its agenda. The chairman is also responsible for ensuring that the directors receive accurate, timely and clear information. The chairman should ensure effective communication with shareholders. The chairman should also facilitate the effective contribution of non-executive directors in particular and ensure constructive relations between executive and non-executive directors.

Code Provisions

A.2.1 The roles of chairman and chief executive should not be exercised by the same individual. The division of responsibilities between the chairman and chief executive should be clearly established, set out in writing and agreed by the board.

A.2.2 The chairman should on appointment meet the independence criteria set out in A.3.1 below. A chief executive should not go on to be chairman of the same company. If exceptionally a board decides that a chief executive should become chairman, the board should consult major shareholders in advance and should set out its reasons to shareholders at the time of the appointment and in the next annual report.

A.3 Board balance and independence

Main Principle

The board should include a balance of executive and non-executive directors (and in particular independent non-executive directors) such that no individual or small group of individuals can dominate the board's decision taking.

Supporting Principles

The board should not be so large as to be unwieldy. The board should be of sufficient size that the balance of skills and experience is appropriate for the requirements of the business and that changes to the board's composition can be managed without undue disruption.

To ensure that power and information are not concentrated in one or two individuals, there should be a strong presence on the board of both executive and non-executive directors.

The value of ensuring that committee membership is refreshed and that undue reliance is not placed on particular individuals should be taken into account in deciding chairmanship and membership of committees.

No one other than the committee chairman and members is entitled to be present at a meeting of the nomination, audit or remuneration committee, but others may attend at the invitation of the committee.

Code Provisions

A.3.1 The board should identify in the annual report each non-executive director it considers to be independent. The board should determine whether the director is independent in character and judgement and whether there are relationships or circumstances which are likely to affect, or could appear to affect, the director's judgement. The board should state its reasons if it determines that a director is independent notwithstanding the existence of relationships or circumstances which may appear relevant to its determination, including if the director:

- has been an employee of the company or group within the last five years;

- has, or has had within the last three years, a material business relationship with the company either directly, or as a partner, shareholder, director or senior employee of a body that has such a relationship with the company;

- has received or receives additional remuneration from the company apart from a director's fee, participates in the company's share option or a performance-related pay scheme, or is a member of the company's pension scheme;

- has close family ties with any of the company's advisers, directors or senior employees;

- holds cross-directorships or has significant links with other directors through involvement in other companies or bodies;

- represents a significant shareholder; or

- has served on the board for more than nine years from the date of their first election.

A.3.2 Except for smaller companies, at least half the board, excluding thechairman, should comprise non-executive directors determined by the board to be independent. A smaller company should have at least two independent non-executive directors.

A.3.3 The board should appoint one of the independent non-executive directors to be the senior independent director. The senior independent director should be available to shareholders if they have concerns which contact through the normal channels of chairman, chief executive or finance director has failed to resolve or for which such contact is inappropriate.

A.4 Appointments to the Board

Main Principle

There should be a formal, rigorous and transparent procedure for the appointment of new directors to the board.

Supporting Principles

Appointments to the board should be made on merit and against objective criteria. Care should be taken to ensure that appointees have enough time available to devote to the job. This is particularly important in the case of chairmanships.

The board should satisfy itself that plans are in place for orderly succession for appointments to the board and to senior management, so as to maintain an appropriate balance of skills and experience within the company and on the board.

Code Provisions

A.4.1 There should be a nomination committee which should lead the process for board appointments and make recommendations to the board. A majority of members of the nomination committee should be independent non-executive directors. The chairman or an independent non-executive director should chair the committee, but the chairman should not chair the nomination committee when it is dealing with the appointment of a successor to the chairmanship. The nomination committee should make available its terms of reference, explaining its role and the authority delegated to it by the board.

A.4.2 The nomination committee should evaluate the balance of skills, knowledge and experience on the board and, in the light of this evaluation, prepare a description of the role and capabilities required for a particular appointment.

A.4.3 For the appointment of a chairman, the nomination committee should prepare a job specification, including an assessment of the time commitment expected, recognising the need for availability in the event of crises. A chairman's other significant commitments should be disclosed to the board before appointment and included in the annual report. Changes to such commitments should be reported to the board as they arise, and their impact explained in the next annual report.

A.4.4 The terms and conditions of appointment of non-executive directors should be made available for inspection. The letter of appointment should set out the expected time commitment. Non-executive directors should undertake that they will have sufficient time to meet what is expected of them. Their other significant commitments should be disclosed to the board before appointment, with a broad indication of the time involved and the board should be informed of subsequent changes.

A.4.5 The board should not agree to a full time executive director taking on more than one non-executive directorship in a FTSE 100 company nor the chairmanship of such a company.

A.4.6 A separate section of the annual report should describe the work of the nomination committee, including the process it has used in relation to board appointments. An explanation should be given if neither an external search consultancy nor open advertising has been used in the appointment of a chairman or a non-executive director.

A.5 Information and professional development

Main Principle

The board should be supplied in a timely manner with information in a form and of a quality appropriate to enable it to discharge its duties. All directors should receive induction on joining the board and should regularly update and refresh their skills and knowledge.

Supporting Principles

The chairman is responsible for ensuring that the directors receive accurate, timely and clear information. Management has an obligation to provide such information but directors should seek clarification or amplification where necessary. The chairman should ensure that the directors continually update their skills and the knowledge and familiarity with the company required to fulfil their role both on the board and on board committees. The company should provide the necessary resources for developing and updating its directors' knowledge and capabilities.

Under the direction of the chairman, the company secretary's responsibilities include ensuring good information flows within the board and its committees and between senior management and non-executive directors, as well as facilitating induction and assisting with professional development as required.

The company secretary should be responsible for advising the board through the chairman on all governance matters.

Code Provisions

A.5.1 The chairman should ensure that new directors receive a full, formal and tailored induction on joining the board. As part of this, the company should offer to major shareholders the opportunity to meet a new non-executive director.

A.5.2 The board should ensure that directors, especially non-executive directors, have access to independent professional advice at the company's expense where they judge it necessary to discharge their responsibilities as directors. Committees should be provided with sufficient resources to undertake their duties.

A.5.3 All directors should have access to the advice and services of the company secretary, who is responsible to the board for ensuring that board procedures are complied with. Both the appointment and removal of the company secretary should be a matter for the board as a whole.

A.6 Performance evaluation

Main Principle

The board should undertake a formal and rigorous annual evaluation of its own performance and that of its committees and individual directors.

Supporting Principle

Individual evaluation should aim to show whether each director continues to contribute effectively and to demonstrate commitment to the role (including commitment of time for board and committee meetings and any other duties). The chairman should act on the results of the performance evaluation by recognising the strengths and addressing the weaknesses of the board and, where appropriate, proposing new members be appointed to the board or seeking the resignation of directors.

Code Provision

A.6.1 The board should state in the annual report how performance evaluation of the board, its committees and its individual directors has been conducted. The non-executive directors, led by the senior independent director, should be responsible for performance evaluation of the chairman, taking into account the views of executive directors.

A.7 Re-election

Main Principle

All directors should be submitted for re-election at regular intervals, subject to continued satisfactory performance. The board should ensure planned and progressive refreshing of the board.

Code Provisions

A.7.1 All directors should be subject to election by shareholders at the first annual general meeting after their appointment, and to re-election thereafter at intervals of no more than three years. The names of directors submitted for election or re-election should be accompanied by sufficient biographical details and any other relevant information to enable shareholders to take an informed decision on their election.

A.7.2 Non-executive directors should be appointed for specified terms subject to re-election and to Companies Acts provisions relating to the removal of a director. The board should set out to shareholders in the papers accompanying a resolution to elect a non-executive director why they believe an individual should be elected. The chairman should confirm to shareholders when proposing re-election that, following formal performance evaluation, the individual's performance continues to be effective and to demonstrate commitment to the role. Any term beyond six years (e.g. two three-year terms) for a non-executive director should be subject to particularly rigorous review, and should take into account the need for progressive refreshing of the board. Non-executive directors may serve longer than nine years (e.g. three three-year terms), subject to annual re-election. Serving more than nine years could be relevant to the determination of a non-executive director's independence (as set out in provision A.3.1).

B. REMUNERATION

B.1 The Level and Make-up of Remuneration

Main Principles

Levels of remuneration should be sufficient to attract, retain and motivate directors of the quality required to run the company successfully, but a company should avoid paying more than is necessary for this purpose. A significant proportion of executive directors' remuneration should be structured so as to link rewards to corporate and individual performance.

Supporting Principle

The remuneration committee should judge where to position their company relative to other companies. But they should use such comparisons with caution, in view of the risk of an upward ratchet of remuneration levels with no corresponding improvement in performance. They should also be sensitive to pay and employment conditions elsewhere in the group, especially when determining annual salary increases.

Code Provisions

Remuneration policy

B.1.1 The performance-related elements of remuneration should form a significant proportion of the total remuneration package of executive directors and should be designed to align their interests with those of shareholders and to give these directors keen incentives to perform at the highest levels. In designing schemes of performance-related remuneration, the remuneration committee should follow the provisions in Schedule A to this Code.

B.1.2 Executive share options should not be offered at a discount save as permitted by the relevant provisions of the Listing Rules.

B.1.3 Levels of remuneration for non-executive directors should reflect the time commitment and responsibilities of the role. Remuneration for non-executive directors should not include share options. If, exceptionally, options are granted, shareholder approval should be sought in advance and any shares acquired by exercise of the options should be held until at least one year after the non-executive director leaves the board. Holding of share options could be relevant to the determination of a non-executive director's independence (as set out in provision A.3.1).

B.1.4 Where a company releases an executive director to serve as a non-executive director elsewhere, the remuneration report should include a statement as to whether or not the director will retain such earnings and, if so, what the remuneration is.

Service Contracts and Compensation

B.1.5 The remuneration committee should carefully consider what compensation commitments (including pension contributions and all other elements) their directors' terms of appointment would entail in the event of early termination. The aim should be to avoid rewarding poor performance. They should take a robust line on reducing compensation to reflect departing directors' obligations to mitigate loss.

B.1.6 Notice or contract periods should be set at one year or less. If it is necessary to offer longer notice or contract periods to new directors recruited from outside, such periods should reduce to one year or less after the initial period.

B.2 Procedure

Main Principle

There should be a formal and transparent procedure for developing policy on executive remuneration and for fixing the remuneration packages of individual directors. No director should be involved in deciding his or her own remuneration.

Supporting Principles

The remuneration committee should consult the chairman and/or chief executive about their proposals relating to the remuneration of other executive directors. The remuneration committee should also be responsible for appointing any consultants in respect of executive director remuneration. Where executive directors or senior management are involved in advising or supporting the remuneration committee, care should be taken to recognise and avoid conflicts of interest.

The chairman of the board should ensure that the company maintains contact as required with its principal shareholders about remuneration in the same way as for other matters.

Code Provisions

B.2.1 The board should establish a remuneration committee of at least three, or in the case of smaller companies two, independent non-executive directors. In addition the company chairman may also be a member of, but not chair, the committee if he or she was considered independent on appointment as chairman. The remuneration committee should make available its terms of reference, explaining its role and the authority delegated to it by the board. Where remuneration consultants are appointed, a statement should be made available of whether they have any other connection with the company.

B.2.2 The remuneration committee should have delegated responsibility for setting remuneration for all executive directors and the chairman, including pension rights and any compensation payments. The committee should also recommend and monitor the level and structure of remuneration for senior management. The definition of 'senior management' for this purpose should be determined by the board but should normally include the first layer of management below board level.

B.2.3 The board itself or, where required by the Articles of Association, the shareholders should determine the remuneration of the non-executive directors within the limits set in the Articles of Association. Where permitted by the Articles, the board may however delegate this responsibility to a committee, which might include the chief executive.

B.2.4 Shareholders should be invited specifically to approve all new long-term incentive schemes (as defined in the Listing Rules) and significant changes to existing schemes, save in the circumstances permitted by the Listing Rules.

C. ACCOUNTABILITY AND AUDIT

C.1 Financial Reporting

Main Principle

The board should present a balanced and understandable assessment of the company's position and prospects.

Supporting Principle

The board's responsibility to present a balanced and understandable assessment extends to interim and other price-sensitive public reports and reports to regulators as well as to information required to be presented by statutory requirements.

Code Provisions

C.1.1 The directors should explain in the annual report their responsibility for preparing the accounts and there should be a statement by the auditors about their reporting responsibilities.

C.1.2 The directors should report that the business is a going concern, with supporting assumptions or qualifications as necessary.

C.2 Internal Control

Main Principle

The board should maintain a sound system of internal control to safeguard shareholders' investment and the company's assets.

Code Provision

C.2.1 The board should, at least annually, conduct a review of the effectiveness of the group's system of internal controls and should report to shareholders that they have done so. The review should cover all material controls, including financial, operational and compliance controls and risk management systems.

C.3 Audit Committee and Auditors

Main Principle

The board should establish formal and transparent arrangements for considering how they should apply the financial reporting and internal control principles and for maintaining an appropriate relationship with the company's auditors.

Code Provisions

C.3.1 The board should establish an audit committee of at least three, or in the case of smaller companies two, independent non-executive directors. In smaller companies the company chairman may be a member of, but not chair, the committee in addition to the independent non-executive directors, provided he or she was considered independent on appointment as chairman. The board should satisfy itself that at least one member of the audit committee has recent and relevant financial experience.

C.3.2 The main role and responsibilities of the audit committee should be set out in written terms of reference and should include:

- to monitor the integrity of the financial statements of the company, and any formal announcements relating to the company's financial performance, reviewing significant financial reporting judgements contained in them;

- to review the company's internal financial controls and, unless expressly addressed by a separate board risk committee composed of independent directors, or by the board itself, to review the company's internal control and risk management systems;

- to monitor and review the effectiveness of the company's internal audit function;

- to make recommendations to the board, for it to put to the shareholders for their approval in general meeting, in relation to the appointment, re-appointment and removal of the external auditor and to approve the remuneration and terms of engagement of the external auditor;

- to review and monitor the external auditor's independence and objectivity and the effectiveness of the audit process, taking into consideration relevant UK professional and regulatory requirements;

- to develop and implement policy on the engagement of the external auditor to supply non-audit services, taking into account relevant ethical guidance regarding the provision of non-audit services by the external audit firm; and to report to the board, identifying any matters in respect of which it considers that action or improvement is needed and making recommendations as to the steps to be taken.

C.3.3 The terms of reference of the audit committee, including its role and the authority delegated to it by the board, should be made available. A separate section of the annual report should describe the work of the committee in discharging those responsibilities.

C.3.4 The audit committee should review arrangements by which staff of the company may, in confidence, raise concerns about possible improprieties in matters of financial reporting or other matters. The audit committee's objective should be to ensure that arrangements are in place for the proportionate and independent investigation of such matters and for appropriate follow-up action.

C.3.5 The audit committee should monitor and review the effectiveness of the internal audit activities. Where there is no internal audit function, the audit committee should consider annually whether there is a need for an internal audit function and make a recommendation to the board, and the reasons for the absence of such a function should be explained in the relevant section of the annual report.

C.3.6 The audit committee should have primary responsibility for making a recommendation on the appointment, reappointment and removal of the external auditors. If the board does not accept the audit committee's recommendation, it should include in the annual report, and in any papers recommending appointment or re-appointment, a statement from the audit committee explaining the recommendation and should set out reasons why the board has taken a different position.

C.3.7 The annual report should explain to shareholders how, if the auditor provides non-audit services, auditor objectivity and independence is safeguarded.

D. RELATIONS WITH SHAREHOLDERS

D.1 Dialogue with Institutional Shareholders

Main Principle

There should be a dialogue with shareholders based on the mutual understanding of objectives. The board as a whole has responsibility for ensuring that a satisfactory dialogue with shareholders takes place.

Supporting Principles

Whilst recognising that most shareholder contact is with the chief executive and finance director, the chairman (and the senior independent director and other directors as appropriate) should maintain sufficient contact with major shareholders to understand their issues and concerns.

The board should keep in touch with shareholder opinion in whatever ways are most practical and efficient.

Code Provisions

D.1.1 The chairman should ensure that the views of shareholders are communicated to the board as a whole. The chairman should discuss governance and strategy with major shareholders. Non-executive directors should be offered the opportunity to attend meetings with major shareholders and should expect to attend them if requested by major shareholders. The senior independent director should attend sufficient meetings with a range of major shareholders to listen to their views in order to help develop a balanced understanding of the issues and concerns of major shareholders.

D.1.2 The board should state in the annual report the steps they have taken to ensure that the members of the board, and in particular the non-executive directors, develop an understanding of the views of major shareholders about their company, for example through direct face-to-face contact, analysts' or brokers' briefings and surveys of shareholder opinion. 20 Nothing in these principles or provisions should be taken to override the general requirements of law to treat shareholders equally in access to information.

D.2 Constructive Use of the AGM

Main Principle

The board should use the AGM to communicate with investors and to encourage their participation.

Code Provisions

D.2.1 At any general meeting, the company should propose a separate resolution on each substantially separate issue, and should in particular propose a resolution at the AGM relating to the report and accounts. For each resolution, proxy appointment forms should provide shareholders with the option to direct their proxy to vote either for or against the resolution or to withhold their vote. The proxy form and any announcement of the results of a vote should make it clear that a 'vote withheld' is not a vote in law and will not be counted in the calculation of the proportion of the votes for and against the resolution.

D.2.2 The company should ensure that all valid proxy appointments received for general meetings are properly recorded and counted. For each resolution, after a vote has been taken, except where taken on a poll, the company should ensure that the following information is given at the meeting and made available as soon as reasonably practicable on a website which is maintained by or on behalf of the company:

- the number of shares in respect of which proxy appointments have been validly made;

- the number of votes for the resolution;

- the number of votes against the resolution; and

- the number of shares in respect of which the vote was directed to be withheld.

D.2.3 The chairman should arrange for the chairmen of the audit, remuneration and nomination committees to be available to answer questions at the AGM and for all directors to attend.

D.2.4 The company should arrange for the Notice of the AGM and related papers to be sent to shareholders at least 20 working days before the meeting.

SECTION 2 INSTITUTIONAL SHAREHOLDERS

E. INSTITUTIONAL SHAREHOLDERS

E.1 Dialogue with companies

Main Principle

Institutional shareholders should enter into a dialogue with companies based on the mutual understanding of objectives.

Supporting Principles

Institutional shareholders should apply the principles set out in the Institutional Shareholders' Committee's "The Responsibilities of Institutional Shareholders and Agents – Statement of Principles", which should be reflected in fund manager contracts.

E.2 Evaluation of Governance Disclosures

Main Principle

When evaluating companies' governance arrangements, particularly those relating to board structure and composition, institutional shareholders should give due weight to all relevant factors drawn to their attention.

Supporting Principle

Institutional shareholders should consider carefully explanations given for departure from this Code and make reasoned judgements in each case. They should give an explanation to the company, in writing where appropriate, and be prepared to enter a dialogue if they do not accept the company's position. They should avoid a box-ticking approach to assessing a company's corporate governance. They should bear in mind in particular the size and complexity of the company and the nature of the risks and challenges it faces.

E.3 Shareholder Voting

Main Principle

Institutional shareholders have a responsibility to make considered use of their votes.

Supporting Principles

Institutional shareholders should take steps to ensure their voting intentions are being translated into practice. Institutional shareholders should, on request, make available to their clients information on the proportion of resolutions on which votes were cast and non-discretionary proxies lodged.

Major shareholders should attend AGMs where appropriate and practicable. Companies and registrars should facilitate this.

© The Financial Reporting Council Limited (FRC). Adapted and reproduced with the kind permission of the Financial Reporting Council. All rights reserved. For further information please visit www.frc.org.uk or call +44 (0)20 7492 2300.

APPENDIX 2

THE COMBINED CODE ON CORPORATE GOVERNANCE (JUNE 2008) SCHEDULE A: PROVISIONS ON THE DESIGN OF PERFORMANCE RELATED REMUNERATION

1. The remuneration committee should consider whether the directors should be eligible for annual bonuses. If so, performance conditions should be relevant, stretching and designed to enhance shareholder value. Upper limits should be set and disclosed. There may be a case for part payment in shares to be held for a significant period.

2. The remuneration committee should consider whether the directors should be eligible for benefits under long-term incentive schemes. Traditional share option schemes should be weighed against other kinds of long-term incentive scheme. In normal circumstances, shares granted or other forms of deferred remuneration should not vest, and options should not be exercisable, in less than three years. Directors should be encouraged to hold their shares for a further period after vesting or exercise, subject to the need to finance any costs of acquisition and associated tax liabilities.

3. Any new long-term incentive schemes which are proposed should be approved by shareholders and should preferably replace any existing schemes or at least form part of a well considered overall plan, incorporating existing schemes. The total rewards potentially available should not be excessive.

4. Payouts or grants under all incentive schemes, including new grants under existing share option schemes, should be subject to challenging performance criteria reflecting the company's objectives. Consideration should be given to criteria which reflect the company's performance relative to a group of comparator companies in some key variables such as total shareholder return.

5. Grants under executive share option and other long-term incentive schemes should normally be phased rather than awarded in one large block.

6. In general, only basic salary should be pensionable.

7. The remuneration committee should consider the pension conse-
    quences and associated costs to the company of basic salary
    increases and any other changes in pensionable remuneration,
    especially for directors close to retirement.

APPENDIX 3

THE REVISED TURNBULL GUIDANCE ON INTERNAL CONTROLS (OCTOBER 2005)

Contents

Financial Reporting Council

Preface

Internal Control: Guidance for Directors on the Combined Code (The Turnbull guidance) was first issued in 1999.

In 2004, the Financial Reporting Council established the Turnbull Review Group to consider the impact of the guidance and the related disclosures and to determine whether the guidance needed to be updated.

In reviewing the impact of the guidance, our consultations revealed that it has very successfully gone a long way to meeting its original objectives. Boards and investors alike indicated that the guidance has contributed to a marked improvement in the overall standard of risk management and internal control since 1999.

Notably, the evidence gathered by the Review Group demonstrated that respondents considered that the substantial improvements in internal control instigated by application of the Turnbull guidance have been achieved without the need for detailed prescription as to how to implement the guidance. The principles-based approach has required boards to think seriously about control issues and enabled them to apply the principles in a way that appropriately dealt with the circumstances of their business. The evidence also supported the proposition that the companies which have derived most benefit from application of the guidance were those whose boards saw embedded risk management and internal control as an integral part of running the business.

Accordingly, the Review Group strongly endorsed retention of the flexible, principles-based approach of the original guidance and has made only a small number of changes.

This however does not mean that there is nothing new for boards to do or that some companies could not make more effective use of the guidance. Establishing an effective system of internal control is not a one-off exercise. No such system remains effective unless it develops to take account of new and emerging risks, control failures, market expectations or changes in the company's circumstances or business objectives. The Review Group reiterates the view of the vast majority of respondents in emphasising the importance of regular and systematic assessment of the risks facing the business and the value of embedding risk management and internal control systems within business processes. It is the board's responsibility to make sure this happens.

Boards should review whether they can make more of the communication opportunity of the internal control statement in the annual report. Investors consider the board's attitude towards risk management and internal control to be an important factor when making investment decisions about a company. Taken together with the Operating and Financial Review, the internal control statement provides an opportunity for the board to help shareholders understand the risk and control issues facing the company, and to explain how the company maintains a framework of internal controls to address these issues and how the board has reviewed the effectiveness of that framework.

It is in this spirit that directors need to exercise their responsibility to review on a continuing basis their application of the revised guidance.

Turnbull Review Group
October 2005

2 Internal Control: Revised Guidance for Directors on the Combined Code (October 2005)

One - Introduction

The importance of internal control and risk management

1   A company's system of internal control has a key role in the management of risks that are significant to the fulfilment of its business objectives. A sound system of internal control contributes to safeguarding the shareholders' investment and the company's assets.

2   Internal control (as referred to in paragraph 19) facilitates the effectiveness and efficiency of operations, helps ensure the reliability of internal and external reporting and assists compliance with laws and regulations.

3   Effective financial controls, including the maintenance of proper accounting records, are an important element of internal control. They help ensure that the company is not unnecessarily exposed to avoidable financial risks and that financial information used within the business and for publication is reliable. They also contribute to the safeguarding of assets, including the prevention and detection of fraud.

4   A company's objectives, its internal organisation and the environment in which it operates are continually evolving and, as a result, the risks it faces are continually changing. A sound system of internal control therefore depends on a thorough and regular evaluation of the nature and extent of the risks to which the company is exposed. Since profits are, in part, the reward for successful risk-taking in business, the purpose of internal control is to help manage and control risk appropriately rather than to eliminate it.

Objectives of the guidance

5   This guidance is intended to:

  •   reflect sound business practice whereby internal control is embedded in the business processes by which a company pursues its objectives;

  •   remain relevant over time in the continually evolving business environment; and

  •   enable each company to apply it in a manner which takes account of its particular circumstances.

The guidance requires directors to exercise judgement in reviewing how the company has implemented the requirements of the Combined Code relating to internal control and reporting to shareholders thereon.

6   The guidance is based on the adoption by a company's board of a risk-based approach to establishing a sound system of internal control and reviewing its effectiveness. This should be incorporated by the company within its normal management and governance processes. It should not be treated as a separate exercise undertaken to meet regulatory requirements.

Internal control requirements of the Combined Code

7   Principle C.2 of the Code states that 'The board should maintain a sound system of internal control to safeguard shareholders' investment and the company's assets'.

8   Provision C.2.1 states that 'The directors should, at least annually, conduct a review of the effectiveness of the group's system of internal control and should report to shareholders that they have done so. The review should cover all material controls, including financial, operational and compliance controls and risk management systems'.

9   Paragraph 9.8.6 of the UK Listing Authority's Listing Rules states that in the case of a listed company incorporated in the United Kingdom, the following items must be included in its annual report and accounts:

*   a statement of how the listed company has applied the principles set out in Section 1 of the Combined Code, in a manner that would enable shareholders to evaluate how the principles have been applied;

*   a statement as to whether the listed company has:

     -    complied throughout the accounting period with all relevant provisions set out in Section 1 of the Combined Code; or

     -    not complied throughout the accounting period with all relevant provisions set out in Section 1 of the Combined Code and if so, setting out:

          (i)   those provisions, if any, it has not complied with;

          (ii) in the case of provisions whose requirements are of a continuing nature, the period within which, if any, it did not comply with some or all of those provisions; and

          (iii) the company's reasons for non-compliance.

4 Internal Control: Revised Guidance for Directors on the Combined Code (October 2005)

Two - Maintaining a sound system of internal control

Responsibilities

15   The board of directors is responsible for the company's system of internal control. It should set appropriate policies on internal control and seek regular assurance that will enable it to satisfy itself that the system is functioning effectively. The board must further ensure that the system of internal control is effective in managing those risks in the manner which it has approved.

16   In determining its policies with regard to internal control, and thereby assessing what constitutes a sound system of internal control in the particular circumstances of the company, the board's deliberations should include consideration of the following factors:

- the nature and extent of the risks facing the company;

- the extent and categories of risk which it regards as acceptable for the company to bear;

- the likelihood of the risks concerned materialising;

- the company's ability to reduce the incidence and impact on the business of risks that do materialise; and

- the costs of operating particular controls relative to the benefit thereby obtained in managing the related risks.

17   It is the role of management to implement board policies on risk and control. In fulfilling its responsibilities management should identify and evaluate the risks faced by the company for consideration by the board and design, operate and monitor a suitable system of internal control which implements the policies adopted by the board.

18   All employees have some responsibility for internal control as part of their accountability for achieving objectives. They, collectively, should have the necessary knowledge, skills, information, and authority to establish, operate and monitor the system of internal control. This will require an understanding of the company, its objectives, the industries and markets in which it operates, and the risks it faces.

6 Internal Control: Revised Guidance for Directors on the Combined Code (October 2005)

10   The Preamble to the Code makes it clear that there is no prescribed form or ⟨
     statement setting out how the various principles in the Code have been appl,
     is that companies should have a free hand to explain their governance policie
     the principles, including any special circumstances which have led to them ad
     particular approach.

11   The guidance in this document applies for accounting periods beginning on or ⟨
     1 January 2006, and should be followed by boards of listed companies in:

     • assessing how the company has applied Code Principle C.2;

     • implementing the requirements of Code Provision C.2.1; and

     • reporting on these matters to shareholders in the annual report and accounts.

12   For the purposes of this guidance, internal controls considered by the board should i⟩
     types of controls including those of an operational and compliance nature, as well as ⟩
     financial controls.

Groups of companies

13   Throughout this guidance, where reference is made to 'company' it should be taken, whe
     applicable, as referring to the group of which the reporting company is the parent compa
     For groups of companies, the review of effectiveness of internal control and the report to ⟨
     shareholders should be from the perspective of the group as a whole.

The Appendix

14   The Appendix to this document contains questions which boards may wish to consider in
     applying this guidance.

Elements of a sound system of internal control

19 An internal control system encompasses the policies, processes, tasks, behaviours and other aspects of a company that, taken together:

- facilitate its effective and efficient operation by enabling it to respond appropriately to significant business, operational, financial, compliance and other risks to achieving the company's objectives. This includes the safeguarding of assets from inappropriate use or from loss and fraud and ensuring that liabilities are identified and managed;

- help ensure the quality of internal and external reporting. This requires the maintenance of proper records and processes that generate a flow of timely, relevant and reliable information from within and outside the organisation;

- help ensure compliance with applicable laws and regulations, and also with internal policies with respect to the conduct of business.

20 A company's system of internal control will reflect its control environment which encompasses its organisational structure. The system will include:

- control activities;

- information and communications processes; and

- processes for monitoring the continuing effectiveness of the system of internal control.

21 The system of internal control should:

- be embedded in the operations of the company and form part of its culture;

- be capable of responding quickly to evolving risks to the business arising from factors within the company and to changes in the business environment; and

- include procedures for reporting immediately to appropriate levels of management any significant control failings or weaknesses that are identified together with details of corrective action being undertaken.

22 A sound system of internal control reduces, but cannot eliminate, the possibility of poor judgement in decision-making; human error; control processes being deliberately circumvented by employees and others; management overriding controls; and the occurrence of unforeseeable circumstances.

23   A sound system of internal control therefore provides reasonable, but not absolute, assurance that a company will not be hindered in achieving its business objectives, or in the orderly and legitimate conduct of its business, by circumstances which may reasonably be foreseen. A system of internal control cannot, however, provide protection with certainty against a company failing to meet its business objectives or all material errors, losses, fraud, or breaches of laws or regulations.

8 Internal Control: Revised Guidance for Directors on the Combined Code (October 2005)

Three - Reviewing the effectiveness of internal control

Responsibilities

24   Reviewing the effectiveness of internal control is an essential part of the board's responsibilities. The board will need to form its own view on effectiveness based on the information and assurances provided to it, exercising the standard of care generally applicable to directors in the exercise of their duties. Management is accountable to the board for monitoring the system of internal control and for providing assurance to the board that it has done so.

25   The role of board committees in the review process, including that of the audit committee, is for the board to decide and will depend upon factors such as the size and composition of the board; the scale, diversity and complexity of the company's operations; and the nature of the significant risks that the company faces. To the extent that designated board committees carry out, on behalf of the board, tasks that are attributed in this guidance document to the board, the results of the relevant committees' work should be reported to, and considered by, the board. The board takes responsibility for the disclosures on internal control in the annual report and accounts.

The process for reviewing effectiveness

26   Effective monitoring on a continuous basis is an essential component of a sound system of internal control. The board cannot, however, rely solely on the embedded monitoring processes within the company to discharge its responsibilities. It should regularly receive and review reports on internal control. In addition, the board should undertake an annual assessment for the purposes of making its public statement on internal control to ensure that it has considered all significant aspects of internal control for the company for the year under review and up to the date of approval of the annual report and accounts.

27   The board should define the process to be adopted for its review of the effectiveness of internal control. This should encompass both the scope and frequency of the reports it receives and reviews during the year, and also the process for its annual assessment, such that it will be provided with sound, appropriately documented, support for its statement on internal control in the company's annual report and accounts.

28   The reports from management to the board should, in relation to the areas covered by them, provide a balanced assessment of the significant risks and the effectiveness of the system of internal control in managing those risks. Any significant control failings or weaknesses identified should be discussed in the reports, including the impact that they have had, or may have, on the company and the actions being taken to rectify them. It is essential that there be openness of communication by management with the board on matters relating to risk and control.

29   When reviewing reports during the year, the board should:

- consider what are the significant risks and assess how they have been identified, evaluated and managed;

- assess the effectiveness of the related system of internal control in managing the significant risks, having regard in particular to any significant failings or weaknesses in internal control that have been reported;

- consider whether necessary actions are being taken promptly to remedy any significant failings or weaknesses; and

- consider whether the findings indicate a need for more extensive monitoring of the system of internal control.

30   Additionally, the board should undertake an annual assessment for the purpose of making its public statement on internal control. The assessment should consider issues dealt with in reports reviewed by it during the year together with any additional information necessary to ensure that the board has taken account of all significant aspects of internal control for the company for the year under review and up to the date of approval of the annual report and accounts.

31   The board's annual assessment should, in particular, consider:

- the changes since the last annual assessment in the nature and extent of significant risks, and the company's ability to respond to changes in its business and the external environment;

- the scope and quality of management's ongoing monitoring of risks and of the system of internal control, and, where applicable, the work of its internal audit function and other providers of assurance;

10 Internal Control: Revised Guidance for Directors on the Combined Code (October 2005)

- the extent and frequency of the communication of the results of the monitoring to the board (or board committee(s)) which enables it to build up a cumulative assessment of the state of control in the company and the effectiveness with which risk is being managed;

- the incidence of significant control failings or weaknesses that have been identified at any time during the period and the extent to which they have resulted in unforeseen outcomes or contingencies that have had, could have had, or may in the future have, a material impact on the company's financial performance or condition; and

- the effectiveness of the company's public reporting processes.

32 Should the board become aware at any time of a significant failing or weakness in internal control, it should determine how the failing or weakness arose and reassess the effectiveness of management's ongoing processes for designing, operating and monitoring the system of internal control.

Four - The board's statement on internal control

33   The annual report and accounts should include such meaningful, high-level information as the board considers necessary to assist shareholders' understanding of the main features of the company's risk management processes and system of internal control, and should not give a misleading impression.

34   In its narrative statement of how the company has applied Code Principle C.2, the board should, as a minimum, disclose that there is an ongoing process for identifying, evaluating and managing the significant risks faced by the company, that it has been in place for the year under review and up to the date of approval of the annual report and accounts, that it is regularly reviewed by the board and accords with the guidance in this document.

35   The disclosures relating to the application of Principle C.2 should include an acknowledgement by the board that it is responsible for the company's system of internal control and for reviewing its effectiveness. It should also explain that such a system is designed to manage rather than eliminate the risk of failure to achieve business objectives, and can only provide reasonable and not absolute assurance against material misstatement or loss.

36   In relation to Code Provision C.2.1, the board should summarise the process it (where applicable, through its committees) has applied in reviewing the effectiveness of the system of internal control and confirm that necessary actions have been or are being taken to remedy any significant failings or weaknesses identified from that review. It should also disclose the process it has applied to deal with material internal control aspects of any significant problems disclosed in the annual report and accounts.

37   Where a board cannot make one or more of the disclosures in paragraphs 34 and 36, it should state this fact and provide an explanation. The Listing Rules require the board to disclose if it has failed to conduct a review of the effectiveness of the company's system of internal control.

38   Where material joint ventures and associates have not been dealt with as part of the group for the purposes of applying this guidance, this should be disclosed.

Five - Appendix

Assessing the effectiveness of the company's risk and control processes

Some questions which the board may wish to consider and discuss with management when regularly reviewing reports on internal control and when carrying out its annual assessment are set out below. The questions are not intended to be exhaustive and will need to be tailored to the particular circumstances of the company.

This Appendix should be read in conjunction with the guidance set out in this document.

Risk assessment

- Does the company have clear objectives and have they been communicated so as to provide effective direction to employees on risk assessment and control issues? For example, do objectives and related plans include measurable performance targets and indicators?

- Are the significant internal and external operational, financial, compliance and other risks identified and assessed on an ongoing basis? These are likely to include the principal risks identified in the Operating and Financial Review.

- Is there a clear understanding by management and others within the company of what risks are acceptable to the board?

Control environment and control activities

- Does the board have clear strategies for dealing with the significant risks that have been identified? Is there a policy on how to manage these risks?

- Do the company's culture, code of conduct, human resource policies and performance reward systems support the business objectives and risk management and internal control system?

- Does senior management demonstrate, through its actions as well as it policies, the necessary commitment to competence, integrity and fostering a climate of trust within the company?

- Are authority, responsibility and accountability defined clearly such that decisions are made and actions taken by the appropriate people? Are the decisions and actions of different parts of the company appropriately co-ordinated?

- Does the company communicate to its employees what is expected of them and the scope of their freedom to act? This may apply to areas such as customer relations; service levels for both internal and outsourced activities; health, safety and environmental protection; security of tangible and intangible assets; business continuity issues; expenditure matters; accounting; and financial and other reporting.

- Do people in the company (and in its providers of outsourced services) have the knowledge, skills and tools to support the achievement of the company's objectives and to manage effectively risks to their achievement?

- How are processes/controls adjusted to reflect new or changing risks, or operational deficiencies?

Information and communication

- Do management and the board receive timely, relevant and reliable reports on progress against business objectives and the related risks that provide them with the information, from inside and outside the company, needed for decision-making and management review purposes? This could include performance reports and indicators of change, together with qualitative information such as on customer satisfaction, employee attitudes etc.

- Are information needs and related information systems reassessed as objectives and related risks change or as reporting deficiencies are identified?

- Are periodic reporting procedures, including half-yearly and annual reporting, effective in communicating a balanced and understandable account of the company's position and prospects?

- Are there established channels of communication for individuals to report suspected breaches of law or regulations or other improprieties?

Monitoring

- Are there ongoing processes embedded within the company's overall business operations, and addressed by senior management, which monitor the effective application of the policies, processes and activities related to internal control and risk management? (Such processes may include control self-assessment, confirmation by personnel of compliance with policies and codes of conduct, internal audit reviews or other management reviews).

14 Internal Control: Revised Guidance for Directors on the Combined Code (October 2005)

- Do these processes monitor the company's ability to re-evaluate risks and adjust controls effectively in response to changes in its objectives, its business, and its external environment?

- Are there effective follow-up procedures to ensure that appropriate change or action occurs in response to changes in risk and control assessments?

- Is there appropriate communication to the board (or board committees) on the effectiveness of the ongoing monitoring processes on risk and control matters? This should include reporting any significant failings or weaknesses on a timely basis.

- Are there specific arrangements for management monitoring and reporting to the board on risk and control matters of particular importance? These could include, for example, actual or suspected fraud and other illegal or irregular acts, or matters that could adversely affect the company's reputation or financial position.

APPENDIX 4

THE SMITH GUIDANCE ON AUDIT COMMITTEES (OCTOBER 2005)

AUTHOR'S NOTE

A new edition of the Smith Guidance was issued by the Financial Reporting Council in October 2008. It contains a limited number of changes pertaining mainly to auditors themselves. The significant changes are:

- audit committees are encouraged to consider the need to include the risk of the withdrawal of their auditor from the market in their risk evaluation and planning;

- companies are encouraged to include in the audit committee's report, information on the appointment, reappointment or removal of the auditor, including supporting information on tendering frequency, the tenure of the incumbent auditor and any contractual obligations that acted to restrict the committee's choice of auditor;

- a small number of detailed changes have been made to the section dealing with the independence of the auditor, to bring the guidance in line with the Auditing Practices Board Ethical Standards for Auditors, which have been issued since the guidance was first published in 2003; and

- an appendix has been added containing guidance on the factors to be considered if a group is contemplating employing firms from more than one network to undertake the audit.

The new edition of the Guidance may be obtained by accessing: www.frc.org.uk/documents/pagemanager/frc/Smith_Guidance/ Guidance%20on%20Audit%20Committees%20October%202008.pdf.

GUIDANCE ON AUDIT COMMITTEES
(The Smith Guidance)

CONTENTS

AUDIT COMMITTEES - COMBINED CODE GUIDANCE

1. Introduction

1.1. This guidance is designed to assist company boards in making suitable arrangements for their audit committees, and to assist directors serving on audit committees in carrying out their role.

1.2. The paragraphs in bold are taken from the Combined Code (Section C3). Listed companies that do not comply with those provisions should include an explanation as to why they have not complied in the statement required by the Listing Rules.

1.3. Best practice requires that every board should consider in detail what arrangements for its audit committee are best suited for its particular circumstances. Audit committee arrangements need to be proportionate to the task, and will vary according to the size, complexity and risk profile of the company.

1.4. While all directors have a duty to act in the interests of the company the audit committee has a particular role, acting independently from the executive, to ensure that the interests of shareholders are properly protected in relation to financial reporting and internal control.

1.5. Nothing in the guidance should be interpreted as a departure from the principle of the unitary board. All directors remain equally responsible for the company's affairs as a matter of law. The audit committee, like other committees to which particular responsibilities are delegated (such as the remuneration committee), remains a committee of the board. Any disagreement within the board, including disagreement between the audit committee's members and the rest of the board, should be resolved at board level.

1.6. The Code provides that a separate section of the annual report should describe the work of the committee. This deliberately puts the spotlight on the audit committee and gives it an authority that it might otherwise lack. This is not incompatible with the principle of the unitary board.

1.7. The guidance contains recommendations about the conduct of the audit committee's relationship with the board, with the executive management and with internal and external auditors. However, the most important features of this relationship cannot be drafted as guidance or put into a code of practice: a frank, open working relationship and a high level of mutual respect are essential, particularly between the audit committee chairman and the board chairman, the chief executive and the finance director. The audit committee must be prepared to take a robust stand, and all parties must be prepared to make information freely available to the audit committee, to listen to their views and to talk through the issues openly.

1.8.   In particular, the management is under an obligation to ensure the audit committee is kept properly informed, and should take the initiative in supplying information rather than waiting to be asked. The board should make it clear to all directors and staff that they must cooperate with the audit committee and provide it with any information it requires. In addition, executive board members will have regard to their common law duty to provide all directors, including those on the audit committee, with all the information they need to discharge their responsibilities as directors of the company.

1.9.   Many of the core functions of audit committees set out in this guidance are expressed in terms of 'oversight', 'assessment' and 'review' of a particular function. It is not the duty of audit committees to carry out functions that properly belong to others, such as the company's management in the preparation of the financial statements or the auditors in the planning or conducting of audits. To do so could undermine the responsibility of management and auditors. Audit committees should, for example, satisfy themselves that there is a proper system and allocation of responsibilities for the day-to-day monitoring of financial controls but they should not seek to do the monitoring themselves.

1.10.   However, the high-level oversight function may lead to detailed work. The audit committee must intervene if there are signs that something may be seriously amiss. For example, if the audit committee is uneasy about the explanations of management and auditors about a particular financial reporting policy decision, there may be no alternative but to grapple with the detail and perhaps to seek independent advice.

1.11.   Under this guidance, audit committees have wide-ranging, time-consuming and sometimes intensive work to do. Companies need to make the necessary resources available. This includes suitable payment for the members of audit committees themselves. They – and particularly the audit committee chairman - bear a significant responsibility and they need to commit a significant extra amount of time to the job. Companies also need to make provision for induction and training for new audit committee members and continuing training as may be required.

1.12.   This guidance applies to all companies to which the Code applies – i.e. UK listed companies. For groups, it will usually be necessary for the audit committee of the parent company to review issues that relate to particular subsidiaries or activities carried on by the group. Consequently, the board of a UK-listed parent company should ensure that there is adequate cooperation within the group (and with internal and external auditors of individual companies within the group) to enable the parent company audit committee to discharge its responsibilities effectively.

2   Establishment and role of the audit committee; membership, procedures and resources

Establishment and role

2.1   **The board should establish an audit committee of at least three, or in the case of smaller companies two, members.**

2.2   **The main role and responsibilities of the audit committee should be set out in written terms of reference and should include:**

+ **to monitor the integrity of the financial statements of the company and any formal announcements relating to the company's financial performance, reviewing significant financial reporting judgements contained in them;**

+ **to review the company's internal financial controls and, unless expressly addressed by a separate board risk committee composed of independent directors or by the board itself, the company's internal control and risk management systems;**

+ **to monitor and review the effectiveness of the company's internal audit function;**

+ **to make recommendations to the board, for it to put to the shareholders for their approval in general meeting, in relation to the appointment of the external auditor and to approve the remuneration and terms of engagement of the external auditor;**

+ **to review and monitor the external auditor's independence and objectivity and the effectiveness of the audit process, taking into consideration relevant UK professional and regulatory requirements;**

+ **to develop and implement policy on the engagement of the external auditor to supply non-audit services, taking into account relevant ethical guidance regarding the provision of non-audit services by the external audit firm;**

and to report to the Board, identifying any matters in respect of which it considers that action or improvement is needed, and making recommendations as to the steps to be taken.

Membership and appointment

2.3   All members of the committee should be independent non-executive directors. The board should satisfy itself that at least one member of the audit committee has recent and relevant financial experience.

2.4   The chairman of the company should not be an audit committee member.

2.5   Appointments to the audit committee should be made by the board on the recommendation of the nomination committee (where there is one), in consultation with the audit committee chairman.

2.6   Appointments should be for a period of up to three years, extendable by no more than two additional three-year periods, so long as members continue to be independent.

Meetings of the audit committee

2.7   It is for the audit committee chairman, in consultation with the company secretary, to decide the frequency and timing of its meetings. There should be as many meetings as the audit committee's role and responsibilities require. It is recommended there should be not fewer than three meetings during the year, held to coincide with key dates within the financial reporting and audit cycle[1]. However, most audit committee chairmen will wish to call more frequent meetings.

2.8   No one other than the audit committee's chairman and members is entitled to be present at a meeting of the audit committee. It is for the audit committee to decide if non-members should attend for a particular meeting or a particular agenda item. It is to be expected that the external audit lead partner will be invited regularly to attend meetings as well as the finance director. Others may be invited to attend.

2.9   Sufficient time should be allowed to enable the audit committee to undertake as full a discussion as may be required. A sufficient interval should be allowed between audit committee meetings and main board meetings to allow any work arising from the audit committee meeting to be carried out and reported to the board as appropriate.

2.10   The audit committee should, at least annually, meet the external and internal auditors, without management, to discuss matters relating to its remit and any issues arising from the audit.

---

[1]   For example, when the audit plans (internal and external) are available for review and when interim statements, preliminary announcements and the full annual report are near completion.

2.11 Formal meetings of the audit committee are the heart of its work. However, they will rarely be sufficient. It is expected that the audit committee chairman, and to a lesser extent the other members, will wish to keep in touch on a continuing basis with the key people involved in the company's governance, including the board chairman, the chief executive, the finance director, the external audit lead partner and the head of internal audit.

Resources

2.12 The audit committee should be provided with sufficient resources to undertake its duties.

2.13 The audit committee should have access to the services of the company secretariat on all audit committee matters including: assisting the chairman in planning the audit committee's work, drawing up meeting agendas, maintenance of minutes, drafting of material about its activities for the annual report, collection and distribution of information and provision of any necessary practical support.

2.14 The company secretary should ensure that the audit committee receives information and papers in a timely manner to enable full and proper consideration to be given to the issues.

2.15 The board should make funds available to the audit committee to enable it to take independent legal, accounting or other advice when the audit committee reasonably believes it necessary to do so.

Remuneration

2.16 In addition to the remuneration paid to all non-executive directors, each company should consider the further remuneration that should be paid to members of the audit committee to recompense them for the additional responsibilities of membership. Consideration should be given to the time members are required to give to audit committee business, the skills they bring to bear and the onerous duties they take on, as well as the value of their work to the company. The level of remuneration paid to the members of the audit committee should take into account the level of fees paid to other members of the board. The chairman's responsibilities and time demands will generally be heavier than the other members of the audit committee and this should be reflected in his or her remuneration.

Skills, experience and training

2.17 It is desirable that the committee member whom the board considers to have recent and relevant financial experience should have a professional qualification from one of the professional accountancy bodies. The need for a degree of financial literacy among the other members will vary according to the nature of the company, but experience of corporate financial matters will normally be required. The availability of appropriate financial expertise will be particularly important where the company's activities involve specialised financial activities.

2.18 The company should provide an induction programme for new audit committee members. This should cover the role of the audit committee, including its terms of reference and expected time commitment by members; and an overview of the company's business, identifying the main business and financial dynamics and risks. It could also include meeting some of the company staff.

2.19 Training should also be provided to members of the audit committee on an ongoing and timely basis and should include an understanding of the principles of and developments in financial reporting and related company law. In appropriate cases, it may also include, for example, understanding financial statements, applicable accounting standards and recommended practice; the regulatory framework for the company's business; the role of internal and external auditing and risk management.

2.20 The induction programme and ongoing training may take various forms, including attendance at formal courses and conferences, internal company talks and seminars, and briefings by external advisers.

3. Relationship with the board

3.1 The role of the audit committee is for the board to decide and to the extent that the audit committee undertakes tasks on behalf of the board, the results should be reported to, and considered by, the board. In doing so it should identify any matters in respect of which it considers that action or improvement is needed, and make recommendations as to the steps to be taken.

3.2 The terms of reference should be tailored to the particular circumstances of the company.

3.3 The audit committee should review annually its terms of reference and its own effectiveness and recommend any necessary changes to the board.

3.4 The board should review the audit committee's effectiveness annually.

3.5   Where there is disagreement between the audit committee and the board, adequate time should be made available for discussion of the issue with a view to resolving the disagreement. Where any such disagreements cannot be resolved, the audit committee should have the right to report the issue to the shareholders as part of the report on its activities in the annual report.

4 Role and responsibilities

Financial reporting

4.1   The audit committee should review the significant financial reporting issues and judgements made in connection with the preparation of the company's financial statements, interim reports, preliminary announcements and related formal statements.

4.2   It is management's, not the audit committee's, responsibility to prepare complete and accurate financial statements and disclosures in accordance with financial reporting standards and applicable rules and regulations. However the audit committee should consider significant accounting policies, any changes to them and any significant estimates and judgements. The management should inform the audit committee of the methods used to account for significant or unusual transactions where the accounting treatment is open to different approaches. Taking into account the external auditor's view, the audit committee should consider whether the company has adopted appropriate accounting policies and, where necessary, made appropriate estimates and judgements. The audit committee should review the clarity and completeness of disclosures in the financial statements and consider whether the disclosures made are set properly in context.

4.3   Where, following its review, the audit committee is not satisfied with any aspect of the proposed financial reporting by the company, it shall report its views to the board.

4.4   The audit committee should review related information presented with the financial statements, including the operating and financial review, and corporate governance statements relating to the audit and to risk management. Similarly, where board approval is required for other statements containing financial information (for example, summary financial statements, significant financial returns to regulators and release of price sensitive information), whenever practicable (without being inconsistent with any requirement for prompt reporting under the Listing Rules) the audit committee should review such statements first.

Internal controls and risk management systems

4.5   The audit committee should review the company's internal financial controls (that is, the systems established to identify, assess, manage and monitor financial risks); and unless expressly addressed by a separate board risk committee comprised of independent directors or by the board itself, the company's internal control and risk management systems.

4.6   The company's management is responsible for the identification, assessment, management and monitoring of risk, for developing, operating and monitoring the system of internal control and for providing assurance to the board that it has done so. Except where the board or a risk committee is expressly responsible for reviewing the effectiveness of the internal control and risk management systems, the audit committee should receive reports from management on the effectiveness of the systems they have established and the conclusions of any testing carried out by internal and external auditors.

4.7   Except to the extent that this is expressly dealt with by the board or risk committee, the audit committee should review and approve the statements included in the annual report in relation to internal control and the management of risk.

Whistleblowing

4.8   **The audit committee should review arrangements by which staff of the company may, in confidence, raise concerns about possible improprieties in matters of financial reporting or other matters. The audit committee's objective should be to ensure that arrangements are in place for the proportionate and independent investigation of such matters and for appropriate follow-up action.**

The internal audit process

4.9   **The audit committee should monitor and review the effectiveness of the company's internal audit function. Where there is no internal audit function, the audit committee should consider annually whether there is a need for an internal audit function and make a recommendation to the board, and the reasons for the absence of such a function should be explained in the relevant section of the annual report.**

4.10   The need for an internal audit function will vary depending on company specific factors including the scale, diversity and complexity of the company's activities and the number of employees, as well as cost/benefit considerations. Senior management and the board may desire objective assurance and advice on risk and control. An adequately resourced internal audit function (or its equivalent where, for example, a third party is contracted to perform some or all of the work concerned) may provide such assurance and advice. There may be other functions within the company that also provide assurance and advice covering specialist areas such as health and safety, regulatory and legal compliance and environmental issues.

4.11 When undertaking its assessment of the need for an internal audit function, the audit committee should also consider whether there are any trends or current factors relevant to the company's activities, markets or other aspects of its external environment, that have increased, or are expected to increase, the risks faced by the company. Such an increase in risk may also arise from internal factors such as organisational restructuring or from changes in reporting processes or underlying information systems. Other matters to be taken into account may include adverse trends evident from the monitoring of internal control systems or an increased incidence of unexpected occurrences.

4.12 In the absence of an internal audit function, management needs to apply other monitoring processes in order to assure itself, the audit committee and the board that the system of internal control is functioning as intended. In these circumstances, the audit committee will need to assess whether such processes provide sufficient and objective assurance.

4.13 The audit committee should review and approve the internal audit function's remit, having regard to the complementary roles of the internal and external audit functions. The audit committee should ensure that the function has the necessary resources and access to information to enable it to fulfil its mandate, and is equipped to perform in accordance with appropriate professional standards for internal auditors[2].

4.14 The audit committee should approve the appointment or termination of appointment of the head of internal audit.

4.15 In its review of the work of the internal audit function, the audit committee should, inter alia:

+ ensure that the internal auditor has direct access to the board chairman and to the audit committee and is accountable to the audit committee;

+ review and assess the annual internal audit work plan;

+ receive a report on the results of the internal auditors' work on a periodic basis;

---

[2] Further guidance can be found in the Institute of Internal Auditors' Code of Ethics and the International Standards for the Professional Practice of Internal Auditing Standards.

+ review and monitor management's responsiveness to the internal auditor's findings and recommendations;

+ meet with the head of internal audit at least once a year without the presence of management; and

+ monitor and assess the role and effectiveness of the internal audit function in the overall context of the company's risk management system.

The external audit process

4.16 The audit committee is the body responsible for overseeing the company's relations with the external auditor.

Appointment

4.17 **The audit committee should have primary responsibility for making a recommendation on the appointment, reappointment and removal of the external auditors. If the board does not accept the audit committee's recommendation, it should include in the annual report, and in any papers recommending appointment or reappointment, a statement from the audit committee explaining its recommendation and should set out reasons why the board has taken a different position.**

4.18 The audit committee's recommendation to the board should be based on the assessments referred to below. If the audit committee recommends considering the selection of possible new appointees as external auditors, it should oversee the selection process.

4.19 The audit committee should assess annually the qualification, expertise and resources, and independence (see below) of the external auditors and the effectiveness of the audit process. The assessment should cover all aspects of the audit service provided by the audit firm, and include obtaining a report on the audit firm's own internal quality control procedures.

4.20 If the external auditor resigns, the audit committee should investigate the issues giving rise to such resignation and consider whether any action is required.

Terms and Remuneration

4.21 The audit committee should approve the terms of engagement and the remuneration to be paid to the external auditor in respect of audit services provided.

4.22 The audit committee should review and agree the engagement letter issued by the external auditor at the start of each audit, ensuring that it has been updated to reflect changes in circumstances arising since the previous year. The scope of the external audit should be reviewed by the audit committee with the auditor. If the audit committee is not satisfied as to its adequacy it should arrange for additional work to be undertaken.

4.23 The audit committee should satisfy itself that the level of fee payable in respect of the audit services provided is appropriate and that an effective audit can be conducted for such a fee.

Independence, including the provision of non-audit services

4.24 The audit committee should have procedures to ensure the independence and objectivity of the external auditor annually, taking into consideration relevant UK professional and regulatory requirements. This assessment should involve a consideration of all relationships between the company and the audit firm (including the provision of non-audit services). The audit committee should consider whether, taken as a whole and having regard to the views, as appropriate, of the external auditor, management and internal audit, those relationships appear to impair the auditor's judgement or independence.

4.25 The audit committee should seek reassurance that the auditors and their staff have no family, financial, employment, investment or business relationship with the company (other than in the normal course of business). The audit committee should seek from the audit firm, on an annual basis, information about policies and processes for maintaining independence and monitoring compliance with relevant requirements, including current requirements regarding the rotation of audit partners and staff.

4.26 The audit committee should agree with the board the company's policy for the employment of former employees of the external auditor, paying particular attention to the policy regarding former employees of the audit firm who were part of the audit team and moved directly to the company. This should be drafted taking into account the relevant ethical guidelines governing the accounting profession. The audit committee should monitor application of the policy, including the number of former employees of the external auditor currently employed in senior positions in the company, and consider whether in the light of this there has been any impairment, or appearance of impairment, of the auditor's judgement or independence in respect of the audit.

4.27   The audit committee should monitor the external audit firm's compliance with applicable United Kingdom ethical guidance relating to the rotation of audit partners, the level of fees that the company pays in proportion to the overall fee income of the firm, office and partner, and other related regulatory requirements.

4.28   The audit committee should develop and recommend to the board the company's policy in relation to the provision of non-audit services by the auditor. The audit committee's objective should be to ensure that the provision of such services does not impair the external auditor's independence or objectivity. In this context, the audit committee should consider:

+   whether the skills and experience of the audit firm make it a suitable supplier of the non audit service;

+   whether there are safeguards in place to ensure that there is no threat to objectivity and independence in the conduct of the audit resulting from the provision of such services by the external auditor;

+   the nature of the non-audit services, the related fee levels and the fee levels individually and in aggregate relative to the audit fee; and

+   the criteria which govern the compensation of the individuals performing the audit.

4.29   The audit committee should set and apply a formal policy specifying the types of non-audit work:

+   from which the external auditors are excluded;

+   for which the external auditors can be engaged without referral to the audit committee; and

+   for which a case-by-case decision is necessary.

In addition, the policy may set fee limits generally or for particular classes of work.

4.30   In the third category, if it is not practicable to give approval to individual items in advance, it may be appropriate to give a general pre-approval for certain classes for work, subject to a fee limit determined by the audit committee and ratified by the board. The subsequent provision of any service by the auditor should be ratified at the next meeting of the audit committee.

4.31   In determining the policy, the audit committee should take into account relevant ethical guidance regarding the provision of non-audit services by the external audit firm, and in principle should not agree to the auditor providing a service if, having regard to the ethical guidance, the result is that:

+ the external auditor audits its own firm's work;

+ the external auditor makes management decisions for the company;

+ a mutuality of interest is created; or

+ the external auditor is put in the role of advocate for the company.

The audit committee should satisfy itself that any safeguards required by ethical guidance are implemented.

4.32 **The annual report should explain to shareholders how, if the auditor provides non-audit services, auditor objectivity and independence is safeguarded.**

Annual audit cycle

4.33 At the start of each annual audit cycle, the audit committee should ensure that appropriate plans are in place for the audit.

4.34 The audit committee should consider whether the auditor's overall work plan, including planned levels of materiality, and proposed resources to execute the audit plan appears consistent with the scope of the audit engagement, having regard also to the seniority, expertise and experience of the audit team.

4.35 The audit committee should review, with the external auditors, the findings of their work. In the course of its review, the audit committee should:
+ discuss with the external auditor major issues that arose during the course of the audit and have subsequently been resolved and those issues that have been left unresolved;

+ review key accounting and audit judgements; and

+ review levels of errors identified during the audit, obtaining explanations from management and, where necessary the external auditors, as to why certain errors might remain unadjusted.

4.36 The audit committee should also review the audit representation letters before signature by management and give particular consideration to matters where representation has been requested that relate to non-standard issues[3]. The audit committee should consider whether the

---

[3] Further guidance can by found in the Auditing Practices Board's Statement of Auditing Standard 440 "Management Representations".

information provided is complete and appropriate based on its own knowledge.

4.37 As part of the ongoing monitoring process, the audit committee should review the management letter (or equivalent). The audit committee should review and monitor management's responsiveness to the external auditor's findings and recommendations.

4.38 At the end of the annual audit cycle, the audit committee should assess the effectiveness of the audit process. In the course of doing so, the audit committee should:

+ review whether the auditor has met the agreed audit plan and understand the reasons for any changes, including changes in perceived audit risks and the work undertaken by the external auditors to address those risks;

+ consider the robustness and perceptiveness of the auditors in their handling of the key accounting and audit judgements identified and in responding to questions from the audit committees, and in their commentary where appropriate on the systems of internal control;

+ obtain feedback about the conduct of the audit from key people involved, e.g. the finance director and the head of internal audit; and

+ review and monitor the content of the external auditor's management letter, in order to assess whether it is based on a good understanding of the company's business and establish whether recommendations have been acted upon and, if not, the reasons why they have not been acted upon.

5   Communication with shareholders

5.1 The terms of reference of the audit committee, including its role and the authority delegated to it by the board, should be made available. A separate section in the annual report should describe the work of the committee in discharging those responsibilities.

5.2 The audit committee section should include, inter alia:

+ a summary of the role of the audit committee;

+ the names and qualifications of all members of the audit committee during the period;

+ the number of audit committee meetings;

+ a report on the way the audit committee has discharged its responsibilities; and

+ the explanation provided for in paragraph 4.29 above.

APPENDIX 5

QUOTED COMPANIES ALLIANCE (QCA) – CORPORATE GOVERNANCE GUIDELINES FOR AIM COMPANIES (JULY 2005): PP 6–15

PURPOSE OF CORPORATE GOVERNANCE

The purpose of good corporate governance is to ensure that the company is managed in an efficient, effective and entrepreneurial manner for the benefit of all shareholders over the longer term.

WHAT FEATURES OF CORPORATE GOVERNANCE ACHIEVE THIS?

Efficient management:

- the governing body must not be so large as to prevent efficient operation;

- the mechanisms by which important decisions are taken should be transparent;

- it should be clear where responsibility lies for the management of the company and for the achievement of key tasks;

- procedures should be in place to protect significant tangible and intangible assets and these need to be regularly reviewed and updated.

Effective management:

- the governing body must have all appropriate skills available to it in order to make the key decisions expected of it;

- decision makers should be provided with the best possible information (accurate, sufficient. timely and clear) on which to constructively challenge recommendations made to them before making their decisions;

- the collective responsibility of the board requires all directors to be involved in the process of arriving at significant decisions;

- ineffective directors (executive and non-executive) must be identified and either helped to become effective or replaced.

Entrepreneurial management:

- there should be a vision of what the company is trying to achieve, over what period, and an understanding of what is required to achieve this ambition.

Benefit of shareholders over the long term:

- vested interests should not be able to act in a manner contrary to the common good of all shareholders; transactions with management. major shareholders and other related parties should be reported in a transparent manner;

- a dialogue should exist between shareholders and board so that the board understands shareholders' objectives;

- a communication mechanism should exist between board and shareholders so that shareholders understand the constraints on the company.

CODE OF BEST PRACTICE FOR AIM COMPANIES – THE QCA GUIDELINES

Matters reserved for the Board

There should be a formal schedule of matters specifically reserved for the Board's decision.

Timely information

The board should be supplied in a timely manner with information (including regular management financial information) in a form and of a quality appropriate to enable it to discharge its duties.

Internal controls review

The board should, at least annually, conduct a review of the effectiveness of the group's system of internal controls and should report to shareholders that they have done so. The review should cover all material controls, including financial, operational and compliance controls and risk management systems.

Chairman and Chief Executive

The roles of chairman and chief executive should not be exercised by the same individual or there should be a clear explanation of how other board procedures provide protection against the risks of concentration of power within the company.

Independent non-executive directors

A company should have at least two independent non-executive directors (one of whom may be the Chairman) and the Board should not be dominated by one person or group of people.

Re-election

All directors should be submitted for re-election at regular intervals, subject to continued satisfactory performance. The board should ensure planned and progressive refreshing of the board.

Audit Committee

The board should establish an audit committee of at least two members, who should all be independent non-executive directors.

Remuneration Committee

The board should establish a remuneration committee of at least two members, who should be independent non-executive directors.

Nomination Committee

Recommendations for appointments to the board should be made by a nomination committee (or the Board as a whole) and should be made after due evaluation.

Dialogue with shareholders

There should be a dialogue with shareholders based on the mutual understanding of objectives. The board as a whole has responsibility for ensuring that a satisfactory dialogue with shareholders takes place.

REPORTING CORPORATE GOVERNANCE

A Corporate Governance statement on the company's web site

Companies should publish a Corporate Governance statement annually that describes how they achieve good governance. We recommend that this report is published on the company's web site (which would also be an appropriate place to make available for inspection the items required to be on display as set out below). It could, alternatively, be published in the annual report and accounts. Where the report is published on the company's web site, the Directors' Report should identify where this information can be found and confirm the (recent) date at which it was reviewed and updated.

Applying the QCA Guidelines

(It is anticipated that all AIM companies will wish to follow good governance and should be able to apply all of the QCA Guidelines set out in this Code. The Corporate Governance statement should, at a minimum, describe how each of the QCA Guidelines is put into practice by the company and also describe any additional corporate governance standards and procedures that the company applies beyond this basic level.

It is anticipated that a company should be able to (and will) apply all of the QCA Guidelines. Where this is not the case, the statement should describe how the features of good governance are being achieved.

Basic disclosures

As well as explaining how the company achieves good governance, the annual report should also include the following 'Basic Disclosures':

- a statement of how the board operates, including a high level statement of which types of decisions are to be taken by the board and which are to be delegated to management;

- the identity of the chairman, the deputy chairman (where there is one), the chief executive, the senior independent director and the chairmen and members of the nomination, audit and remuneration committees;

- the identity of those directors the Board considers to be independent and the reasons why it has determined a director to be independent notwithstanding factors which may appear to impair that status.

- the board should describe any performance evaluation procedures it applies;

- the names of directors, accompanied by sufficient biographical details (with any other relevant information) to enable shareholders to take an informed decision on the balance of the Board and the re-election of certain of them;

- the number of meetings of the Board (normally monthly) and of the Committees and individual directors' attendance at them;

- an explanation of the directors' responsibility for preparing the accounts and a statement by the auditors about their reporting responsibilities;

- a statement by the directors that the business is a going concern, with supporting assumptions or qualifications as necessary;

- an explanation to shareholders of how, if the auditor provides significant non-audit services, auditor objectivity and independence is safeguarded.

Available for inspection

The following items should be available for inspection on the company's web site or by shareholders on request:

- the terms and conditions of appointment of non-executive directors should be made available for inspection.

- the audit committee should make available its terms of reference, explaining its role and the authority delegated to it by the board.

- the remuneration committee should make available its terms of reference, explaining its role and the authority delegated to it by the board.

- the nomination committee should make available its terms of reference, explaining its role and the authority delegated to it by the board, or the board should explain its processes where it acts as the nomination committee.

RELATING FEATURES OF GOOD GOVERNANCE, THE QCA GUIDELINES AND BASIC REPORTING

The purpose of good corporate governance is to ensure that the company is managed in an efficient, effective and entrepreneurial manner for the benefit of all shareholders over the longer term.

Feature	QCA Guideline	Additional disclosure guidance
Efficient Management		
The governing body must not be so large as to prevent efficient operation		The identity of the chairman, the deputy chairman (where there is one), the chief executive, the senior independent director and the chairmen and members of the nomination, audit and remuneration committees.
The mechanisms by which important decisions are taken should be transparent.	There should be a formal schedule of matters specifically reserved for the Board's decision. It should establish an audit committee of at least two members, who should all be independent non-executive directors. The board should establish a remuneration committee of at least two members, who should all be independent non-executive directors.	A statement of how the board operates, including a high level statement of which types of decisions are to be taken by the board and which are to be delegated to management.

A statement of where the terms of reference of the principal board committees can be accessed. |

Feature	QCA Guideline	Additional disclosure guidance
It should be clear where responsibility lies for the management of the company and for the achievement of key tasks.	The roles of chairman and chief executive should not be exercised by the same individual or there should be a clear explanation of how other board procedures provide protection from the risks of concentration of power within the company.	An overview of the responsibilities of the Chairman and each of the executive directors and explanation of the directors' responsibility for preparing the accounts and a state-ment by the auditors about their reporting responsibilities.
Procedures should be in place to protect significant tangible and intangible assets and these need to be regularly reviewed and updated.	The board should, at least annually, conduct a review of the effectiveness of the group's system of internal controls and should report to shareholders that they have done so. The review should cover all material controls, including financial, operational and compliance controls and risk management systems.	Report to shareholders that a review has been conducted. A statement by the directors that the business is a going concern, with supporting assumptions or qualifications as necessary.

Effective Management

The governing body must have all appropriate skills available to it in order to make the key decisions expected of it.	Recommendations for appointments to the board should be made by a nomination committee (or the Board as a whole) and should be made after due evaluation.	The names of directors, accompanied by sufficient biographical details (with any other relevant information) to enable shareholders to take an informed decision on the balance of the Board.

Feature	QCA Guideline	Additional disclosure guidance
Decision makers should be provided with the best possible information (accurate, sufficient, timely and clear) on which to challenge constructively recommendations made to them before making their decisions.	The board should be supplied in a timely manner with Information (including regular management financial information) in a form and of a quality appropriate to enable it to discharge its duties	
The collective responsibility of the board requires all directors to be involved in the process of arriving at significant decisions.	There should be a formal schedule of matters specifically reserved for the Board's decision.	The number of meetings of the Board (normally monthly) and of the Committees and individual directors attendance at them.
Ineffective directors (executive and non-executive) must be identified and either helped to become effective or replaced.	All directors should be submitted for re-election at regular intervals, subject to continued satisfactory performance. The board should ensure planned and progressive refreshing of the board.	The board should describe any performance evaluation procedures it applies.

Entrepreneurial Management

| There should be a vision of what the company is trying to achieve, over what period, and an understanding of what is required to achieve this ambition. | There should be a dialogue with shareholders based on the mutual understanding of objectives. The board as a whole has responsibility for ensuring that a satisfactory dialogue with shareholders takes place. | This should already be a key part of the chairman's statement and other directors' statements in the annual report. |

Feature	QCA Guideline	Additional disclosure guidance
Benefit of shareholders over the longer term		
Vested interests should not be able to act in a manner contrary to the common good of all shareholders: transactions with management, major shareholders and other related parties should be reported in a transparent manner.	The roles of chairman and chief executive should not be exercised by the same individual or there should be a clear explanation of how other board procedures provide protection from the risks of concentration of power within the company. A company should have at least two independent non-executive directors and not be dominated by one person or group of people.	The identity of those directors the Board considers to be independent and the reasons why it has determined a director to be independent, notwithstanding factors which may appear to impair that status. An explanation to shareholders of how, if the auditor provides significant non-audit services, auditor objectivity and independence is safeguarded.
A dialogue should exist between shareholders and board so that (i) the board understands shareholders' objectives and (ii) shareholders understand the constraints on the company.	There should be a dialogue with shareholders based on the mutual understanding of objectives. The board as a whole has responsibility for ensuring that a satisfactory dialogue with shareholders takes place.	

APPENDIX 6

NATIONAL ASSOCIATION OF PENSION FUNDS (NAPF) – CORPORATE GOVERNANCE POLICY: POLICY AND VOTING GUIDELINES FOR AIM COMPANIES (MARCH 2007): PP 5–10

DISCLOSURE STANDARDS

Directors are appointed by shareholders who are the owners of companies and it is therefore important that they report to the owners regularly on the company's performance and the development of its business, and that governance structures are in place to ensure that the company is led by an effective board.

However, it has not been unusual for smaller companies to publish annual reports that provide little, or no, explanation of their governance structure, or remuneration policy and practice. Consequently, it can be very difficult for shareholders to make an informed evaluation of a company's governance.

Companies should seek to apply the disclosure standards set by the Combined Code. However, this may be inappropriate for some smaller companies and therefore as a minimum we expect companies to disclose:

- Directors' names, other directorships and brief biographical details (including executive or non-executive status);

- The names of the chairman, the deputy chairman (where there is one), the chief executive, the senior independent director and the chairmen and members of the nomination, audit and remuneration committees (where these committees exist); and

- The names of the non-executive directors whom the board determines to be independent, with reasons where necessary.

These requirements are broadly similar to those of the latest AIM Rules. We encourage companies to include them in their annual report, but as a minimum they should refer shareholders to the company website.

NAPF AIM Policy

The **NAPF AIM Policy** expects a company to disclose its corporate governance policies, including biographical details of its directors and details of board committees.

COMBINED ROLES OF CHAIRMAN AND CHIEF EXECUTIVE

The Combined Code states that companies must provide a clear explanation of the respective roles and responsibilities of the Chairman and Chief Executive. The Main Principle emphasises that no one individual should have unfettered powers of decision, hence the roles of Chairman and CEO should be separated.

The QCA Guidelines state the roles of chairman and chief executive should not be exercised by the same individual or there should be a clear explanation of how other board procedures provide protection from the risks of concentration of power within the company.

The NAPF policy considers that the functions of Chairman and CEO are different. They should be clearly distinguished and not confused or compromised by being combined. However, where this is not the case the Company should provide details of the exceptional circumstances which caused the roles to become combined as well as a forward looking statement explaining its intentions to separate the roles.

NAPF AIM Policy

The **NAPF AIM Policy** does not deviate from the NAPF Policy. However a pragmatic approach is justified if a vote against the director combining these roles might be considered detrimental to the company.

CEO BECOMING CHAIRMAN

The Combined Code states that a CEO should not go on to be Chairman of the same company.

The QCA Guidelines do not address this point.

The NAPF policy supports the Combined Code principle that the CEO should not become Chairman. However should this happen, the

Company must disclose in the annual report its reasons for the appointment and describe the selection process.

NAPF AIM Policy

The **NAPF AIM Policy** does not deviate from the NAPF Policy.

APPOINTMENT OF A SENIOR INDEPENDENT DIRECTOR

The Combined Code states that companies should appoint a recognised senior independent non-executive director, other than the board Chairman.

The QCA Guidelines do not address this point.

The NAPF policy supports the Combined Code principle.

NAPF AIM Policy

The **NAPF AIM Policy** requires the appointment of a Senior Independent Director where a company has a combined Chairman and CEO, to ensure an independent voice on the board who can provide a communication channel for the Company's shareholders if needed. In other circumstances a Senior Independent Director is to be encouraged but is not required.

BALANCE OF THE BOARD

The Combined Code states that a smaller company should have at least two independent non-executive directors on its board.

The Combined Code provisions for board balance, along with committee composition, are the areas where smaller companies have most problems in complying. The make-up of smaller company boards varies considerably. AIM comprises a broad spectrum of companies, some of which are more mature and have an advanced corporate governance framework that includes larger boards and established board committees, whilst other less mature companies may have as few as three directors, typically, a Chairman, CEO and a non-executive director.

In addition to the size of a board, the Combined Code definition of independence presents a further hindrance towards compliance, since some of the criteria may be unachievable for smaller companies.

The QCA Guidelines state that a company should have at least two independent non-executive directors and not be dominated by one person or group of people.

The NAPF policy supports the Combined Code principle and encourages companies to provide a detailed explanation in the event of non-compliance.

NAPF AIM Policy

For larger boards the **NAPF AIM Policy** does not deviate from the NAPF Policy, which requires at least two independent directors, excluding the Chairman.

For smaller boards the **NAPF AIM Policy** requires that boards have at least two independent non-executive directors to comprise not less than one third of the board, one of whom may be the Chairman.

This less stringent requirement is appropriate for AIM companies who have boards comprising of no more than four directors. Such boards might consist of the Chairman, the CEO and, at most, two non-executive directors, of which one should be independent. These provisions safeguard independent representation on the board whilst providing sufficient flexibility for those companies with smaller boards.

COMPOSITION OF THE AUDIT, REMUNERATION AND NOMINATION COMMITTEES

The Combined Code requires that the Nomination Committee should be made up of a majority of independent non-executive directors.

The QCA Guidelines state that there should be a Nomination Committee which should lead the process for board appointments and make recommendations to the board. The Committee could comprise the whole board.

A majority of members of the Committee should be independent non-executive directors. The chairman or an independent non-executive director should chair the Committee, but the chairman should not chair the Nomination Committee when it is dealing with the appointment of a successor to the chairmanship.

The Combined Code requires that:

Audit and Remuneration Committees comprise at least two non-executive directors, all of whom are considered independent.

At least one member of the Audit Committee should have 'recent and relevant' financial experience.

The QCA Guidelines are aligned with the Combined Code provision with regard to the composition of the Audit and Remuneration Committees.

NAPF AIM Policy

The **NAPF AIM policy** supports the Combined Code principle. However, it recognises that the lack of independent membership, compounded with the insufficient number of non-executive directors on a board, could make compliance unachievable.

The Audit, Remuneration and Nomination Committees ideally should comprise solely independent non-executive directors. At the least there should be a majority of independent directors on all committees.

The Chairman may be a member of the Audit, Remuneration or Nomination Committees (not as Chairman) provided that, other than his chairmanship, he/she fulfils the test of independence, in which case he/she will be viewed as an independent director.

REMUNERATION ARRANGEMENTS

NAPF AIM Policy

The **NAPF AIM Policy** does not deviate from the NAPF Policy. Companies should also generally adhere to current best practice guidelines (ABI & NAPF Remuneration Guidelines). A significant component of senior management's remuneration should be linked to performance and there should be disclosure of the performance conditions attaching to any bonuses or long-term incentive plans. Companies are strongly encouraged to put their Remuneration Reports to a vote at the AGM.

DIRECTOR INDEPENDENCE

The NAPF Policy and the QCA Guidelines encourage all companies to be rigorous in the assessment of independence using the criteria of independence defined in the Combined Code.

However, when applied to AIM companies some of the stated criteria require more flexibility due to the particular circumstances faced by such companies. A significant shareholding, option grants and tenure are among the most common problems faced by AIM companies.

For FTSE All-Share companies, NAPF considers personal shareholdings in excess of one percent of a company's issued share capital to be material and consequently considers that such a shareholding may affect independence.

However. we believe that the threshold should be increased for AIM companies, because they have a smaller share capital and they may pay non-executive directors' fees in shares rather than cash, due to cash flow pressures.

NAPF AIM Policy

The **NAPF AIM Policy** is that independence may be compromised if a director has a beneficial or non-beneficial share holding of more than three percent of the Company's issued share capital.

NAPF believes that remuneration other than fees paid in cash or shares may compromise independence. This includes participation in the company's share option scheme or a performance-related pay scheme, or membership of a company's pension scheme.

It is most common for smaller AIM companies to have issued options to non-executive directors, either historically upon Initial Public Offering (IPO) or as a one-off grant (due to cash flow constraints).

The **NAPF AIM Policy** excludes historical one-off grants, if the quantum is not considered to be material, from the assessment of independence. However, should this practice become routine or a director actively participates in an option scheme then the director's independence may be judged to have been compromised. Companies can use fully-paid shares as part of the remuneration for non-executive directors.

The **NAPF AIM Policy** is flexible in cases where tenure is between nine and twelve years and tenure is the only factor affecting a director's independence. The board evaluation process and succession planning policy are important when reviewing independence and should be disclosed in the Annual Report.

PRE-EMPTION RIGHTS

NAPF AIM Policy

The **NAPF AIM Policy** is to support the Pre-emption Principles published in 2006 by the Pre-emption Group. Companies should seek annual approval from shareholders for issuance on a non-pre-emptive basis.

However, it is recognised that there will more often be good reasons for waiving pre-emption rights among smaller companies; for example, for reasons of cost, shareholder structure or speed. Companies should, in keeping with the spirit of the principles, consult with leading shareholders in advance, provide them with a full justification for a decision to seek authority to issue stock above the 5% annual limit and should account for its usage in the subsequent Annual Report.

APPENDIX 7

THE INSTITUTE OF CHARTERED ACCOUNTANTS OF SCOTLAND (ICAS) – AVOIDING THE PITFALLS IN RUNNING A PRIVATE COMPANY: A PRACTICAL GUIDE FOR DIRECTORS (APRIL 2008): PP 8–18

INTRODUCTION

Corporate governance looks at the way in which a company is governed, focusing on the relationships between board members, and evaluating internal controls. Good corporate governance should support the leadership of the company by setting good standards of business behaviour and, in doing so, improve the long term value of the company. It should assist in bringing discipline and accountability.

The Institute of Chartered Accountants of Scotland is pleased to publish this guide to corporate governance for the use of individual directors and for boards of smaller companies as they develop and grow. Although corporate governance codes have been developed for publicly listed companies, we believe that the key principles and benefits are important to businesses of all sizes.

The Combined Code on Corporate Governance (the Code) sets out principles that need to be applied, and provisions with which listed companies are expected to comply, or to explain why they have not. However, for a smaller, private company, compliance with some or all aspects of the Code may not be practical or even appropriate. This guide considers those principles of the Code that we believe are the most relevant to private companies and discusses the manner in which they might be usefully applied.

This guide is for:

* directors of a company who wish to apply a sound system of management and control as the company grows and develops;

* individuals who are asked to join a business as a director to help them to assess the level of governance in the business;

- shareholders of privately owned companies to benchmark the governance in the company against best practice; and

- external investors to assess what might be an appropriate level of governance for unlisted companies.

This guide is not intended to be prescriptive but simply to suggest ways in which private companies may develop good practice in governing their affairs. For the growing company it also provides a pathway to the framework set out in the Combined Code. The guide considers the collective responsibilities of the board, the role of each director, and risk management and internal controls. The practical implications of how each topic can be applied depending on the company's ownership are also considered.

The different stages of ownership of a company specifically identified in this guide are:

1. 100% private ownership, either start-up or mature situation, i.e. the owner-managed company.

2. 100% private ownership, but with external commitments such as bank loans.

3. Private ownership but with some shareholders who are not involved in the management.

4. No longer in private ownership, for example, due to an AIM or full listing.

This guide focuses on the first three stages.

1. THE COLLECTIVE RESPONSIBILITIES OF THE BOARD

'Every company should be headed by an effective board, which is collectively responsible for the success of the company', according to the Combined Code. This is equally relevant for the private company. The board needs clarity of its role and responsibilities. The simplest way of doing this is to set these out in a board 'charter' which can be monitored and revisited on an ongoing basis. The responsibility of the board is to direct the affairs of the company to maximise its value for its shareholders and stakeholders as a whole. In doing so, the board must ensure the company complies with its articles as well as relevant legal, regulatory and governance requirements. The following paragraphs outline the collective responsibilities of a board and how they may apply in practice to the private company.

The Responsibilities of the Board

The board's key responsibilities are to:

- establish clear purpose, vision and values;

- set appropriate strategy and structure;

- delegate day-to-day authority to manage the business to management, monitor management's performance and hold them to account;

- establish proper risk management and internal control frameworks; and

- provide leadership.

Practical considerations for the private company:

- In an owner-managed company the distinction between the board and the management may be blurred or non-existent. Nevertheless, time should be allowed for consideration of purpose, strategy and structure, risks and internal control.

- The growing company, with increasing staff numbers and external financing, should be encouraged to formalise the key responsibilities by discussing the board's role and setting it out in a clear statement.

- Any non-executive directors on the board should lead the monitoring of management performance, the challenge to the vision, values, strategy, risk management and internal controls, and should ensure that the board provides appropriate leadership.

- A company is unlikely to remain static and therefore its strategy and direction will evolve, meaning that the key responsibilities should be revisited on a regular basis.

- The board should have appropriate documentation to reflect and communicate the company's mission, business plan, and delegations.

Matters Reserved for the Board

To make sure the board can exercise its oversight responsibilities, it retains approval authority for certain specific matters. These should be formally documented in a schedule of matters reserved and, in our view, would reserve to the board the approval of:

- Changes to capital.

- Payment of dividends.

- Corporate objectives, strategies and structure.

- Corporate plans and all material changes to the corporate plans.

- Operating and capital budgets and all material changes to these budgets.

- Material transactions (e.g. acquisitions, disposals, starting or ceasing a business activity).

- The financial statements.

- Any borrowings or guarantees.

- Relevant external communications e.g. with any regulator or shareholders.

- The appointment and remuneration of directors.

- Any authorities delegated to management.

- Political and charitable donations.

- Company policies.

- Compliance with legislation, for example in the areas of company law, employment, environmental matters, health and safety, wrongful trading and competition laws.

Practical considerations for the private company:

- Arguably, the smaller the company, the more important it is to identify someone else, such as the person providing company secretarial services, who can undertake the necessary oversight and operational decisions if need be, or in case of an emergency such as when the director(s) are not available. Alternatively, the owner manager may wish to appoint a power of attorney in case of such emergencies.

- In an owner-managed company those responsibilities undertaken by the owner manager and those delegated to staff should be clearly distinguished and understood.

- As the company grows there should be a regular review of which matters are reserved and which authorities are delegated.

Delegations of Authority

Operational matters need to be delegated in order to ensure the smooth running of the business and to allow the board to focus on its primary role. A schedule of delegations of authority should be established, which sets out the parameters of the delegated authority and particularly any financial limits. Areas that could be covered in the scheme of delegation include:

- Opening bank accounts and authorising payments.

- General purchasing powers/budgets.

- Signing of leases.

- Signing of regulatory documents.

- Powers of attorney.

- External communication.

- Staff recruitment and remuneration.

- Health and safety responsibilities.

- Compliance with current legislation, in particular, employment, health and safety and tax.

Practical considerations for the private company:

- In a smaller company the owner-manager usually retains responsibility for many of the above matters. It should be clear what areas are delegated, if any.

- As the company grows the owner/board needs to develop a systematic means of delegating authority and formalising this.

- Delegated authorities ought to be reviewed periodically to ensure that they are complied with and that the authorities remain appropriate for the size of the enterprise and its management structure.

Board Meetings

The board should meet often enough to complete its statutory and regulatory responsibilities and to exercise its oversight role properly. Good practice can be summarised as:

- An agenda should be prepared by the chairman and company secretary.

- The agenda and any supporting papers should be circulated with sufficient time to allow directors to prepare for the meeting.

- Formal minutes should be taken of the meeting, ensuring all decisions are recorded and giving a flavour of the challenges and questioning raised by directors.

- The minutes should include an action plan to ensure decisions are followed up in a reasonable timescale.

- The meeting should monitor progress against the approved plans and budgets and ensure proper coverage of the matters reserved.

Practical considerations for the private company:

- In an owner-managed company it is good practice to set aside time for regular formal board meetings (and not just extend informal management meetings), at least to consider those aspects set out above.

- As a company grows, and particularly when external finance is introduced, the board may be expected to meet more frequently; for example on a monthly basis or around times when key reporting requirements are to be met (e.g. completion of annual report).

- It is also helpful to have documented procedures to deal with urgent issues which require board approval and arise between timetabled board meetings.

- Despite the Companies Act 2006 no longer requiring a private company to hold an AGM, companies with shareholders who are not involved in the management of the business may benefit from the discipline of a formal meeting to review the past year's activities and results, and the future prospects of the company.

Implementation and Compliance Schedules

The company should prepare, and keep updated, implementation schedules which show when the various financial, legal and regulatory requirements require to be completed and who is responsible for completing them. The schedules may include:

- Preparation of accounts and their approval by the board.

- Filing accounts with Companies House and HMRC.

- Tax returns and payments.

- Preparation and submission of annual return with Companies House.

- Health and safety reviews and risk assessments.

- Employment matters.

Practical considerations for the private company:

- These principles are relevant regardless of the size or ownership of the company.

- Matters to be addressed in a compliance schedule are included at Appendix A.

- A specific individual should be responsible for monitoring the compliance schedule on a monthly basis. It is important to be aware that criminal penalties can arise from failure to comply with the submission deadlines. It is the directors who are responsible for company compliance and passing this work on to an adviser does not transfer this responsibility.

2. THE ROLE AND RESPONSIBILITIES OF INDIVIDUAL BOARD MEMBERS

An effective board should have a balance of skills and experience that is appropriate for the size and requirements of the business. In the smallest owner-managed companies it is probable that all responsibilities will fall on one or two people but as the company grows, so should the board. At the stage when a company wishes to list, the Combined Code expects a balance of executive and non-executive directors, and that the chairman should be separate from the chief executive. The following paragraphs outline the individual board members' responsibilities and how they may be undertaken in the private company as it grows and develops.

The Chairman

The chairman is appointed by the board and his duties include responsibility for:

- leadership of the board;

- setting the board agenda and ensuring that directors have accurate and clear information;

- the effectiveness of board meetings, including the induction, training and development of members of the board;

- ensuring the company has an appropriate strategy, objectives, and risk controls; and

- communications with the shareholders.

Practical considerations for the private company:

- In a private company without external shareholders it is unusual to find the roles of chairman and chief executive as separate appointments. However, the individual fulfilling these two roles should remember that the responsibilities of each are separate and distinct.

- An independent chairman may be best practice but in a small company this is unusual and may not be commercially justifiable.

- Once a company has external financing and/or shareholders who are not involved in the management, it should have a chairman who is separate from the chief executive.

The Chief Executive

The chief executive is appointed by the board, and is responsible for managing the day to day business of the company and should have clear authority from the board to do so.

Practical considerations for the private company:

- A smaller company is usually run by its owner who assumes a range of roles. As the company grows it is best practice for the decision-making in the company to be spread between several (executive) directors or management.

- When a company seeks external financing, the role of the chief executive should be more clearly defined to be responsible for overall management of the business. With external financing there are new responsibilities on the management team and the board should consider whether it needs to recruit new directors.

- Once a company has shareholders who are not involved in the management, the chief executive should have a clearly defined role reporting to a board of directors.

The Secretary

Despite the fact that under the 2006 Companies Act a private company no longer needs to appoint a company secretary, the functions that the company secretary carries out remain. These consist of fulfilling the legal necessities and administration associated with running the company.

Practical considerations for the private company:

- In an owner-managed small company it may appear unnecessary to appoint a secretary; however, all the associated tasks should be included on a compliance schedule and allocated to a specific individual or individuals.

- A private company with only one director should consider appointing a company secretary so that there is more than one officer of the company in order to act if the director is incapacitated.

- With external shareholders, one person should have overall responsibility for shareholder information and dealing with shareholder communications.

Executive Directors and Non-Executive Directors

Executive directors have day-to-day management responsibilities, in addition to their responsibilities as members of the board. They are usually employed on a full-time basis by the company.

The role of non-executive directors is to participate fully in the functioning of the board, advising, supporting and challenging management as appropriate. Usually they will be independent, in other words have no other links with the company. In particular, a non-executive director should:

- have suitable experience;

- challenge and contribute to the development of strategy;

- scrutinise the performance of management against the objectives of the company;

- seek to ensure the integrity of financial information; and

- determine appropriate levels of remuneration and consider succession planning.

Practical considerations for the private company:

- In an owner-managed company a non-executive director may bring different experience and an external, more objective, viewpoint to the board.

- As a company grows, with wider responsibilities and external commitments, this should be reflected by giving consideration to introducing and/or increasing the number of non-executive directors.

- External investors will frequently insist on a non-executive director and the investor may assist in the appointment.

The Appointment of Non-Executive Directors

In selecting someone for appointment as a non-executive director, it is appropriate to consider the following:

- Skills and experience.

- Professional qualifications.

- References.

- Other appointments.

- Potential conflicts of interest.

- Sufficient time available to devote to the role.

- Likely remuneration package.

- Role and specific responsibilities on the board.

There should be a formal letter of appointment of the non-executive director which should detail the amount of time expected to be committed to the company and the basis of remuneration. (An executive director should have a service contract detailing his or her terms and conditions.)

Practical considerations for the private company:

- A letter of appointment.

- Length of period of appointment: Companies may appoint a non-executive director for a fixed period such as an initial three-year period, which can be renewed for further three year periods, as recommended in the Code. However, other companies may prefer the flexibility of an open ended agreement and this is common in private companies.

- The overall length of service should be carefully considered from the points of view of external perceptions and value to the company. In a highly specialised industry it may take a period of time for a non-executive director to become familiar with the business.

3. RISK AND INTERNAL CONTROL

The board's responsibilities identified earlier include the key elements of risk management and internal controls. Risk is an inherent part of being in business, and risk management is concerned with identifying, assessing, monitoring and mitigating risk, not necessarily removing it. An effective system of internal control is key to robust risk management. There should be a set of clearly documented procedures that tell those responsible what they must do or not do and, as part of an effective control system, there need to be regular checks to ensure that the procedures are operating effectively. The Combined Code states 'the board should maintain a sound system of internal control to safeguard shareholders' investment and the company's assets'.

The following paragraphs outline key aspects of risk management and internal control and how these may apply in the private company. The practical application will depend on a number of factors including the number of employees, the levels of delegation, the nature of the business and geographical spread, and the complexity of the company's practices and procedures.

Risk Management

A company should ensure that it has a continuous risk management process. This involves:

- agreeing the company's appetite for risk, for example, in some industry sectors the business model may be based on taking a higher degree of risk than competitors in order to achieve a premium price or other market advantage;

- identifying the risks in the company's strategy; including strategic, operational, financial;

- regulatory, environmental or political risks;

- taking appropriate measures to mitigate the risks identified;

- establishing controls and review procedures to ensure that risk management is effective; and

- updating and improving these processes in the light of experience.

Practical considerations for the private company:

- In an owner-managed company risk management is generally addressed by the owner but is rarely documented, although making notes of even simple assessments can provide a focus to decision making and risk mitigation.

- A simple SWOT (strengths, weaknesses, opportunities and threats) analysis can be beneficial to identify key risks and opportunities.

- Understanding risk should be a company-wide responsibility but often in a smaller company it will be either the chief executive or finance director who will shoulder most of this responsibility. Where possible, involvement of other staff will almost always add to the effectiveness of the process.

- Professional advisers may be of assistance in identifying key risks and controls.

- In the growing company, reporting and monitoring procedures should be put in place so that the senior management team, board, and ultimately the shareholders, can be confident that risks are being properly identified and managed.

- In larger companies the creation of a risk management committee involving senior managers and directors should create the basis for more effective analysis of risks.

- A risk management policy needs to be constantly revisited to ensure that the company learns from its own experience, makes use of relevant industry knowledge, and takes account of changes in the external business environment.

Company Policies and Internal Controls

Company policies and procedures set out standards of behaviour and responsibilities for staff and the internal controls are the checks to ensure they are being properly applied. Policies are likely to be required across all aspects of the business to varying degrees depending on the scale and nature of the company's operations. These policies may cover the following:

- Anti-fraud.

- Anti money-laundering.

- Business continuity.

- Internal and external communications.

- Human resources, remuneration, allowable expenses, and compliance with current legislation.

- Information security and reliability.

- Outside appointments.

- Purchasing/ procurement.

- Records management.

- Regulatory compliance.

- Health and safety compliance.

An internal control system should consist of policies, procedures, allocation of responsibilities, and checks to ensure these are functioning. The system is unlikely to remain effective, however, unless it is reviewed regularly, and developed as the business grows to take account of new and emerging risks, control failures and market expectations or changes. Internal controls should include some or all of the following:

- Authorisation limits.

- Segregation of duties.

- Accounting reconciliations and monitoring of cash flow.

- Suitable qualifications and training.

- Budgetary controls.

- Controls over incoming funds, expenditure and access to bank accounts.

- Security of premises and control over assets.

Practical considerations for the private company:

- Smaller owner-managed companies with few employees handle risks and controls quite informally but as a company grows a more formal system of internal control will become necessary.

- Basic control policies usually start with financial controls, insurance requirements, and health and safety.

- Strong financial controls and the ability to monitor any covenants will be essential if external financing is sought.

- Without regular review and monitoring of cash management, particularly in cash strapped companies there may be exposure to wrongful trading or insolvency.

- As the company grows, the basic controls can be extended and, thereafter, the company should evaluate the level of risk attached to the above topics and the way in which these are controlled.

Business Continuity

A continuity plan should identify the key people and processes in an organisation which could place the company at risk if they were not available for whatever reason. The key areas are likely to include:

- Key personnel – directors, managers, staff with specific skills, knowledge or licences.

- Premises.

- IT systems.

- Supply chain.

- Customer, staff and supplier communication channels.

- Payroll, banking and financial systems.

The continuity plan should include an action plan for the company to continue to operate if something should happen in one of the identified key risk areas, including a timescale within which a back up resource must be made available. Reasons could include:

- Unexpected death or serious illness of a key member or members of staff.

- IT system crash or virus attack.

- An unforeseen incident at any point in a company's supply chain.

- Loss of a single supplier, distributor, or customer.

- Payroll or financial system crash.

- Fire at company's premises.

The company should consider back-up procedures, which could include:

- Regular back-up to a remote server for IT systems.

- Delegating key tasks to nominated alternative company personnel in the event of an emergency, with training to ensure alternative personnel are well briefed and competent.

- Ensuring that key company processes do not rely solely on one person within the organisation especially, for example, access to the company bank account or payroll system.

- Documenting emergency plans and alternative procedures if a company's supply chain or customer communications is affected, to minimise down-time, or if a company's premises are destroyed or otherwise unavailable.

Practical considerations for the private company:

- These principles are relevant to all private companies.

- In an owner-managed company, whilst it is good practice and advisable to consider business continuity this is not always undertaken due to time and cost restraints. Nevertheless a basic plan covering the key areas could possibly save the company if something unexpectedly goes wrong.

- Any business plan should be tested to establish as far as possible whether it works in practice, with any learning points identified in the test reflected in a revised plan. Testing might usefully involve third parties who have been identified as key elements of the continuity strategy.

- Many well run companies have a company manual, which consists of a documented record of the elements which have been discussed in this section, including key personnel and their responsibilities, the main company policy documents, and a risk register. Creating a comprehensive manual, and then reviewing it regularly, assists the board in governing the company in a structured manner. A company manual should also enable a person to cover someone else's responsibilities if necessary and therefore provide part of the contingency planning.

- In any private company, and in particular in an owner-managed company, it is important to consider a succession plan. This may need to be revisited periodically and plans are required to work towards its fulfilment. For example, will a younger member of the family take over, or do the owners have an ambition to sell to a rival, or float on AIM? If a company is seeking external investment or for the shareholders to sell out it is beneficial to have had, for example, a non-executive director, minuted board meetings, regular budgeting and so on to show that there is a proven record from which to negotiate.

Code of Business Conduct

Successful companies benefit from the highest standards of professional and ethical conduct from all directors and employees. A code of business conduct sets out these standards and supports and enhances a company's core values and culture. The existence of such a code also presents the company favourably externally. The principles of effective business conduct include:

- Compliance with all applicable laws, regulations, and professional conduct standards.

- High standards of service.

- Avoiding personal or financial conflicts of interest.

- Not being compromised through any unwarranted preferential treatment given to or accepted from customers, suppliers, or others.

- Communicating honestly and accurately with all stakeholders.

- Integrity and honest, ethical business practice.

- Contributing to the social and economic wellbeing of the community.

- Treating customers, suppliers and employees fairly and supporting employees' learning and development.

Practical considerations for the private company:

- Whilst this may initially appear to be an exercise for the larger company, all companies can benefit from formally considering and documenting the manner in which they wish to conduct their business and ensuring the company's values are applied in all the company's operations.

- With increasing numbers of staff it is useful to have the ethos of the company clearly expounded for induction, training and even disciplinary action purposes.

APPENDIX 8

COMPANIES ACT 2006, PART 10
CHAPTER 2 – GENERAL DUTIES OF
DIRECTORS: SECTIONS 170–180

INTRODUCTORY

170 Scope and nature of general duties

(1) The general duties specified in sections 171 to 177 are owed by a director of a company to the company.

(2) A person who ceases to be a director continues to be subject—
   (a) to the duty in section 175 (duty to avoid conflicts of interest) as regards the exploitation of any property, information or opportunity of which he became aware at a time when he was a director, and
   (b) to the duty in section 176 (duty not to accept benefits from third parties) as regards things done or omitted by him before he ceased to be a director.
   To that extent those duties apply to a former director as to a director, subject to any necessary adaptations.

(3) The general duties are based on certain common law rules and equitable principles as they apply in relation to directors and have effect in place of those rules and principles as regards the duties owed to a company by a director.

(4) The general duties shall be interpreted and applied in the same way as common law rules or equitable principles, and regard shall be had to the corresponding common law rules and equitable principles in interpreting and applying the general duties.

(5) The general duties apply to shadow directors where, and to the extent that, the corresponding common law rules or equitable principles so apply.

THE GENERAL DUTIES

171 Duty to act within powers

A director of a company must—
  (a) act in accordance with the company's constitution, and
  (b) only exercise powers for the purposes for which they are conferred.

172 Duty to promote the success of the company

(1) A director of a company must act in the way he considers, in good faith, would be most likely to promote the success of the company for the benefit of its members as a whole, and in doing so have regard (amongst other matters) to—
  (a) the likely consequences of any decision in the long term,
  (b) the interests of the company's employees,
  (c) the need to foster the company's business relationships with suppliers, customers and others,
  (d) the impact of the company's operations on the community and the environment,
  (e) the desirability of the company maintaining a reputation for high standards of business conduct, and
  (f) the need to act fairly as between members of the company.

(2) Where or to the extent that the purposes of the company consist of or include purposes other than the benefit of its members, subsection (1) has effect as if the reference to promoting the success of the company for the benefit of its members were to achieving those purposes.

(3) The duty imposed by this section has effect subject to any enactment or rule of law requiring directors, in certain circumstances, to consider or act in the interests of creditors of the company.

173 Duty to exercise independent judgment

(1) A director of a company must exercise independent judgment.

(2) This duty is not infringed by his acting—
  (a) in accordance with an agreement duly entered into by the company that restricts the future exercise of discretion by its directors, or
  (b) in a way authorised by the company's constitution.

174 Duty to exercise reasonable care, skill and diligence

(1) A director of a company must exercise reasonable care, skill and diligence.

(2) This means the care, skill and diligence that would be exercised by a reasonably diligent person with—
    (a) the general knowledge, skill and experience that may reasonably be expected of a person carrying out the functions carried out by the director in relation to the company, and
    (b) the general knowledge, skill and experience that the director has.

175 Duty to avoid conflicts of interest

(1) A director of a company must avoid a situation in which he has, or can have, a direct or indirect interest that conflicts, or possibly may conflict, with the interests of the company.

(2) This applies in particular to the exploitation of any property, information or opportunity (and it is immaterial whether the company could take advantage of the property, information or opportunity).

(3) This duty does not apply to a conflict of interest arising in relation to a transaction or arrangement with the company.

(4) This duty is not infringed—
    (a) if the situation cannot reasonably be regarded as likely to give rise to a conflict of interest; or
    (b) if the matter has been authorised by the directors.

(5) Authorisation may be given by the directors—
    (a) where the company is a private company and nothing in the company's constitution invalidates such authorisation, by the matter being proposed to and authorised by the directors; or
    (b) where the company is a public company and its constitution includes provision enabling the directors to authorise the matter, by the matter being proposed to and authorised by them in accordance with the constitution.

(6) The authorisation is effective only if—
    (a) any requirement as to the quorum at the meeting at which the matter is considered is met without counting the director in question or any other interested director, and
    (b) the matter was agreed to without their voting or would have been agreed to if their votes had not been counted.

(7) Any reference in this section to a conflict of interest includes a conflict of interest and duty and a conflict of duties.

176 Duty not to accept benefits from third parties

(1) A director of a company must not accept a benefit from a third party conferred by reason of—
    (a) his being a director, or
    (b) his doing (or not doing) anything as director.

(2) A "third party" means a person other than the company, an associated body corporate or a person acting on behalf of the company or an associated body corporate.

(3) Benefits received by a director from a person by whom his services (as a director or otherwise) are provided to the company are not regarded as conferred by a third party.

(4) This duty is not infringed if the acceptance of the benefit cannot reasonably be regarded as likely to give rise to a conflict of interest.

(5) Any reference in this section to a conflict of interest includes a conflict of interest and duty and a conflict of duties.

177 Duty to declare interest in proposed transaction or arrangement

(1) If a director of a company is in any way, directly or indirectly, interested in a proposed transaction or arrangement with the company, he must declare the nature and extent of that interest to the other directors.

(2) The declaration may (but need not) be made—
    (a) at a meeting of the directors, or
    (b) by notice to the directors in accordance with—
        (i) section 184 (notice in writing), or
        (ii) section 185 (general notice).

(3) If a declaration of interest under this section proves to be, or becomes, inaccurate or incomplete, a further declaration must be made.

(4) Any declaration required by this section must be made before the company enters into the transaction or arrangement.

(5) This section does not require a declaration of an interest of which the director is not aware or where the director is not aware of the

transaction or arrangement in question. For this purpose a director is treated as being aware of matters of which he ought reasonably to be aware.

(6)   A director need not declare an interest—
  (a)   if it cannot reasonably be regarded as likely to give rise to a conflict of interest;
  (b)   if, or to the extent that, the other directors are already aware of it (and for this purpose the other directors are treated as aware of anything of which they ought reasonably to be aware); or
  (c)   If, or to the extent that, it concerns terms of his service contract that have been or are to be considered—
      (i)   by a meeting of the directors, or
      (ii) by a committee of the directors appointed for the purpose under the company's constitution.

SUPPLEMENTARY PROVISIONS

178 Civil consequences of breach of general duties

(1)   The consequences of breach (or threatened breach) of sections 171 to 177 are the same as would apply if the corresponding common law rule or equitable principle applied.

(2)   The duties in those sections (with the exception of section 174 (duty to exercise reasonable care, skill and diligence)) are, accordingly, enforceable in the same way as any other fiduciary duty owed to a company by its directors.

179 Cases within more than one of the general duties

Except as otherwise provided, more than one of the general duties may apply in any given case.

180 Consent, approval or authorisation by members

(1)   In a case where—
  (a)   section 175 (duty to avoid conflicts of interest) is complied with by authorisation by the directors, or
  (b)   section 177 (duty to declare interest in proposed transaction or arrangement) is complied with,
  the transaction or arrangement is not liable to be set aside by virtue of any common law rule or equitable principle requiring the consent or approval of the members of the company. This is without prejudice to any enactment, or provision of the company's constitution, requiring such consent or approval.

(2)   The application of the general duties is not affected by the fact that the case also falls within Chapter 4 (transactions requiring approval of members), except that where that Chapter applies and—
      (a)   approval is given under that Chapter, or
      (b)   the matter is one as to which it is provided that approval is not needed,
      it is not necessary also to comply with section 175 (duty to avoid conflicts of interest) or section 176 (duty not to accept benefits from third parties).

(3)   Compliance with the general duties does not remove the need for approval under any applicable provision of Chapter 4 (transactions requiring approval of members).

(4)   The general duties—
      (a)   have effect subject to any rule of law enabling the company to give authority, specifically or generally, for anything to be done (or omitted) by the directors, or any of them, that would otherwise be a breach of duty, and
      (b)   where the company's articles contain provisions for dealing with conflicts of interest, are not infringed by anything done (or omitted) by the directors, or any of them, in accordance with those provisions.

(5)   Otherwise, the general duties have effect (except as otherwise provided or to context otherwise requires) notwithstanding any enactment or rule of law.

APPENDIX 9

HIGGS REVIEW (JANUARY 2003) – SAMPLE LETTER OF NON-EXECUTIVE DIRECTOR APPOINTMENT

On [date], upon the recommendation of the nomination committee, the board of [company] ('the Company') has appointed you as non-executive director. I am writing to set out the terms of your appointment. It is agreed that this is a contract for services and is not a contract of employment.

Appointment – Your appointment will be for an initial term of three years commencing on [date], unless otherwise terminated earlier by and at the discretion of either party upon [one month's] written notice. Continuation of your contract of appointment is contingent on satisfactory performance and re-election at forthcoming AGMs. Non-executive directors are typically expected to serve two three-year terms, although the board may invite you to serve an additional period.

Time commitment – Overall we anticipate a time commitment of [number] days per months after the induction phase. This will include attendance at [monthly] board meetings, the AGM, [one] annual board away day, and [at least one] site visit per year. In addition, you will be expected to devote appropriate preparation time ahead of each meeting.

By accepting this appointment, you have confirmed that you are able to allocate sufficient time to meet the expectations of your role. The agreement of the chairman should be sought before accepting additional commitments that might impact on the time you are able to devote to your role as a non-executive director of the company.

Fees – You will be paid a fee of £[amount] gross per annum which will be paid monthly in arrears, [plus [number] ordinary shares of the company per annum, both of] which will be subject to an annual review by the board. The company will reimburse you for all reasonable and properly documented expenses you incur in performing the duties of your office.

Outside interests – It is accepted and acknowledged that you have business interests other than those of the company and have declared any conflicts that are apparent at present. In the event that you become aware of any potential conflicts of interest, these should be disclosed to the chairman and company secretary as soon as apparent.

[The board of the Company have determined you to be independent according to provision A.3.1 of the Code.]

Confidentiality – All information acquired during your appointment is confidential to the Company and should not be released, either during your appointment or following termination (by whatever means), to third parties without prior clearance from the chairman.

Your attention is also drawn to the requirements under both legislation and regulation as to the disclosure of price sensitive information. Consequently you should avoid making any statements that might risk a breach of these requirements without prior clearance from the chairman or company secretary.

Induction – Immediately after appointment, the Company will provide a comprehensive, formal and tailored induction. This will include the information pack recommended by the Institute of Chartered Secretaries and Administrators (ICSA), available at www.icsa.org.uk. We will also arrange for site visits and meetings with senior and middle management and the Company's auditors. We will also offer to major shareholders the opportunity to meet you.

Review process – The performance of individual directors and the whole board and its committees is evaluated annually. If, in the interim, there are any matters which cause you concern about your role you should discuss them with the chairman as soon as is appropriate.

Insurance – The Company has directors' and officers' liability insurance and it is intended to maintain such cover for the full term of your appointment. The current indemnity limit is £[amount]; a copy of the policy document is attached.

Independent professional advice – Occasions may arise when you consider that you need professional advice in the furtherance of your duties as a director. Circumstances may occur when it will be appropriate for you to seek advice from independent advisors at the company's expense. A copy of the board's agreed procedure under which directors may obtain such independent advice is attached. The company will reimburse the full cost of expenditure incurred in accordance with the attached policy.

Committees – This letter refers to your appointment as a non-executive director of the Company. In the event that you are also asked to serve on one or more of the board committees this will be covered in a separate communication setting out the committee(s)'s terms of reference, any specific responsibilities and any additional fees that may be involved.

APPENDIX 10

QCA GUIDANCE FOR SMALLER QUOTED COMPANIES (AUGUST 2004): P 20 APPENDIX A: MATTERS WHICH SHOULD BE PRESENTED TO THE BOARD

1. Management structure and Appointments

- Senior management responsibilities

- Board and other senior management appointments or removals

- Board and senior management succession, training, development and appraisal

- Appointment or removal of Company Secretary

- Appointment or removal of internal auditor

- Remuneration, contracts, grants of options and incentive arrangements for senior management

- Delegation of the Board's powers

- Agreeing membership and terms of reference of board committees and task forces

- Establishment of managerial authority limits for smaller transactions

- Matters referred to the Board by the board committees

2. Strategic/Policy Considerations

- Business strategy

- Diversification/retrenchment policy

- Specific risk management policies including insurance, hedging, borrowing limits and corporate security

- Agreement of codes of ethics and business practices

- Receive and review regular reports on internal controls

- Annual assessment of significant risks and effectiveness of internal controls

- Calling of shareholders' meetings

- Avoidance of wrongful or fraudulent trading

3. Transactions

- Acquisitions and disposals of subsidiaries or other assets or liabilities over, say, 5% of net assets/profits

- Investment and other capital projects over a similar level

- Substantial commitments including:
  - pension funding
  - contracts in excess of one year's duration
  - giving security over significant group assets (including mortgages and charges over the group's property)

- Contracts not in the ordinary course of business

- Actions or transactions where there may be doubt over propriety

- Approval of prospectuses, circulars and similar documents

- Disclosure of directors' interests

- Transactions with directors or other related parties

4. Finance

- Raising new capital and confirmation of major financing facilities

- Treasury policies including foreign currency and interest rate exposure

- Discussion of any proposed qualification to the accounts

- Final approval of annual and interim reports and accounts and accounting policies

- Appointment/proposal of auditors

- Charitable and political donations

- Approval and recommendation of dividends

- Operating budgets

5. General

- Governance of company pension schemes and appointment of company nominees as trustees

- Allotment, calls or forfeiture of shares

APPENDIX 11

INSTITUTE OF CHARTERED SECRETARIES AND ADMINISTRATORS (ICSA) GUIDANCE ON TERMS OF REFERENCE – REMUNERATION COMMITTEE

ICSA Guidance on Terms of Reference
– Remuneration Committee

Contents

If using online, click on the headings below to go to the related sections.

A   Introduction

This guidance note proposes model terms of reference for the remuneration committee of a quoted company in the UK seeking to comply fully with the requirements of the Combined Code on Corporate Governance (the Combined Code). It draws on the experience of senior company secretaries and is based on best practice as carried out in some of the UK's top listed companies.

B   The Combined Code

The Combined Code states that:

> There should be a formal and transparent procedure for developing policy on executive remuneration and for fixing the remuneration packages of individual directors.'[1]

It goes on to state that:

> The board should establish a remuneration committee ... [which] should make available its terms of reference, explaining its role and the authority delegated to it by the board.'[2]

It is clear therefore that the Combined Code not only requires companies to go through a formal process of considering executive remuneration, but to be seen to be doing so, and that establishing clear terms of reference for the remuneration committee, and making them available,[3] is an essential part of this process.

The Combined Code also states that the chairman of the committee should attend the AGM prepared to respond to any questions that may be raised by shareholders on matters within the committee's area of responsibility.[4]

C   Notes on the terms of reference

The list of duties we have proposed are based on those contained within the *Summary of Principal Duties of the Remuneration Committee* which ICSA helped compile for the Higgs Review.[5] Some companies may wish to add to this list and some smaller companies may need to modify it in other ways.

The Combined Code recommends that the committee should comprise of at least three independent non-executive directors (although two is permissible for smaller companies).[6] In addition to the independent non-executives, the company chairman may also be a member of the committee if he or she was considered independent on appointment as chairman, but may not chair it.[7]

---

1 The Combined Code, June 2006, B.2
2 The Combined Code, June 2006, B.2.1
3 Footnote 4 to the Combined Code clarifies that the requirement to make the terms of reference available would be met by including the information on a website maintained by or on behalf of the company.
4 The Combined Code, June 2006 D.2.3
5 The Higgs Report list of duties was originally appended to 2003 version of the Combined Code but is now incorporated in a document entitled *Suggestions for Good Practice from the Higgs Report*, available from the FRC website *www.frc.org.uk* as associated guidance.
6 A smaller company is defined in footnote 3 to the Combined Code as one which is below the FTSE 350 throughout the year immediately prior to the reporting year.
7 The Combined Code, June 2006, B.2.1. This code provision was amended in 2006 to allow the company chairman to serve on the committee.

Although not a provision in the Combined Code, the Higgs Review states as a matter of good practice in its non-code recommendations, that the company secretary (or their designee) should act as secretary to the committee.[8] In this regard, the company secretary has a responsibility to ensure that the board and its committees are properly constituted and advised and would normally act as an intermediary between the main board and the various committees to ensure clear co-ordination.

The frequency with which the committee needs to meet will vary from company to company and may change from time to time. It is clear, however, that it must meet close to the year end to review the directors' remuneration report which quoted companies must now submit to shareholders for approval at the AGM. We would recommend that the committee should meet at least twice a year in order to discharge its responsibilities properly.

References to 'the committee' are to 'the remuneration committee'.
References to 'the board' are to 'the board of directors'.
Square brackets contain recommendations which are in line with best practice but which may need to be changed to suit the circumstances of the particular organisation.

D   Model terms of reference

1.   Membership

1.1. Members of the committee shall be appointed by the board, on the recommendation of the nomination committee and in consultation with the chairman of the remuneration committee. The committee shall be made up of at least [3] members, all of whom shall be independent non-executive directors. The chairman of the board may also serve on the committee as an additional member if he or she was considered independent on appointment as chairman.
1.2. Only members of the committee have the right to attend committee meetings. However, other individuals such as the chief executive, the head of human resources and external advisers may be invited to attend for all or part of any meeting as and when appropriate.
1.3. Appointments to the committee shall be for a period of up to three years, which may be extended for two further three-year periods, provided the director still meets the criteria for membership of the committee.
1.4. The board shall appoint the committee chairman who shall be an independent non-executive director. In the absence of the committee chairman and/or an appointed deputy, the remaining members present shall elect one of themselves to chair the meeting. The chairman of the board shall not be chairman of the committee.

2.   Secretary

2.1. The company secretary or their nominee shall act as the secretary of the committee.

3.   Quorum

3.1. The quorum necessary for the transaction of business shall be [2]. A duly convened meeting of the committee at which a quorum is present shall be competent to exercise all or any of the authorities, powers and discretions vested in or exercisable by the committee.

---

8   *Higgs Review of the Role and Effectiveness of Non-executive Directors*, January 2003 para 11.30

4. Meetings

4.1. The committee shall meet [at least twice a year][quarterly on the first Wednesday in each of January, April, July and October] and at such other times as the chairman of the committee shall require.[9]

5. Notice of meetings

5.1. Meetings of the committee shall be summoned by the secretary of the committee at the request of any of its members.

5.2. Unless otherwise agreed, notice of each meeting confirming the venue, time and date together with an agenda of items to be discussed, shall be forwarded to each member of the committee, any other person required to attend and all other non-executive directors, no later than [5] working days before the date of the meeting. Supporting papers shall be sent to committee members and to other attendees as appropriate, at the same time.

6. Minutes of meetings

6.1. The secretary shall minute the proceedings and resolutions of all committee meetings, including the names of those present and in attendance.

6.2. Minutes of committee meetings shall be circulated promptly to all members of the committee and, once agreed, to all members of the board, unless a conflict of interest exists.

7. Annual general meeting

7.1. The chairman of the committee shall attend the annual general meeting prepared to respond to any shareholder questions on the committee's activities.

8. Duties

The committee shall

8.1. determine and agree with the board the framework or broad policy for the remuneration of the company's chief executive, chairman, the executive directors, the company secretary and such other members of the executive management as it is designated to consider.[10] The remuneration of non-executive directors shall be a matter for the chairman and the executive members of the board. No director or manager shall be involved in any decisions as to their own remuneration

8.2. in determining such policy, take into account all factors which it deems necessary. The objective of such policy shall be to ensure that members of the executive management of the company are provided with appropriate incentives to encourage enhanced performance and are, in a fair and responsible manner, rewarded for their individual contributions to the success of the company

8.3. review the ongoing appropriateness and relevance of the remuneration policy

---

9   The frequency and timing of meetings will differ according to the needs of the company. Meetings should be organised so that attendance is maximised (for example by timetabling them to coincide with board meetings).

10 Some companies require the remuneration committee to consider the packages of all executives at or above a specified level, such as those reporting to a main board director, while others require the committee to deal with all packages above a certain figure.

8.4. approve the design of, and determine targets for, any performance related pay schemes operated by the company and approve the total annual payments made under such schemes

8.5. review the design of all share incentive plans for approval by the board and shareholders. For any such plans, determine each year whether awards will be made, and if so, the overall amount of such awards, the individual awards to executive directors and other senior executives and the performance targets to be used

8.6. determine the policy for, and scope of, pension arrangements for each executive director and other senior executives

8.7. ensure that contractual terms on termination, and any payments made, are fair to the individual, and the company, that failure is not rewarded and that the duty to mitigate loss is fully recognised

8.8. within the terms of the agreed policy and in consultation with the chairman and/or chief executive as appropriate, determine the total individual remuneration package of each executive director and other senior executives including bonuses, incentive payments and share options or other share awards

8.9. in determining such packages and arrangements, give due regard to any relevant legal requirements, the provisions and recommendations in the Combined Code and the UK Listing Authority's Listing Rules and associated guidance

8.10. review and note annually the remuneration trends across the company or group

8.11. oversee any major changes in employee benefits structures throughout the company or group

8.12. agree the policy for authorising claims for expenses from the chief executive and chairman[11]

8.13. ensure that all provisions regarding disclosure of remuneration, including pensions, are fulfilled

8.14. be exclusively responsible for establishing the selection criteria, selecting, appointing and setting the terms of reference for any remuneration consultants who advise the committee

8.15. obtain reliable, up-to-date information about remuneration in other companies. The committee shall have full authority to commission any reports or surveys which it deems necessary to help it fulfil its obligations

9. Reporting responsibilities

9.1. The committee chairman shall report formally to the board on its proceedings after each meeting on all matters within its duties and responsibilities

9.2. The committee shall make whatever recommendations to the board it deems appropriate on any area within its remit where action or improvement is needed

9.3. The committee shall produce an annual report of the company's remuneration policy and practices which will form part of the company's annual report and ensure each year that it is put to shareholders for approval at the AGM

10. Other

10.1. The committee shall, at least once a year, review its own performance, constitution and terms of reference to ensure it is operating at maximum effectiveness and recommend any changes it considers necessary to the board for approval.

---

11 It is suggested that the more common arrangement is for the chairman of the board to authorise the chief executive's expenses and for the chairman of the remuneration committee to authorise the chairman's claims. An alternative would be for the committee to authorise the expenses of both.

11. Authority

11.1. The committee is authorised by the board to seek any information it requires from any employee of the company in order to perform its duties.

11.2. In connection with its duties the committee is authorised by the board, at the company's expense

11.2.1 to obtain any outside legal or other professional advice

11.2.2 within any budgetary restraints imposed by the board, to appoint remuneration consultants, and to commission or purchase any relevant reports, surveys or information which it deems necessary to help fulfil its duties

October 2007

BACK TO THE TOP

The information given in this Guidance Note is provided in good faith with the intention of furthering the understanding of the subject matter. Whilst we believe the information to be accurate at the time of publication, ICSA and its staff cannot, however, accept any liability for any loss or damage occasioned by any person or organisation acting or refraining from action as a result of any views expressed therein. If the reader has any specific doubts or concerns about the subject matter they are advised to seek legal advice based on the circumstances of their own situation.

© Institute of Chartered Secretaries & Administrators
16 Park Crescent · London · W1B 1AH · Phone: 020 7580 4741 · Fax: 020 7323 1132 · Web: www.icsa.org.uk | 6 of

APPENDIX 12

INSTITUTE OF CHARTERED SECRETARIES AND ADMINISTRATORS (ICSA) GUIDANCE ON TERMS OF REFERENCE – AUDIT COMMITTEE

ICSA Guidance on Terms of Reference
– Audit Committee

Contents

If using online, click on the headings below to go to the related sections.

A   Introduction

This guidance note proposes model terms of reference for the audit committee of a company seeking to comply fully with the requirements of the Combined Code on Corporate Governance. It draws on the experience of senior company secretaries and is based on best practice as carried out in some of the UK's top listed companies. Companies with a US listing may need to amend the terms of reference in light of US requirements introduced pursuant to the Sarbanes-Oxley Act.

Although the guidance note is aimed primarily at the corporate sector, the doctrine of good governance, including the adoption of audit committees, is increasingly being embraced by other organisations particularly in the public and not for profit sectors. The principles underlying the content of this guidance note are likely to be applicable regardless of the size or type of organisation and should be useful across all sectors.

B   The Combined Code

The Combined Code on Corporate Governance (the Combined Code) states as a principle that:

> The board should establish formal and transparent arrangements for considering how they should apply the financial reporting and internal control principles and for maintaining an appropriate relationship with the company's auditors.'[1]

It goes on to clarify that, in practical terms, this means that: 'The board should establish an audit committee....'[2] Listed companies throughout Europe will soon be required by EU legislation to establish an audit committee.[3] Other influential organisations such as the Commonwealth Association for Corporate Governance and the International Corporate Governance Network also support the establishment of audit committees.

The Combined Code recommends that the main role and responsibilities of the audit committee should be 'set out in written terms of reference'[4] and be made 'available'[5] (e.g. by including them on a website maintained by or on behalf of the company).[6]

In addition, it recommends that the work of the committee should be described in a separate section of the annual report[7] and that the committee chairman should attend the AGM prepared to respond to any questions on the committee's area of responsibility.[8] So, as with most aspects of corporate governance, companies are not only required to go through a formal process of considering their internal audit and control procedures and evaluating their relationship with their external auditor, but must also be seen to be doing so in a fair and thorough manner. As part of this process, it is essential that the audit committee is properly constituted with a clear remit and identified authority.

---

1   The Combined Code, June 2006, C.3
2   The Combined Code, June 2006, C.3.1
3   Directive 2006/43/EC on Statutory Audits of Annual and Consolidated Accounts must be implemented by 29 June 2008.
4   The Combined Code, June 2006, C.3.2
5   The Combined Code, June 2006, C.3.3
6   See footnote 4 to the Combined Code, June 2006.
7   The Combined Code, June 2006, C.3.3
8   The Combined Code, June 2006 D.2.3

C   Notes on the terms of reference

The Smith Guidance[9] recognises that 'audit committee arrangements need to be proportionate to the task, and will vary according to the size, complexity and risk profile of the company'.[10]

As regards the make up of the committee, we have followed the Combined Code and recommend a minimum of three independent non-executive directors (although two is permissible for smaller companies).[11] The board should satisfy itself that at least one member of the committee has recent and relevant financial experience. We have made specific recommendations that others may be required to assist the committee from time to time, according to the particular items being considered and discussed.

Although not a provision in the Code the Higgs Review states as good practice, in its non-code recommendations, that the company secretary, or their designee, should act as secretary to the committee.[12] The Smith Guidance states that the audit committee should have access to the services of the company secretariat on all audit committee matters including: assisting the chairman in planning the audit committee's work, drawing up meeting agendas, maintenance of minutes, drafting of material about its activities for the annual report, collection and distribution of information and provision of any necessary practical support. It also states that the company secretary should ensure that the audit committee receives information and papers in a timely manner to enable full and proper consideration to be given to the issues.[13]

The frequency with which the committee needs to meet will vary from company to company and may change from time to time. As a general rule, most audit committees would be expected to meet quarterly – the Combined Code provides that the committee should meet at least three times a year.

The list of duties we have proposed are those which we believe all audit committees should consider. Some companies may wish to add to this list[14] and some smaller companies may need to modify it in other ways.

The Combined Code includes a provision for a report on the audit committee to be included in the company's annual report.[15] Such report will need to disclose the following:

- Role and main responsibilities of the audit committee
- Composition of committee, including relevant qualifications and experience; the appointment process; and any fees paid in respect of membership
- Number of meetings and attendance levels
- A description of the main activities of the year to
  - Monitor the integrity of the financial statements
  - Review the integrity of the internal financial control and risk management systems
  - Review the independence of the external auditors, and the provision of non-audit services
  - Describe the oversight of the external audit process, and how its effectiveness was assessed
  - Explain the recommendation to the board on the appointment of auditors

---

9   *Guidance on Audit Committees (The Smith Guidance)*, January 2003. This report was originally included as an appendix in the Combined Code but can now be obtained separately from the FRC website www.frc.org.uk.
10   *Guidance on Audit Committees (The Smith Guidance)*, January 2003, para. 1.3.
11   A smaller company is defined in footnote 3 to the Combined Code as one which is below the FTSE 350 throughout the year immediately prior to the reporting year.
12   *Higgs Review of the Role and Effectiveness of Non-executive Directors*, January 2003 para 11.30.
13   *Guidance on Audit Committees (The Smith Guidance)*, January 2003, paras. 2.13 and 2.14.
14   For example, some companies also require the committee to monitor/make recommendations on the potential implications of legal actions being taken against the company, the adequacy of arrangements for managing conflicts of interest, the expenses incurred by the chairman and treasury management policies.
15   The Combined Code, June 2006 C.3.3 and *Guidance on Audit Committees (The Smith Guidance)*, January 2003, para. 5.2.

References to 'the committee' are to 'the audit committee'.
References to 'the board' are to 'the board of directors'.
The square brackets contain recommendations which are in line with best practice but which may need to be changed to suit the circumstances of the particular organisation.

D   Model terms of reference

1.   Membership

1.1   Members of the committee shall be appointed by the board, on the recommendation of the nomination committee in consultation with the chairman of the audit committee. The committee shall be made up of at least [3] members.

1.2   All members of the committee shall be independent non-executive directors[16] at least one of whom shall have recent and relevant financial experience. The chairman of the board shall not be a member of the committee.[17]

1.3   Only members of the committee have the right to attend committee meetings. However, other individuals such as the chairman of the board, chief executive, finance director, other directors, the heads of risk, compliance and internal audit and representatives from the finance function may be invited to attend all or part of any meeting as and when appropriate.

1.4   The external auditors will be invited to attend meetings of the committee on a regular basis.

1.5   Appointments to the committee shall be for a period of up to three years, which may be extended for two further three year periods, provided the director remains independent.

1.6   The board shall appoint the committee chairman who shall be an independent non-executive director. In the absence of the committee chairman and/or an appointed deputy, the remaining members present shall elect one of themselves to chair the meeting.

2.   Secretary

2.1   The company secretary or their nominee shall act as the secretary of the committee.

3.   Quorum

3.1   The quorum necessary for the transaction of business shall be [2] members. A duly convened meeting of the committee at which a quorum is present shall be competent to exercise all or any of the authorities, powers and discretions vested in or exercisable by the committee.

4.   Frequency of meetings

4.1   The committee shall meet [at least three times a year at appropriate times in the reporting and audit cycle] [quarterly on the first Wednesday in each of January, April, July and October] and otherwise as required.[18]

---

16   An independent non-executive director is defined in Combined Code provision A.3.1
17   Except on appointment, the Chairman of the company is not considered to meet the test of independence. Combined Code provision A.3.1
18   The frequency and timing of meetings will differ according to the needs of the company. Meetings should be organised so that attendance is maximised (for example by timetabling them to coincide with board meetings).

5. Notice of meetings

5.1 Meetings of the committee shall be called by the secretary of the committee at the request of any of its members or at the request of external or internal auditors if they consider it necessary.

5.2 Unless otherwise agreed, notice of each meeting confirming the venue, time and date together with an agenda of items to be discussed, shall be forwarded to each member of the committee, any other person required to attend and all other non-executive directors, no later than [5] working days before the date of the meeting. Supporting papers shall be sent to committee members and to other attendees as appropriate, at the same time.

6. Minutes of meetings

6.1 The secretary shall minute the proceedings and resolutions of all meetings of the committee, including recording the names of those present and in attendance.

6.2 The secretary shall ascertain, at the beginning of each meeting, the existence of any conflicts of interest and minute them accordingly.

6.3 Minutes of committee meetings shall be circulated promptly to all members of the committee and, once agreed, to all members of the board, unless a conflict of interest exists.

7. Annual General Meeting

7.1 The chairman of the committee shall attend the Annual General Meeting prepared to respond to any shareholder questions on the committee's activities.

8. Duties

The committee should carry out the duties below for the parent company, major subsidiary undertakings and the group as a whole, as appropriate.

8.1 Financial reporting

8.1.1 The committee shall monitor the integrity of the financial statements of the company, including its annual and half-yearly reports, interim management statements, [preliminary results' announcements] and any other formal announcement relating to its financial performance, reviewing significant financial reporting issues and judgements which they contain. The committee shall also review summary financial statements, significant financial returns to regulators and any financial information contained in certain other documents, such as announcements of a price sensitive nature.

8.1.2 The committee shall review and challenge where necessary

     8.1.2.1 the consistency of, and any changes to, accounting policies both on a year on year basis and across the company/group

     8.1.2.2 the methods used to account for significant or unusual transactions where different approaches are possible

     8.1.2.3 whether the company has followed appropriate accounting standards and made appropriate estimates and judgements, taking into account the views of the external auditor

8.1.2.4 the clarity of disclosure in the company's financial reports and the context in which statements are made; and

8.1.2.5 all material information presented with the financial statements, such as the operating and financial review and the corporate governance statement (insofar as it relates to the audit and risk management);

8.1.3   The committee shall review the annual financial statements of the pension funds where not reviewed by the board as a whole.

8.2 Internal controls and risk management systems

The committee shall

8.2.1   keep under review the effectiveness of the company's internal controls and risk management systems; and

8.2.2   review and approve the statements to be included in the annual report concerning internal controls and risk management[19]

8.3 Whistleblowing and fraud

The committee shall

8.3.1. review the company's arrangements for its employees to raise concerns, in confidence, about possible wrongdoing in financial reporting or other matters. The committee shall ensure that these arrangements allow proportionate and independent investigation of such matters and appropriate follow up action; and

8.3.2. review the company's procedures for detecting fraud

8.4 Internal audit

The committee shall

8.4.1   monitor and review the effectiveness of the company's internal audit function in the context of the company's overall risk management system[20]

8.4.2   approve the appointment and removal of the head of the internal audit function

8.4.3   consider and approve the remit of the internal audit function and ensure it has adequate resources and appropriate access to information to enable it to perform its function effectively and in accordance with the relevant professional standards. The committee shall also ensure the function has adequate standing and is free from management or other restrictions

8.4.4   review and assess the annual internal audit plan

8.4.5   review promptly all reports on the company from the internal auditors

8.4.6   review and monitor management's responsiveness to the findings and recommendations of the internal auditor; and

8.4.7   meet the head of internal audit at least once a year, without management being present, to discuss their remit and any issues arising from the internal audits carried out. In addition, the head of internal audit shall be given the right of direct access to the chairman of the board and to the committee

---

19 Unless this is done by the board as a whole.
20 If the company does not have an internal audit function, the Committee should consider annually whether there should be one and make a recommendation to the board accordingly. The absence of such a function should be explained in the annual report.

8.5 External Audit

The committee shall
8.5.1 consider and make recommendations to the board, to be put to shareholders for
approval at the AGM, in relation to the appointment, re-appointment and removal
of the company's external auditor. The committee shall oversee the selection process
for new auditors and if an auditor resigns the committee shall investigate the issues
leading to this and decide whether any action is required
8.5.2 oversee the relationship with the external auditor including (but not limited to)
    8.5.2.1 approval of their remuneration, whether fees for audit or non-audit services
and that the level of fees is appropriate to enable an adequate audit to be
conducted
    8.5.2.2 approval of their terms of engagement, including any engagement letter
issued at the start of each audit and the scope of the audit
    8.5.2.3 assessing annually their independence and objectivity taking into account
relevant [UK] professional and regulatory requirements and the relationship
with the auditor as a whole, including the provision of any non-audit
services
    8.5.2.4 satisfying itself that there are no relationships (such as family, employment,
investment, financial or business) between the auditor and the company
(other than in the ordinary course of business)
    8.5.2.5 agreeing with the board a policy on the employment of former employees of
the company's auditor, then monitoring the implementation of this policy
    8.5.2.6 monitoring the auditor's compliance with relevant ethical and professional
guidance on the rotation of audit partners, the level of fees paid by the
company compared to the overall fee income of the firm, office and partner
and other related requirements
    8.5.2.7 assessing annually their qualifications, expertise and resources and the
effectiveness of the audit process which shall include a report from the
external auditor on their own internal quality procedures
    8.5.2.8 seeking to ensure co-ordination with the activities of the internal audit
function
8.5.3 meet regularly with the external auditor, including once at the planning stage before
the audit and once after the audit at the reporting stage. The committee shall meet
the external auditor at least once a year, without management being present, to
discuss their remit and any issues arising from the audit
8.5.4 review and approve the annual audit plan and ensure that it is consistent with the
scope of the audit engagement
8.5.5 review the findings of the audit with the external auditor. This shall include but not
be limited to, the following

    8.5.5.1 a discussion of any major issues which arose during the audit
    8.5.5.2 any accounting and audit judgements
    8.5.5.3 levels of errors identified during the audit

The committee shall also review the effectiveness of the audit
8.5.6 review any representation letter(s) requested by the external auditor before they are
signed by management
8.5.7 review the management letter and management's response to the auditor's findings
and recommendations
8.5.8 develop and implement a policy on the supply of non-audit services by the external
auditor, taking into account any relevant ethical guidance on the matter

8.6 Reporting responsibilities

8.6.1   The committee chairman shall report formally to the board on its proceedings after each meeting on all matters within its duties and responsibilities.

8.6.2   The committee shall make whatever recommendations to the board it deems appropriate on any area within its remit where action or improvement is needed.

8.6.3   The committee shall compile a report to shareholders on its activities to be included in the company's annual report.

8.7 Other matters

The committee shall

8.7.1   have access to sufficient resources in order to carry out its duties, including access to the company secretariat for assistance as required

8.7.2   be provided with appropriate and timely training, both in the form of an induction programme for new members and on an ongoing basis for all members

8.7.3   give due consideration to laws and regulations, the provisions of the Combined Code and the requirements of the UK Listing Authority's Listing, Prospectus and Disclosure and Transparency Rules as appropriate

8.7.4   be responsible for co-ordination of the internal and external auditors

8.7.5   oversee any investigation of activities which are within its terms of reference and act for internal purposes as a court of the last resort

8.7.6   at least once a year, review its own performance, constitution and terms of reference to ensure it is operating at maximum effectiveness and recommend any changes it considers necessary to the board for approval

9. Authority

The committee is authorised

9.1   to seek any information it requires from any employee of the company in order to perform its duties

9.2   to obtain, at the company's expense, outside legal or other professional advice on any matter within its terms of reference

9.3   to call any employee to be questioned at a meeting of the committee as and when required

October 2007

BACK TO THE TOP

The information given in this Guidance Note is provided in good faith with the intention of furthering the understanding of the subject matter. Whilst we believe the information to be accurate at the time of publication, ICSA and its staff cannot, however, accept any liability for any loss or damage occasioned by any person or organisation acting or refraining from action as a result of any views expressed therein. If the reader has any specific doubts or concerns about the subject matter they are advised to seek legal advice based on the circumstances of their own situation.

© Institute of Chartered Secretaries & Administrators

APPENDIX 13

INSTITUTE OF CHARTERED SECRETARIES AND ADMINISTRATORS (ICSA) GUIDANCE ON TERMS OF REFERENCE – NOMINATION COMMITTEE

ICSA Guidance on Terms of Reference
– Nomination Committee

Contents

If using online, click on the headings below to go to the related sections.

A   Introduction

This guidance note proposes model terms of reference for the nomination committee of a company seeking to comply fully with the requirements of the Combined Code on Corporate Governance (the Combined Code). It draws on the experience of senior company secretaries and is based on best practice as carried out in some of the UK's top listed companies.

B   The Combined Code

The Combined Code states that:

'There should be a formal, rigorous and transparent procedure for the appointment of new directors to the board.'[1]

It also provides that:

'There should be a nomination committee which should lead the process for board appointments and make recommendations to the board.'[2]

Previous guidance has permitted smaller listed companies to allow the board to act as a nomination committee. This is no longer the case and, although the Higgs Review recognised that it may take time for smaller companies to comply, it states 'there should be no differentiation in the Code's provision for larger and smaller companies.'[3]

The Combined Code recommends that companies go through a formal process of reviewing the balance and effectiveness of the board, identifying the skills needed and those individuals who might best provide them. In particular the nomination committee should assess the time commitments of the board posts and ensure that the individual has sufficient available time to undertake them.

As with most aspects of corporate governance, the company must be seen to be doing all these things in a fair and thorough manner. The chairman of the nomination committee is required to attend the AGM prepared to respond to any questions which may be raised by shareholders on matters within the committee's area of responsibility.[4] The Combined Code also requires the terms of reference of the nomination committee, explaining its role and the authority delegated to it by the board, to be made publicly available (e.g. by placing them on a website maintained by or on behalf of the company).[5] It is, therefore, essential that the nomination committee be properly constituted with a clear remit and identified authority.

C   Notes on the terms of reference

The list of duties we have proposed are based on those contained in the *Summary of the Principal Duties of the Nomination Committee* which ICSA drew up for the Higgs Review.[6] Some companies may wish to add to this list and some smaller companies may need to modify it in other ways.

---

1   The Combined Code, June 2006 A.4
2   The Combined Code, June 2006 A.4.1
3   *Higgs Review of the Role and Effectiveness of Non-executive Directors*, January 2003, para. 16.8
4   The Combined Code, June 2006 D.2.3
5   The Combined Code, June 2006 A.4.1 (see also footnote 4 to the Combined Code)
6   The Higgs Report list of duties was originally appended to 2003 version of the Combined Code but is now incorporated in a document entitled *Suggestions for Good Practice from the Higgs Report*, available from the FRC website *www.frc.org.uk* as associated guidance.

The Combined Code states that the majority of members serving on the nomination committee should be independent non-executive directors although it gives no guidance on the overall size of the committee.[7] We have recommended a committee of three but companies with larger boards may wish to consider increasing this to four or five.

Although not a provision in the Combined Code, the Higgs review states as good practice, in its non-code recommendations, that the company secretary (or their designee) should act as secretary to the committee.[8] In this regard, it is the company secretary's responsibility to ensure that the board and its committees are properly constituted and advised. There also needs to be a clear co-ordination between the board and the various committees where the company secretary would normally act as a valued intermediary.

The frequency with which the committee needs to meet will vary considerably from company to company and may change from time to time. It is, however, clear that it must meet close to the year-end to consider whether or not directors retiring by rotation should be put forward for re-appointment at the annual general meeting (AGM) and to review the statement in the annual report concerning its activities. We would recommend that it should meet at least twice a year in order to discharge its responsibilities properly.

References to 'the committee' are to the nomination committee.
References to 'the board' are to the board of directors.
Square brackets contain recommendations which are in line with best practice but which may need to be changed to suit the circumstances of the particular organisation.

D   Model terms of reference

1.   Membership

1.1. The committee shall comprise of at least [3] directors. A majority of the members of the committee should be independent non-executive directors. All appointments to the committee shall be made by the board.

1.2. Only members of the committee have the right to attend committee meetings. However, other individuals such as the chief executive, the head of human resources and external advisers may be invited to attend for all or part of any meeting, as and when appropriate.

1.3. Appointments to the committee shall be for a period of up to three years, which may be extended for two further three-year periods provided that the majority of the committee members remain independent.

1.4. The board shall appoint the committee chairman who should be either the chairman of the board or an independent non-executive director. In the absence of the committee chairman and/or an appointed deputy, the remaining members present shall elect one of their number to chair the meeting from those who would qualify under these terms of reference to be appointed to that position by the board. The chairman of the board shall not chair the committee when it is dealing with the matter of succession to the chairmanship.

---

7   The Combined Code, June 2006 A.4.1. The definition of independence is given in Combined Code provision A.3.1.
8   *Review of the Role and Effectiveness of Non-executive Directors*, para 11.30

2. Secretary

2.1. The company secretary or their nominee shall act as the secretary of the committee.

3. Quorum

3.1. The quorum necessary for the transaction of business shall be [2] [both of whom must be independent non-executive directors]. A duly convened meeting of the committee at which a quorum is present shall be competent to exercise all or any of the authorities, powers and discretions vested in or exercisable by the committee.

4. Frequency of meetings

4.1. The committee shall meet [at least twice a year][quarterly on the first Wednesday in each of January, April, July and October] and at such other times as the chairman of the committee shall require.[9]

5. Notice of meetings

5.1. Meetings of the committee shall be called by the secretary of the committee at the request of the committee chairman.

5.2. Unless otherwise agreed, notice of each meeting confirming the venue, time and date, together with an agenda of items to be discussed, shall be forwarded to each member of the committee, any other person required to attend and all other non-executive directors, no later than [5] working days before the date of the meeting. Supporting papers shall be sent to committee members and to other attendees as appropriate, at the same time.

6. Minutes of meetings

6.1. The secretary shall minute the proceedings and resolutions of all committee meetings, including the names of those present and in attendance.

6.2. Minutes of committee meetings shall be circulated promptly to all members of the committee and the chairman of the board and, once agreed, to all other members of the board, unless a conflict of interest exists.

7. Annual General Meeting

7.1. The committee chairman shall attend the annual general meeting prepared to respond to any shareholder questions on the committee's activities.

---

9   The frequency and timing of meetings will differ according to the needs of the company. Meetings should be organised so that attendance is maximised (for example by timetabling them to coincide with board meetings).

8.   Duties

8.1. The committee shall

8.1.1. regularly review the structure, size and composition (including the skills, knowledge and experience) required of the board compared to its current position and make recommendations to the board with regard to any changes

8.1.2. give full consideration to succession planning for directors and other senior executives in the course of its work, taking into account the challenges and opportunities facing the company, and what skills and expertise are therefore needed on the board in the future

8.1.3. be responsible for identifying and nominating for the approval of the board, candidates to fill board vacancies as and when they arise

8.1.4. before any appointment is made by the board, evaluate the balance of skills, knowledge and experience on the board, and, in the light of this evaluation prepare a description of the role and capabilities required for a particular appointment. In identifying suitable candidates the committee shall

    8.1.4.1 use open advertising or the services of external advisers to facilitate the search

    8.1.4.2 consider candidates from a wide range of backgrounds

    8.1.4.3 consider candidates on merit and against objective criteria, taking care that appointees have enough time available to devote to the position

8.1.5. keep under review the leadership needs of the organisation, both executive and non-executive, with a view to ensuring the continued ability of the organisation to compete effectively in the marketplace

8.1.6. keep up to date and fully informed about strategic issues and commercial changes affecting the company and the market in which it operates

8.1.7. review annually the time required from non-executive directors. Performance evaluation should be used to assess whether the non-executive directors are spending enough time to fulfil their duties

8.1.8. ensure that on appointment to the board, non-executive directors receive a formal letter of appointment setting out clearly what is expected of them in terms of time commitment, committee service and involvement outside board meetings

8.2. The committee shall also make recommendations to the board concerning

8.2.1. formulating plans for succession for both executive and non-executive directors and in particular for the key roles of chairman and chief executive

8.2.2. suitable candidates for the role of senior independent director

8.2.3. membership of the audit and remuneration committees, in consultation with the chairmen of those committees

8.2.4. the re-appointment of any non-executive director at the conclusion of their specified term of office having given due regard to their performance and ability to continue to contribute to the board in the light of the knowledge, skills and experience required

8.2.5. the continuation (or not) in service of any director who has reached the age of [70] if required by the articles

8.2.6. the re-election by shareholders of any director under the 'retirement by rotation' provisions in the company's articles of association having due regard to their performance and ability to continue to contribute to the board in the light of the knowledge, skills and experience required

8.2.7. any matters relating to the continuation in office of any director at any time including the suspension or termination of service of an executive director as an employee of the company subject to the provisions of the law and their service contract

8.2.8. the appointment of any director to executive or other office

9. Reporting responsibilities

9.1. The committee chairman shall report formally to the board on its proceedings after each meeting on all matters within its duties and responsibilities.

9.2. The committee shall make whatever recommendations to the board it deems appropriate on any area within its remit where action or improvement is needed.

9.3. The committee shall make a statement in the annual report about its activities, the process used to make appointments and explain if external advice or open advertising has not been used.

10. Other

10.1. The committee shall, at least once a year, review its own performance, constitution and terms of reference to ensure it is operating at maximum effectiveness and recommend any changes it considers necessary to the board for approval.

11. Authority

11.1. The committee is authorised to seek any information it requires from any employee of the company in order to perform its duties.

11.2. The committee is authorised to obtain, at the company's expense, outside legal or other professional advice on any matters within its terms of reference.

October 2007

BACK TO THE TOP

The information given in this Guidance Note is provided in good faith with the intention of furthering the understanding of the subject matter. Whilst we believe the information to be accurate at the time of publication, ICSA and its staff cannot, however, accept any liability for any loss or damage occasioned by any person or organisation acting or refraining from action as a result of any views expressed therein. If the reader has any specific doubts or concerns about the subject matter they are advised to seek legal advice based on the circumstances of their own situation.

© Institute of Chartered Secretaries & Administrators

APPENDIX 14

THE COMBINED CODE (JUNE 2008), SCHEDULE C: DISCLOSURE OF CORPORATE GOVERNANCE ARRANGEMENTS

DISCLOSURE AND TRANSPARENCY RULES (DTR)

Section 7.1 of the Disclosure and Transparency Rules concerns audit committees or bodies carrying out equivalent functions.

DTR 7.1.1 R to 7.1.3 R sets out requirements relating to the composition and functions of the committee or equivalent body:

- DTR 7.1.1 R states than an issuer must have a body which is responsible for performing the functions set out in DTR 7.1.3 R, and that least one member of that body must be independent and at least one member must have competence in accounting and/or auditing.

- DTR 7.1.2 G states that the requirements for independence and competence in accounting and/or auditing may be satisfied by the same member or by different members of the relevant body.

- DTR 7.1.3 R states that an issuer must ensure that, as a minimum, the relevant body must:
  (1) monitor the financial reporting process;
  (2) monitor the effectiveness of the issuer's internal control, internal audit where applicable, and risk management systems;
  (3) monitor the statutory audit of the annual and consolidated accounts;
  (4) review and monitor the independence of the statutory auditor, and in particular the provision of additional services to the issuer.

DTR 7.1.5 R to 7.1.7 R explain what disclosure is required:

- DTR 7.1.5 R states that the issuer must make a statement available to the public disclosing which body carries out the functions required by DTR 7.1.3 R and how it is composed.

- DTR 7.1.6 G states that this can be included in the corporate governance statement required under DTR 7.2 (see below).

- DTR 7.1.7 R states that compliance with the relevant provisions of the Combined Code (as set out in the Appendix to this Schedule) will result in compliance with DTR 7.1.1 R to 7.1.5 R.

Section 7.2 concerns corporate governance statements. Issuers are required to produce a corporate governance statement that must be either included in the directors' report (DTR 7.2.1 R); or in a separate report published together with the annual report; or on the issuer's website, in which case there must be a cross-reference in the directors' report (DTR 7.2.9 R).

DTR 7.2.2 R requires that the corporate governance statements must contain a reference to the corporate governance code to which the company is subject (for listed companies incorporated in the UK this is the Combined Code). DTR 7.2.3 R requires that, to the extent that it departs from that code, the company must explain which parts of the code it departs from and the reasons for doing so. DTR 7.2.4 G states that compliance with LR 9.8.6R (6) (the 'comply or explain' rule in relation to the Combined Code) will also satisfy these requirements.

DTR 7.2.5 R to 7.2.7 R and DTR 7.2.10 R set out certain information that must be disclosed in the corporate governance statement:

- DTR 7.2.5 R states that the corporate governance statement must contain a description of the main features of the company's internal control and risk management systems in control and risk management systems in relation to the financial reporting process. DTR 7.2.10 R states that an issuer which is required to prepare a group directors' report within the meaning of Section 415(2) of the Companies Act 2006 must include in that report a description of the main features of the group's internal control and risk management systems in relation to the process for preparing consolidated accounts.

- DTR 7.2.6 R states that the corporate governance statement must contain the information required by paragraph 13(2)(c), (d), (f), (h) and (i) of Schedule 7 to the Large and Medium-sized Companies and Groups (Accounts and Reports) Regulations 2008 (SI 2008/410) where the issuer is subject to the requirements of that paragraph.

- DTR 7.2.7 R states that the corporate governance statement must contain a description of the composition and operation of the issuer's administrative, management and supervisory bodies and their committees. DTR 7.2.8 G states that compliance with the relevant provisions of the Combined Code (as set out in the

"Overlap between the Disclosure and Transparency Rules and the Combined Code" below) will satisfy the requirements of DTR 7.2.7 R.

THE COMBINED CODE

In addition the Code includes specific requirements for disclosure which are set out below:

The <u>annual report should record</u>:

- a statement of how the board operates, including a high level statement of which types of decisions are to be taken by the board and which are to be delegated to management (A.1.1);

- the names of the chairman, the deputy chairman (where there is one), the chief executive, the senior independent director and the chairmen and members of the nomination, audit and remuneration committees (A.1.2);

- the number of meetings of the board and those committees and individual attendance by directors (A.1.2);

- the names of the non-executive directors whom the board determines to be independent, with reasons where necessary (A.3.1);

- the other significant commitments of the chairman and any changes to them during the year (A.4.3);

- how performance evaluation of the board, its committees and its directors has been conducted (A.6.1);

- the steps the board has taken to ensure that members of the board, and in particular the non-executive directors, develop an understanding of the views of major shareholders about their company (0.1 .2).

The <u>annual report should also include</u>:

- a separate section describing the work of the nomination committee, including the process it has used in relation to board appointments and an explanation if neither external search consultancy nor open advertising has been used in the appointment of a chairman or a non-executive director (A.4.6);

- a description of the work of the remuneration committee as required under the Directors' Remuneration Report Regulations 2002, and including, where an executive director serves as a non-executive director elsewhere, whether or not the director will retain such earnings and, if so, what the remuneration is (8.1.4);

- an explanation from the directors of their responsibility for preparing the accounts and a statement by the auditors about their reporting responsibilities (C.1.1);

- a statement from the directors that the business is a going concern, with supporting assumptions or qualifications as necessary (C.1.2);

- a report that the board has conducted a review of the effectiveness of e group's system of internal controls (C.2.1);

- a separate section describing the work of the audit committee in discharging its responsibilities (C.3.3);

- where there is no internal audit function, the reasons for the absence of such a function (C.3.S);

- where the board does not accept the audit committee's recommendation on the appointment, reappointment or removal of an external auditor, a statement from the audit committee explaining the recommendation and the reasons why the board has taken a different position (C.3.6); and

- an explanation of how, if the auditor provides non-audit services, auditor objectivity and independence is safeguarded (C.3.7).

The following information should be made available (which may be met by placing the information on a website that is maintained by or on behalf of the company):

- the terms of reference of the nomination, remuneration and audit committees, explaining their role and the authority delegated to them by the board (*AA.1*, B.2.1 and C.3.3);

- the terms and conditions of appointment of non-executive directors (*AAA*) (see footnote 8 on page 10); and

- where remuneration consultants are appointed, a statement of whether they have any other connection with the company (B.2.1).

The board should set out to shareholders in the papers accompanying a resolution to elect or re-elect directors:

- sufficient biographical details to enable shareholders to take an informed decision on their election or re-election (A. 7.1);

- why they believe an individual should be elected to a non-executive role (A.7.2); and

- on re-election of a non-executive director, confirmation from the chairman that, following formal performance evaluation, the individual's performance continues to be effective and to demonstrate commitment to the role, including commitment of time for board and committee meetings and any other duties (A.7.2).

The board should <u>set out to shareholders in the papers recommending appointment or reappointment of an external auditor</u>:

- if the board does not accept the audit committee's recommendation, a statement from the audit committee explaining the recommendation and from the board setting out reasons why they have taken a different position (C.3.6).

APPENDIX – OVERLAP BETWEEN THE DISCLOSURE AND TRANSPARENCY RULES AND THE COMBINED CODE

DISCLOSURE AND TRANSPARENCY RULES	COMBINED CODE
D.T.R 7.1.1 R	**Provision C.3.1**
Sets out minimum requirements on composition of the audit committee or equivalent body.	Sets out recommended composition of the audit committee.
D.T.R 7.1.3 R	**Provision C.3.2**
Sets out minimum functions of the audit committee or equivalent body.	Sets out the recommended minimum terms of reference for the committee.
D.T.R 7.1.5 R	**Provision A.1.2:**
The composition and function of the audit committee or equivalent body must be disclosed in the annual report.	The annual report should identify members of the board committees.
	Provision C.3.3
OTR 7.1.7 R *states that compliance with Code provisions A. 1.2, C.3.1, C.3.2 and* C.3.3 *will result in compliance with OTR* 7.1.1 *R to OTR* 7.1.5 *R.*	The annual report should describe the work of the audit committee. Further recommendations on the content of the audit committee report are set out in the Smith Guidance.

D.T.R 7.2.5 R

The corporate governance statement must include a description of the main features of the company's internal control and risk management systems in relation to the financial reporting process.

While this requirement differs from the requirement in the Combined Code, it is envisaged that both could be met by a single internal control statement.

DTR 7.2.7 R

The corporate governance statement must include a description of the composition and operation of the administrative, management and supervisory bodies and their committees.

DTR 7.2.8 R states that compliance with Code provisions A.1.1, A.1.2, A.4.6, B.2.1 and C.3.3 will result in compliance with DTR 7.2.7.R.

Provision C.2.1

The Board must report that a review of the effectiveness of the internal control system has been carried out. Further recommendations on the content of the internal control statement are set out in the Turnbull Guidance.

This requirement overlaps with a number of different provisions of the Code:

A.1.1: the annual report should include a statement of how the board operates.

A.1.2: the annual report should identify members of the board and board committees.

A.4.6: the annual report should describe the work of the nomination committee.

B.2.1: a description of the work of the remuneration committee should be made available. [Note: in order to comply with DTR 7.2.7 R this information will need to be included in the corporate governance statement].

C.3.3: the annual report should describe the work of the audit committee.

APPENDIX 15

COMBINED CODE CHECKLIST

A checklist of the Main Principles and the Code Provisions for corporate governance reporting to assist with the corporate governance narrative on application of the Principles and the statement on compliance or non-compliance with the Provisions.

SECTION 1 – COMPANIES

Main Principles

A.   DIRECTORS

A.1   The Board

Every company should be headed by an effective board, which is collectively responsible for the success of the company.

A.2   Chairman and Chief Executive

There should be a clear division of responsibilities at the head of the company between the running of the board and the executive responsibility for the running of the company's business. No one individual should have unfettered powers of decision.

A.3   Board Balance and Independence

The board should include a balance of executive and non-executive directors (and in particular independent non-executive directors) such that no individual or small group of individuals can dominate the board's decision taking.

A.4   Appointments to the Board

There should be a formal, rigorous and transparent procedure for the appointment of new directors to the board.

A.5	Information and Professional Development	The board should be supplied in a timely manner with information in a form and of a quality appropriate to enable it to discharge its duties. All directors should receive induction on joining the board and should regularly update and refresh their skills and knowledge.
A.6	Performance Evaluation	The board should undertake a formal and rigorous annual evaluation of its own performance and that of its committees and individual directors.
A.7	Re-election	All directors should be submitted for re-election at regular intervals, subject to continued satisfactory performance. The board should ensure planned and progressive refreshing of the board.

B.   REMUNERATION

B.1	The Level and Make-up of Remuneration	Levels of remuneration should be sufficient to attract, retain and motivate directors of the quality required to run the company successfully, but a company should avoid paying more than is necessary for this purpose. A significant proportion of executive directors' remuneration should be structured so as to link rewards to corporate and individual performance.
B.2	Procedure	There should be a formal and transparent procedure for developing policy on executive remuneration and for fixing the remuneration packages of individual directors. No director should be involved in deciding his or her own remuneration.

C.   ACCOUNTABILITY AND AUDIT

C.1	Financial Reporting	The board should present a balanced and understandable assessment of the company's position and prospects.
C.2	Internal Control	The board should maintain a sound system of internal control to safeguard shareholders' investment and the company's assets.

C.3 Audit Committees and Auditors   The board should establish formal and transparent arrangements for considering how they should apply the financial reporting and internal control principles and for maintaining an appropriate relationship with the company's auditors.

D.   RELATIONS WITH SHAREHOLDERS

D.1 Dialogue with Institutional Shareholders   There should be a dialogue with shareholders based on the mutual understanding of objectives. The board as a whole has responsibility for ensuring that a satisfactory dialogue with shareholders takes place.

D.2 Constructive Use of the AGM   The board should use the AGM to communicate with investors and to encourage their participation.

Code Provisions

A.   DIRECTORS

A.1 THE BOARD   Yes No Explanation
                                                                 if 'No'

A.1.1 The board should meet sufficiently   ☐ ☐
regularly to discharge its duties effectively.
There should be a formal schedule of
matters specifically reserved for its
decision. The annual report should include
a statement of how the board operates,
including a high level statement of which
types of decisions are to be taken by the
board and which are to be delegated to
management.

A.1.2 The annual report should identify the   ☐ ☐
chairman, the deputy chairman (where
there is one), the chief executive, the senior
independent director and the chairmen
and members of the nomination, audit
and remuneration committees. It should
also set out the number of meetings of the
board and those committees and
individual attendance by directors.

A.1.3 The chairman should hold meetings with □ □
the non-executive directors without the
executives present. Led by the senior
independent director, the non-executive
directors should meet without the
chairman present at least annually to
appraise the chairman's performance (as
described in A.6.1) and on such other
occasions as are deemed appropriate.

A.1.4 Where directors have concerns which □ □
cannot be resolved about the running of
the company or a proposed action, they
should ensure that their concerns are
recorded in the board minutes. On
resignation, a nonexecutive director should
provide a written statement to the
chairman, for circulation to the board, if
they have any such concerns.

A.1.5 The company should arrange appropriate □ □
insurance cover in respect of legal action
against its directors.

A.2 CHAIRMAN AND CHIEF EXECUTIVE   Yes No Explanation
if 'No'

A.2.1 The roles of chairman and chief executive □ □
should not be exercised by the same
individual. The division of responsibilities
between the chairman and chief executive
should be clearly established, set out in
writing and agreed by the board.

A.2.2 The chairman should on appointment □ □
meet the independence criteria set out in
A.3.1 below. A chief executive should not
go on to be chairman of the same
company. If exceptionally a board decides
that a chief executive should become
chairman, the board should consult major
shareholders in advance and should set out
its reasons to shareholders at the time of
the appointment and in the next annual
report.

A.3 BOARD BALANCE AND
INDEPENDENCE

A.3.1 The board should identify in the annual report each non-executive director it considers to be independent. The board should determine whether the director is independent in character and judgement and whether there are relationships or circumstances which are likely to affect, or could appear to affect, the director's judgement. The board should state its reasons if it determines that a director is independent notwithstanding the existence of relationships or circumstances which may appear relevant to its determination, including if the director:

- has been an employee of the company or group within the last five years;

- has, or has had within the last three years, a material business relationship with the company either directly, or as a partner, shareholder, director or senior employee of a body that has such a relationship with the company;

- has received or receives additional remuneration from the company apart from a director's fee, participates in the company's share option or a performance-related pay scheme, or is a member of the company's pension scheme;

- has close family ties with any of the company's advisers, directors or senior employees;

- holds cross-directorships or has significant links with other directors through involvement in other companies or bodies;

- represents a significant shareholder; or

- has served on the board for more than nine years from the date of their first election.

A.3.2 Except for smaller companies, at least half   ☐ ☐
      the board, excluding the chairman, should
      comprise non-executive directors
      determined by the board to be
      independent. A smaller company should
      have at least two independent
      non-executive directors.

A.3.3 The board should appoint one of the   ☐ ☐
      independent non-executive directors to be
      the senior independent director. The senior
      independent director should be available to
      shareholders if they have concerns which
      contact through the normal channels of
      chairman, chief executive or finance
      director has failed to resolve or for which
      such contact is inappropriate.

A.4   APPOINTMENTS TO THE BOARD   **Yes No Explanation
                                                   if 'No'**

A.4.1 There should be a nomination committee   ☐ ☐
      which should lead the process for board
      appointments and make recommendations
      to the board. A majority of members of
      the nomination committee should be
      independent non-executive directors. The
      chairman or an independent non-executive
      director should chair the committee, but
      the chairman should not chair the
      nomination committee when it is dealing
      with the appointment of a successor to the
      chairmanship. The nomination committee
      should make available its terms of
      reference, explaining its role and the
      authority delegated to it by the board.

A.4.2 The nomination committee should   ☐ ☐
      evaluate the balance of skills, knowledge
      and experience on the board and, in the
      light of this evaluation, prepare a
      description of the role and capabilities
      required for a particular appointment.

A.4.3 For the appointment of a chairman, the ☐ ☐
nomination committee should prepare a
job specification, including an assessment
of the time commitment expected,
recognising the need for availability in the
event of crises. A chairman's other
significant commitments should be
disclosed to the board before appointment
and included in the annual report.
Changes to such commitments should be
reported to the board as they arise, and
their impact explained in the next annual
report.

A.4.4 The terms and conditions of appointment ☐ ☐
of non-executive directors should be made
available for inspection. The letter of
appointment should set out the expected
time commitment. Non-executive directors
should undertake that they will have
sufficient time to meet what is expected of
them. Their other significant commitments
should be disclosed to the board before
appointment, with a broad indication of
the time involved and the board should be
informed of subsequent changes.

A.4.5 The board should not agree to a full time ☐ ☐
executive director taking on more than one
non-executive directorship in a FTSE 100
company nor the chairmanship of such a
company.

A.4.6 A separate section of the annual report ☐ ☐
should describe the work of the
nomination committee, including the
process it has used in relation to board
appointments. An explanation should be
given if neither an external search
consultancy nor open advertising has been
used in the appointment of a chairman or
a non-executive director.

A.5 INFORMATION AND PROFESSIONAL DEVELOPMENT	Yes	No	**Explanation if 'No'**
A.5.1 The chairman should ensure that new directors receive a full, formal and tailored induction on joining the board. As part of this, the company should offer to major shareholders the opportunity to meet a new nonexecutive director.	☐	☐	
A.5.2 The board should ensure that directors, especially non-executive directors, have access to independent professional advice at the company's expense where they judge it necessary to discharge their responsibilities as directors. Committees should be provided with sufficient resources to undertake their duties.	☐	☐	
A.5.3 All directors should have access to the advice and services of the company secretary, who is responsible to the board for ensuring that board procedures are complied with. Both the appointment and removal of the company secretary should be a matter for the board as a whole.	☐	☐	
A.6 PERFORMANCE EVALUATION	Yes	No	**Explanation if 'No'**
A.6.1 The board should state in the annual report how performance evaluation of the board, its committees and its individual directors has been conducted. The non-executive directors, led by the senior independent director, should be responsible for performance evaluation of the chairman, taking into account the views of executive directors.	☐	☐	

A.7 RE-ELECTION

Yes No Explanation if 'No'

A.7.1 All directors should be subject to election by shareholders at the first annual general meeting after their appointment, and to re-election thereafter at intervals of no more than three years. The names of directors submitted for election or re-election should be accompanied by sufficient biographical details and any other relevant information to enable shareholders to take an informed decision on their election.

☐ ☐

A.7.2 Non-executive directors should be appointed for specified terms subject to re-election and to Companies Acts provisions relating to the removal of a director. The board should set out to shareholders in the papers accompanying a resolution to elect a non-executive director why they believe an individual should be elected. The chairman should confirm to shareholders when proposing re-election that, following formal performance evaluation, the individual's performance continues to be effective and to demonstrate commitment to the role. Any term beyond six years (e.g. two three-year terms) for a non-executive director should be subject to particularly rigorous review, and should take into account the need for progressive refreshing of the board. Non-executive directors may serve longer than nine years (e.g. three three-year terms), subject to annual re-election. Serving more than nine years could be relevant to the determination of a non-executive director's independence (as set out in provision A.3.1).

☐ ☐

B.   REMUNERATION

B.1 THE LEVEL AND MAKE-UP OF REMUNERATION	**Yes No Explanation if 'No'**

B.1.1 The performance-related elements of
        remuneration should form a significant
        proportion of the total remuneration
        package of executive directors and should
        be designed to align their interests with
        those of shareholders and to give these
        directors keen incentives to perform at the
        highest levels. In designing schemes of
        performance-related remuneration, the
        remuneration committee should follow the
        provisions in Schedule A to this Code.
☐ ☐

B.1.2 Executive share options should not be
        offered at a discount save as permitted by
        the relevant provisions of the Listing
        Rules.
☐ ☐

B.1.3 Levels of remuneration for non-executive
        directors should reflect the time
        commitment and responsibilities of the
        role. Remuneration for nonexecutive
        directors should not include share options.
        If, exceptionally, options are granted,
        shareholder approval should be sought in
        advance and any shares acquired by
        exercise of the options should be held until
        at least one year after the non-executive
        director leaves the board. Holding of share
        options could be relevant to the
        determination of a non-executive director's
        independence (as set out in Provision
        A.3.1).
☐ ☐

B.1.4 Where a company releases an executive
        director to serve as a non-executive
        director elsewhere, the remuneration report
        should include a statement as to whether
        or not the director will retain such
        earnings and, if so, what the remuneration
        is.
☐ ☐

Service Contracts and Compensation

B.1.5 The remuneration committee should   ☐ ☐
carefully consider what compensation
commitments (including pension
contributions and all other elements) their
directors' terms of appointment would
entail in the event of early termination.
The aim should be to avoid rewarding
poor performance. They should take a
robust line on reducing compensation to
reflect departing directors' obligations to
mitigate loss.

B.1.6 Notice or contract periods should be set at   ☐ ☐
one year or less. If it is necessary to offer
longer notice or contract periods to new
directors recruited from outside, such
periods should reduce to one year or less
after the initial period.

B.2 PROCEDURE   **Yes No Explanation**
                                            if 'No'

B.2.1 The board should establish a remuneration   ☐ ☐
committee of at least three, or in the case
of smaller companies two, independent
non-executive directors. In addition the
company chairman may also be a member
of, but not chair, the committee if he or
she was considered independent on
appointment as chairman. The
remuneration committee should make
available its terms of reference, explaining
its role and the authority delegated to it by
the board. Where remuneration
consultants are appointed, a statement
should be made available of whether they
have any other connection with the
company.

B.2.2 The remuneration committee should have ☐ ☐
delegated responsibility for setting
remuneration for all executive directors
and the chairman, including pension rights
and any compensation payments. The
committee should also recommend and
monitor the level and structure of
remuneration for senior management. The
definition of 'senior management' for this
purpose should be determined by the
board but should normally include the
first layer of management below board
level.

B.2.3 The board itself or, where required by the ☐ ☐
Articles of Association, the shareholders
should determine the remuneration of the
non-executive directors within the limits
set in the Articles of Association. Where
permitted by the Articles, the board may
however delegate this responsibility to a
committee, which might include the chief
executive.

B.2.4 Shareholders should be invited specifically ☐ ☐
to approve all new long-term incentive
schemes (as defined in the Listing Rules)
and significant changes to existing
schemes, save in the circumstances
permitted by the Listing Rules.

C. ACCOUNTABILITY AND AUDIT

C.1 FINANCIAL REPORTING

**Yes No Explanation
if 'No'**

C.1.1 The directors should explain in the annual ☐ ☐
report their responsibility for preparing the
accounts and there should be a statement
by the auditors about their reporting
responsibilities.

C.1.2 The directors should report that the ☐ ☐
business is a going concern, with
supporting assumptions or qualifications
as necessary.

C.2 INTERNAL CONTROL   **Yes No Explanation if 'No'**

C.2.1 The board should, at least annually,   ☐ ☐
conduct a review of the effectiveness of the
group's system of internal controls and
should report to shareholders that they
have done so. The review should cover all
material controls, including financial,
operational and compliance controls and
risk management systems.

C.3 AUDIT COMMITTEE AND AUDITORS   **Yes No Explanation if 'No'**

C.3.1 The board should establish an audit   ☐ ☐
committee of at least three, or in the case
of smaller companies two, independent
non-executive directors. In smaller
companies the company chairman may be
a member of, but not chair, the committee
in addition to the independent
non-executive directors, provided he or she
was considered independent on
appointment as chairman. The board
should satisfy itself that at least one
member of the audit committee has recent
and relevant financial experience.

C.3.2 The main role and responsibilities of the   ☐ ☐
audit committee should be set out in
written terms of reference and should
include:

- to monitor the integrity of the financial
  statements of the company, and any
  formal announcements relating to the
  company's financial performance,
  reviewing significant financial reporting
  judgements contained in them;

- to review the company's internal
  financial controls and, unless expressly
  addressed by a separate board risk
  committee composed of independent
  directors, or by the board itself, to
  review the company's internal control
  and risk management systems;

- to monitor and review the effectiveness
  of the company's internal audit
  function;

- to make recommendations to the board, for it to put to the shareholders for their approval in general meeting, in relation to the appointment, re-appointment and removal of the external auditor and to approve the remuneration and terms of engagement of the external auditor;

- to review and monitor the external auditor's independence and objectivity and the effectiveness of the audit process, taking into consideration relevant UK professional and regulatory requirements;

- to develop and implement policy on the engagement of the external auditor to supply non-audit services, taking into account relevant ethical guidance regarding the provision of non-audit services by the external audit firm; and to report to the board, identifying any matters in respect of which it considers that action or improvement is needed and making recommendations as to the steps to be taken.

C.3.3 The terms of reference of the audit ☐ ☐
committee, including its role and the authority delegated to it by the board, should be made available. A separate section of the annual report should describe the work of the committee in discharging those responsibilities.

C.3.4 The audit committee should review ☐ ☐
arrangements by which staff of the company may, in confidence, raise concerns about possible improprieties in matters of financial reporting or other matters. The audit committee's objective should be to ensure that arrangements are in place for the proportionate and independent investigation of such matters and for appropriate follow-up action.

C.3.5 The audit committee should monitor and ☐ ☐
review the effectiveness of the internal
audit activities. Where there is no internal
audit function, the audit committee should
consider annually whether there is a need
for an internal audit function and make a
recommendation to the board, and the
reasons for the absence of such a function
should be explained in the relevant section
of the annual report.

C.3.6 The audit committee should have primary ☐ ☐
responsibility for making a
recommendation on the appointment,
reappointment and removal of the external
auditors. If the board does not accept the
audit committee's recommendation, it
should include in the annual report, and in
any papers recommending appointment or
re-appointment, a statement from the audit
committee explaining the recommendation
and should set out reasons why the board
has taken a different position.

C.3.7 The annual report should explain to ☐ ☐
shareholders how, if the auditor provides
non-audit services, auditor objectivity and
independence is safeguarded.

D. RELATIONS WITH SHAREHOLDERS

D.1 DIALOGUE WITH INSTITUTIONAL   **Yes No Explanation**
SHAREHOLDERS   **if 'No'**

D.1.1 The chairman should ensure that the views ☐ ☐
of shareholders are communicated to the
board as a whole. The chairman should
discuss governance and strategy with
major shareholders. Non-executive
directors should be offered the opportunity
to attend meetings with major
shareholders and should expect to attend
them if requested by major shareholders.
The senior independent director should
attend sufficient meetings with a range of
major shareholders to listen to their views
in order to help develop a balanced
understanding of the issues and concerns
of major shareholders.

D.1.2 The board should state in the annual ☐ ☐
report the steps they have taken to ensure
that the members of the board, and in
particular the non-executive directors,
develop an understanding of the views of
major shareholders about their company,
for example through direct face-to-face
contact, analysts' or brokers' briefings and
surveys of shareholder opinion. Nothing
in these principles or provisions should be
taken to override the general requirements
of law to treat shareholders equally in
access to information.

D.2   CONSTRUCTIVE USE OF THE AGM   **Yes No Explanation**
                                                if 'No'

D.2.1 At any general meeting, the company ☐ ☐
should propose a separate resolution on
each substantially separate issue, and
should in particular propose a resolution
at the AGM relating to the report and
accounts. For each resolution, proxy
appointment forms should provide
shareholders with the option to direct their
proxy to vote either for or against the
resolution or to withhold their vote. The
proxy form and any announcement of the
results of a vote should make it clear that
a 'vote withheld' is not a vote in law and
will not be counted in the calculation of
the proportion of the votes for and against
the resolution.

D.2.2 The company should ensure that all valid ☐ ☐
proxy appointments received for general
meetings are properly recorded and
counted. For each resolution, after a vote
has been taken, except where taken on a
poll, the company should ensure that the
following information is given at the
meeting and made available as soon as
reasonably practicable on a website which
is maintained by or on behalf of the
company:

- the number of shares in respect of
  which proxy appointments have been
  validly made;

- the number of votes for the resolution;

- the number of votes against the resolution; and

- the number of shares in respect of which the vote was directed to be withheld.

D.2.3 The chairman should arrange for the chairmen of the audit, remuneration and nomination committees to be available to answer questions at the AGM and for all directors to attend. ☐ ☐

D.2.4 The company should arrange for the Notice of the AGM and related papers to be sent to shareholders at least 20 working days before the meeting. ☐ ☐

APPENDIX 16

INSTITUTE OF CHARTERED SECRETARIES AND ADMINISTRATORS (ICSA) GUIDANCE NOTE: LISTED COMPANY REPORTING REQUIREMENTS FOR DIRECTORS REMUNERATION

Companies must comply with reporting requirements for directors' remuneration or face the prospect of a fine. For the listed company, these requirements fall into three categories:

- statutory (those required under the Companies Act 1985 as amended from time to time);

- regulatory (those required under the Listing Rules of the UK Listing Authority – the Financial Services Authority);

- best practice (those required by the Combined Code on Corporate Governance, which is appended to the Listing Rules).

The requirements are both detailed and complex. The fact that the categories overlap – and there is much duplication of provisions – causes further confusion. This guidance note aims to give a clear and concise picture of a company's obligations.

DISCLOSURE RULES

The statutory rules were amended in July by the Directors' Remuneration Report Regulations 2002. The new rules apply as from the financial year ending on or after 31 December 2002. The Regulations use the term 'quoted' company so that the requirement to prepare a Remuneration report applies only to companies that have equity listed on the Official List of the London Stock Exchange, and not e.g. to AIM listed companies or companies that have only debt listed. The rules however do apply to companies that have securities listed on an official exchange of an EEA state, the New York Stock Exchange or on NASDAQ.

The board must prepare a directors' remuneration report, which must be approved by the board and signed on its behalf. The report is to be circulated in the same manner as the annual report and accounts and laid before the members in the general meeting, save that members will be given the right to a separate advisory vote on the directors' remuneration report. The report must include:

- Details naming each director who was or had been a member of the Remuneration Committee and specific information on and about the use of any remuneration consultants. Such information includes: the name of any person providing consultancy services to the Remuneration Committee in its deliberations over directors' pay; where that person is not also a director of the company, details of any other service provided by him to the company in that year; and whether that person was appointed by the Remuneration Committee.

- A forward-looking policy statement on the remuneration of directors, including, for each director: (i) a summary of any performance conditions attaching to any entitlement to share options or under a long-term incentive scheme; (ii) an explanation as to why those conditions were selected; (iii) a summary of the methods to be used in determining whether those conditions are met and reasons for choosing those methods; (iv) if any performance condition requires comparisons to be made with factors external to the company, information about those factors and, if those factors relate to one or more other company or an index, the identity of the other company or index; (v) a description of and explanation about any significant amendment proposed to be made concerning the entitlement of any director to share options or under a long-term incentive scheme; (vi) an explanation of why any entitlement to any share options or under a long-term incentive scheme is not subject to any performance conditions, if that is the case; and (vii) an explanation on each remuneration package as to the relative importance of each element that is performance-linked. The policy statement must also disclose details on duration of, notice periods in and termination payments under service contracts.

- A line graph to compare share price performance of the company (by reference to total shareholder return, fairly calculated according to specified criteria) with that of other shares on a named equity market index, over a five-year period, and giving reasons for choosing that comparator index.

- Disclosure for each director on information regarding service contracts including: date of the contract, the unexpired term and details of any notice periods; and any provision for compensation payable upon early termination together with other information necessary to calculate an estimate of liability in the event of early termination.

- Disclosure of remuneration packages for each director. The directors must be named and the packages split into the component parts: basic salary and fees (including 'golden hellos'); bonuses; expenses allowance and benefits in kind (those chargeable to UK income tax); compensation for loss of office and/or other payments connected with early termination or breach of contract; and other non-cash benefits not falling under one of the prescribed heads. The amounts above must be totalled, appear in tabular form together with the previous year's comparatives. The nature and the estimated value of 'other non-cash benefits' must be stated.

- A policy statement on the granting of executive options or awards under any SAYE or other long-term incentive scheme. (Any departure from or change to the previous year's policy must be explained and justified.)

- Disclosure of share options and SAYE options for each director, as at the end of the financial year and until a date not more than one month before the circulation of the annual report and accounts. Total interests must be shown and a distinction made between those that are beneficial and those that are non-beneficial. (Beneficial means shares either held in the director's name or the name of a person or persons 'connected' to him – e.g. spouse, children under 18 – or held by a company controlled by him or a 'connected person'.) Specific information requiring disclosure include: share options that were awarded or exercised in the year; options that expired unexercised in the year; and any variation to terms and conditions (including to any performance criteria) relating to the award or exercise of share options. For all unexpired share options, disclosure is required of the price paid for its award, if any, the exercise price (if applicable), the date from which the options may be exercised and date on which the options expire, as well as the market price at the end of the year and the highest and lowest prices during that year. In respect of share options exercised, the disclosures must show market price as at time when the options were exercised. (Certain aggregation is permitted to avoid excessive length, but professional advice should be sought.)

- Details for each director of any long-term incentive schemes (other than share options). Interests in such schemes at both the start and the end of the year under review should be shown. Entitlements and awards granted during the year must also be made public – and the year in which year such entitlements and awards can be taken up specified, together with any variations made to any scheme terms.

- Details of contributions to and entitlements in any defined benefit scheme for each director – the amount of retirement benefits accruing in the year, the accumulated accrued benefits (pension and lump sum) as at the end of the year under review, information on or necessary to determine transfer values, early retirement rights and any discretionary benefits.

- For money purchase schemes, details of contributions made or payable during the year under review.

- Aggregate of excess retirement benefits receivable by directors, past directors or their nominees or dependents. Details of the estimated money value and the nature of any non-cash benefits must be given.

- Disclosure of significant payments made to former directors during the year.

- Aggregate of consideration payable to third parties for the services of any director. Details of the estimated money value and the nature of any noncash benefits must be given.

- An explanation and justification for any element of remuneration that is pensionable other than basic salary.

A distinction should be made between those amounts paid for services as a director of a company or its subsidiaries, and those paid under a contract of employment either with the company or its subsidiaries. A director of a parent company must also disclose in the parent company's accounts amounts of emoluments paid to him/her by subsidiaries. Finally, the 'aggregate amount of directors' emoluments etc' (*CA85, para 1 of Sch. 6*) disclosed in the notes to the accounts are still required – but only for those items in para 1.

DISCLOSURE RECOMMENDATIONS

In addition to the above mandatory requirements, the following points arise under the Code of Best Practice:

- Shareholders should be asked to approve all new long-term incentive schemes.

- If grants under any executive share option or any long-term incentive plan are awarded in one block rather than phased, this should be explained and justified.

October 2002

APPENDIX 17

CORPORATE GOVERNANCE STATEMENT – RICARDO PLC

CORPORATE GOVERNANCE IN PRACTICE

The Combined Code on Corporate Governance

The Combined Code on Corporate Governance issued by the Financial Reporting Council in July 2003 ('the Code') applies to reporting periods beginning on or after 1 November 2003. Section 1 of the Code applies to companies. Under the UK Listing Authority's Listing Rules which apply to the London Stock Exchange's main market, Ricardo plc is required to report on how it has applied the principles set out in Section 1 of the Code, and either to confirm that it has complied with the provisions of Section 1 of the Code or to provide an explanation of where it has not.

This part of the Annual Report, together with the Directors' Remuneration Report set out on pages 50 to 57, describes how the Company has applied the principles contained in Section 1 of the Code. An explanation of the few areas where the Company has not complied with Section 1 of the Code during the twelve months ended 30 June 2007 is given on page 49. In June 2006, the Code was revised, effective for reporting years beginning on or after 1 November 2006. The directors consider that the Company has been fully compliant with Section 1 of the June 2006 version of the Code since October 2006 when the Chairman stood down as a member of the Audit Committee, in line with the Code's guidance that the chairman of a company should not be a member of its audit committee.

The Board of Directors

The Board, which is headed by the non-executive Chairman, Marcus Beresford, also included three other non-executive and three executive members as at 30 June 2007, and throughout the period complied with the Code's provision that a smaller company should have at least two independent directors. (Ricardo was below the FTSE 350 throughout the year immediately prior to the year ended 30 June 2007.) The Board met regularly throughout the year with ad hoc meetings also being held.

The role of the Board is to provide entrepreneurial leadership of the Company within a framework of effective controls which enables risk to be assessed and managed. The Board sets strategic aims, reviews management performance and ensures that the necessary financial and human resources are in place to meet its objectives and its obligations to its shareholders and others. The Board has agreed a schedule of matters reserved for the Board, which includes approval of the Group's strategy, acquisitions and disposals of businesses, the annual financial budgets, major capital expenditure, major proposals and certain key policies. The Board approves interim dividends and recommends final dividends. It receives recommendations from the Audit Committee in relation to the appointment of auditors, their remuneration and the policy relating to non-audit services and from the Nomination Committee it receives recommendations regarding Board appointments. The Board agrees the policy for executive directors' remuneration with the Remuneration Committee and determines fees paid to non-executive directors. Board papers are circulated before Board meetings in sufficient time to be meaningful. The Board delegates to management, through the Chief Executive Officer, the implementation of strategy, the overall performance of the Group and the management of the business in a fit and proper manner in keeping with its values and policies.

The division of responsibilities between the Chairman and the Chief Executive Officer is clearly defined and has been approved by the Board. The Chairman's primary responsibility is ensuring the effectiveness of the Board and setting its agenda. The Chief Executive has direct charge of the Group on a day to day basis and is accountable to the Board for the financial and operational performance of the Group. The Chief Executive also chairs the Ricardo Operating Board which deals with operational issues. It usually meets quarterly and includes the Managing Directors of subsidiary companies and other senior executives. The minutes of the meetings are circulated to the Board.

The performance of the Board is evaluated each year by a rigorous process based around a detailed questionnaire which each director completes. The areas covered include: the quality of leadership and the setting of strategy and values; the board's setting of its own objectives and review of its progress against those objectives; the composition of the Board, the appropriateness of its skill level and mix of experience and the effectiveness of the various roles; how well the board members work and communicate together and with others; the appropriateness of board and senior management succession planning and the induction and training of board members; the way Board meetings are conducted, the content of those meetings and related processes; the effectiveness of the various committees; and the appropriateness of its risk and control frameworks. The questionnaire also reviews the performance of each individual non-executive director. The results of the questionnaire are analysed and reviewed by the Board and appropriate improvements agreed and implemented.

Each director is appraised through the normal appraisal process. The Chief Executive Officer is appraised by the Chairman, the other executive Board members are appraised by the Chief Executive Officer, and the non-executive Board members other than the Chairman are appraised by the Chairman. Under the leadership of the senior independent director, the non-executive Board members hold a meeting without the Chairman being present to appraise the Chairman's performance.

A new director, on appointment, is briefed on the activities of the Company, and receives a full, formal and tailored induction. Non-executive directors are briefed on issues arising at Board meetings if required and non-executive directors have access to the Chairman and the Chief Executive Officer at any time. Ongoing training is provided as needed including presentations by the operating units on specific aspects of the business, supplemented by visits to key locations and meetings with key senior executives. Directors are updated continually on the Group's business and by means of Board presentations on matters including insurance, pensions, social, ethical, environmental and health and safety issues. In the furtherance of their duties or in relation to acts carried out by the Board or the Company, each director has been informed that they are entitled to seek independent professional advice at the expense of the Company. The Company maintains appropriate cover under a Directors' and Officers' liability insurance policy for legal action taken against any director. Each director has access to the services of the Company Secretary if required.

The non-executive directors are considered by the Board to be independent of management and are free to exercise independence of judgement. They have never been employees of the Company nor have they participated in any of the Company's share schemes, pension schemes or bonus arrangements. They receive no other remuneration from the Company other than the directors' fees and travel expenses. Confirmation has been sought and received from each non-executive director that he:

- does not have, and has not had within the last three years, a material business relationship with the Company, either directly or as a partner, shareholder, director or senior employee of a body that has such a relationship with the Company;

- has no close family ties with any of the Company's advisers, directors or senior employees;

- holds no cross-directorships or significant links with other directors through involvement in other companies or bodies; and

- does not represent a significant shareholder.

Confirmation of the above was also sought and received from the Chairman at the date of his appointment. Directors are subject to election at the Annual General Meeting following their appointment and are subject to re-election at least every three years.

The Chairman met during the year with the other non-executives and without the executive directors being present. The non-executive Deputy Chairman, Ian Percy, is the senior independent director who is available to shareholders if contact through normal channels is inappropriate or has failed to resolve an issue.

	Board meet-ings	Committee meetings		
		Audit	Remunera-tion	Nomina-tion
Number of meetings in the year	8	3	4	2
Number attended by each member:				
Marcus Beresford	8	1	4	2
Ian Percy	8	3	4	2
Michael Harper	8	3	4	2
David Hall	8	3	3	1
Dave Shemmans	8			2
Paula Bell (appointed 9 October 2006)	6			
Steve Parker	8			
Andrew Goodburn (resigned 5 January 2007)	4			
Jeremy Holt (resigned 16 May 2007)	7			

The table above shows the number of Board meetings (excluding those held to deal with minor administrative matters) and Audit, Remuneration and Nomination Committee meetings held during the year and the attendance of each director.

The Audit Committee

The Audit Committee is established by and is responsible to the Board. It has written terms of reference. Its main responsibilities are:

- to monitor and be satisfied with the truth and fairness of the Company's financial statements before submission to the Board for approval, ensuring their compliance with the appropriate accounting standards, the law and the Listing Rules of the UK Listing Authority;

- to review the Company's internal financial controls and internal control and risk management systems, and to review the effectiveness of the internal audit function and ensure that it is adequately resourced;

- to make recommendations to the Board in relation to the appointment and re-appointment of the external auditors and their remuneration, following appointment or re-appointment by the shareholders in general meeting, and to review the scope and planning of the audit and be satisfied with the auditors' independence, objectivity and effectiveness on an ongoing basis; and

- to implement the policy relating to any non-audit services performed by the external auditors.

Ian Percy, the Chairman of the Audit Committee, has wide experience as Chairman of audit committees, was recently Chairman of Companies House and was formerly Chairman of the Accounts Commission for Scotland and President of the Institute of Chartered Accountants of Scotland. He therefore has recent and relevant experience. The other members of the Audit Committee, Michael Harper and David Hall, who are both non-executive directors, have gained wide experience in regulatory and risk issues. In October 2006, following the satisfactory induction of David Hall as a fourth non-executive member of the Ricardo board, Marcus Beresford stood down as a member of the Audit Committee, in line with the Code's guidance that the chairman of a company should not be a member of its audit committee. Appointments to the Audit Committee are made by the Board on the recommendation of the Nomination Committee which takes into account the particular skills and attributes required to fulfil particular roles. The Audit Committee is authorised by the Board to seek and obtain any information it requires from any officer or employee of the Company and to obtain external legal or other independent professional advice as is deemed necessary by it. Audit Committee meetings are attended by the Chairman, the Chief Executive Officer and the Group Finance Director, where the Chairman of the Audit Committee considers it appropriate.

Meetings of the Audit Committee are held at least three times a year to coincide with the review of the scope of the external and internal audit and observations arising from their work in relation to internal control and to review the financial statements in September and February each year. The external auditors are normally invited to all meetings and meet with the Audit Committee without management being present at least once a year. At the Audit Committee meeting in September it carries out a full review of the year end financial statements and of the audit, using as a basis the Report to the Audit Committee prepared by the external auditors and taking into account any significant accounting policies, any changes to them and any significant estimates or judgments. Questions are asked of management of any significant or unusual transactions where the accounting treatment could be open to different interpretations. A similar but less detailed review is carried out in February when the Half Year Report is considered.

The Audit Committee receives reports from management and internal audit on the effectiveness of the system of internal controls and risk management systems. It also receives from the external auditors a report of matters arising during the course of the audit which the auditors deem to be of significance for the Audit Committee's attention.

The external auditors are required to give the Audit Committee information about policies and processes for maintaining their independence and compliance with requirements regarding the rotation of audit partners and staff. The Audit Committee considers all relationships between the external auditors and the Company to ensure that they do not compromise the auditors' judgement or independence particularly with the provision of non-audit services where a policy relating to these has been agreed by the Board. Essentially the external auditors would be excluded from carrying out non-audit services if they are put in the position of auditing their own work, making management decisions for the Company, if a mutual interest between the Company and the auditors is created or if the auditors take on the role of an advocate for the Company. If the external auditors carry out non-audit services and the cost of these services is estimated to exceed £20,000, prior approval by the Audit Committee is required.

The internal audit function is centrally managed. Internal audits are led by suitably skilled staff from head office or parts of the business independent from the business or function being audited, and are resourced by staff from around the Group with suitable skills, experience and independence for the area they are auditing. This approach not only ensures independence in the process but also the relevance of the recommendations and the sharing of best practice around the Group. During the year a review of the internal audit process was carried out. The audit plan for the year was reviewed as was the staffing to carry out the audits. The resources were considered adequate. The internal audit reports were reviewed as was management's response to the findings and recommendations. The Audit Committee considers that the internal audit process is an effective tool in the overall context of the Company's risk management system. The Audit Committee meets annually with the head of Internal Audit without the management being present.

The 1998 Public Interest Disclosure Act ('the Act') aims to promote greater openness in the workplace and ensure that 'whistle blowers' are protected. The Company maintains a policy in accordance with the Act which allows employees to raise concerns on a confidential basis if they have reasonable grounds for believing that there is serious malpractice within the Company. The policy is designed to deal with concerns, which must be raised without malice and in good faith, in relation to specific issues which are in the public interest and which fall outside the scope of other Company policies and procedures. There is a specific procedure laid down and action will be taken in those cases where the concern is shown or considered to be justified. The individual making the disclosure will be informed of what action is to be taken and a formal written record will be kept of each stage of the procedure. The whistle blowing policy is published internally on the Company's intranet site.

The Remuneration Committee

The Remuneration Committee, which is chaired by Michael Harper, comprises the non-executive directors and is described in the Directors' Remuneration Report on pages 50 to 57.

The Nomination Committee

The Nomination Committee, having evaluated the balance of skills, knowledge and experience on the Board, makes recommendations to the Board of executive and non-executive appointments. Before such recommendations are made, descriptions of the roles and skills required in fulfilling these roles are prepared for particular appointments. To attract suitable candidates, appropriate external advice is taken and interviews conducted by at least two members of the Nomination Committee to ensure a balanced view. Prior to her appointment by the Board as Group Finance Director to replace Andrew Goodburn when he retired in January 2007, Paula Bell along with other potential candidates went through a rigorous interview process with an external agency. When an appointment of a non-executive director is made, a formal letter is sent setting out clearly what is expected regarding time commitment, committee membership and involvement outside Board meetings. The chosen candidate is required to disclose to the Board any other significant commitments before the appointment can be ratified. The Committee has written terms of reference, and comprises Marcus Beresford (Chairman), the other non-executive directors (Ian Percy, Michael Harper and David Hall) and Dave Shemmans (Chief Executive Officer) and meets at least once a year and at other times as appropriate. The Chairman of the Committee is the Chairman of the Board, Marcus Beresford, except when a new Chairman of the Board is being sought, when it is the senior independent director, Ian Percy. The leadership needs and succession planning of the Company are regularly monitored as are the size and structure of the Board with consideration being given to the training needs of the executive and non-executive members. Non-executive directors are subject to rigorous review when they are continuing to serve on the Board for any term beyond six years.

Boards of subsidiary companies

The Group has a policy of appointing industry experts to participate in its local operating boards, thus bringing broader global experience to the Group. Sivert Hiljemark, formerly at Volvo Cars (UK), Walter Aspatore of Amherst Partners, LLC, Professor Wallentowitz of Aachen University and Akira Kijima, formerly at Mitsubishi Motor Corporation, are members of the UK, US, German and Japanese local operating boards respectively.

Shareholder communications

The Chief Executive Officer and the Group Finance Director regularly meet with institutional shareholders to foster a mutual understanding of objectives. Additionally the Chairman and the senior independent director are available for discussions with major shareholders if required. Surveys of shareholder opinion are normally carried out following announcements of results and are circulated to the Board.

The Annual General Meeting ('AGM') in November 2006 was attended by all directors in office at the time of the meeting. The directors encourage the participation of all shareholders, including private investors, at the AGM and as a matter of policy the level of proxy votes (for, against and vote withheld) lodged on each resolution is declared at the meeting and displayed on the Company's website. The Annual Report and Accounts is mailed to shareholders and others who request it and is published on our website www.ricardo.com.

Going Concern

After making enquiries, the directors have confidence that the Company and the Group have adequate resources to continue in operational existence for the foreseeable future. For this reason they continue to adopt the going concern basis in preparing the Report and Accounts.

Internal control and risk management

The Board is responsible for the Group's system of internal controls and risk management systems and for reviewing their effectiveness. Such systems are designed to manage rather than eliminate the risk of failure to achieve business objectives and can only provide reasonable and not absolute assurance against material misstatement or loss.

Each part of the Group highlights potential financial and non-financial risks which may impact on the business as part of the monthly management reporting procedures. The Board receives these monthly management reports and monitors the position at Board meetings.

As part of the risk management process, directors and senior managers are required to certify on a bi-annual basis that they have established effective controls to manage risk and to comply with legislation and Group procedures. Procedures are in place to ensure that effective control and risk management is embedded in the Group and that the Group is in a position to react as appropriate as new risks arise. The Board confirms that there are ongoing processes for identifying, evaluating and mitigating the significant risks faced by the Group. The processes have been in place during the year under review and up to the date of approval of the Annual Report and Accounts, consistent with the most recent Turnbull Committee guidance for directors on internal control.

The Group's internal control and monitoring procedures include:

- clear responsibility on the part of line and financial management for the maintenance of good financial controls and the production of accurate and timely management information;

- the control of key financial risks through clearly laid down authorisation levels and appropriate segregation of accounting duties, the control of key project risks through project delivery and review systems and the control of other key business risks via a number of processes and activities recorded in the Group's risk register;

- detailed monthly budgeting and reporting of trading results, balance sheets and cash flows, with regular review by management of variances from budget;

- reporting on compliance with internal financial controls and procedures by Group internal audit; and

- review of reports issued by the external auditors.

The Audit Committee, on behalf of the Board, reviews reports from both the internal and external auditors together with management's response regarding proposed actions. In this manner they have reviewed the effectiveness of the system of internal controls for the period covered by the Accounts.

Compliance with the Code

During the year ended 30 June 2007, the Company did not comply with Section 1 of the Code with respect to:

- The Chairman's membership of the Remuneration Committee: the Code's guidance has been that the Chairman should not sit on the Remuneration Committee. However the Board takes the view that his membership of the Remuneration Committee is important. The Chairman does not chair this Committee. It is noted that the June 2006 revision to the Code now states that the Chairman where considered independent on appointment may be a member of the Remuneration Committee provided he is not also the chair of the Committee.

- The Chairman's membership of the Audit Committee: it is recognised that the Code does not treat the Chairman as independent after appointment and therefore the Chairman should not sit on the Audit Committee. As explained above, the Chairman stepped down from the Audit Committee in October 2006, but attends where necessary at the request of the Chairman of the Audit Committee.

In all other respects the directors consider that the Company has complied with the provisions of Section 1 of the Code during the year ended 30 June 2007, and that the Company has been fully compliant with Section 1 of the June 2006 version of the Code since October 2006.

On behalf of the Board

Marcus Beresford   **Ian Percy**

Chairman   Senior Independent Director
                                      and Chairman of the Audit
                                      Committee

17 September 2007

APPENDIX 18

INSTITUTIONAL SHAREHOLDERS' COMMITTEE (UPDATED JUNE 2007): THE RESPONSIBILITIES OF INSTITUTIONAL SHAREHOLDERS AND AGENTS – STATEMENT OF PRINCIPLES

1. INTRODUCTION AND SCOPE

This Statement of Principles has been drawn up by the Institutional Shareholders' Committee.[1] It develops the principles set out in its 1991 statement 'The Responsibilities of Institutional Shareholders in the UK' and expands on the Combined Code on Corporate Governance of June 1998. It sets out best practice for institutional shareholders and/or agents in relation to their responsibilities in respect of investee companies in that they will:

- set out their policy on how they will discharge their responsibilities – clarifying the priorities attached to particular issues and when they will take action – see 2 below;

- monitor the performance of, and establish, where necessary, a regular dialogue with investee companies – see 3 below;

- intervene where necessary – see 4 below;

- evaluate the impact of their engagement – see 5 below; and

- report back to clients/beneficial owners – see 5 below.

In this statement the term 'institutional shareholder' includes pension funds, insurance companies, and investment trusts and other collective

---

[1] In 1991 the members of the Institutional Shareholders' Committee were: the Association of British Insurers; the Association of Investment Trust Companies; the British Merchant Banking and Securities Houses Association; the National Association of Pension Funds; and the Unit Trust Association. In 2005, the members are: the Association of British Insurers; the Association shareholders and agents should keep under review how far the principles in this statement can be applied to other equity investments of Investment Trust Companies; the National Association of Pension Funds; and the Investment Management Association.

investment vehicles. Frequently, agents such as investment managers are appointed by institutional shareholders to invest on their behalf.

This statement covers the activities of both institutional shareholders and those that invest as agents, including reporting by the latter to their institutional shareholder clients. The actions described in this statement in general apply only in the case of UK listed companies. They can be applied to any such UK company, irrespective of market capitalisation, although institutional shareholders' and agents' policies may indicate de minimis limits for reasons of cost-effectiveness or practicability. Institutional shareholders and agents should keep under review how far the principles in this statement can be applied to other equity investments.

The policies of engagement set out below do not constitute an obligation to micro-manage the affairs of investee companies, but rather relate to procedures designed to ensure that shareholders derive value from their investments by dealing effectively with concerns over under-performance. Nor do they preclude a decision to sell a holding, where this is the most effective response to such concerns.

Fulfilling fiduciary obligations to end-beneficiaries in accordance with the spirit of this statement may have implications for institutional shareholders' and agents' resources. They should devote appropriate resources, but these should be commensurate with the benefits for beneficiaries. The duty of institutional shareholders and agents is to the end beneficiaries and not to the wider public.

2. SETTING OUT THEIR POLICY ON HOW THEY WILL DISCHARGE THEIR RESPONSIBILITIES

Both institutional shareholders and agents will have a clear statement of their policy on engagement and on how they will discharge the responsibilities they assume. This policy statement will be a public document. The responsibilities addressed will include each of the matters set out below.

- How investee companies will be monitored. In order for monitoring to be effective, where necessary, an active dialogue may need to be entered into with the investee company's board and senior management.

- The policy for meeting with an investee company's board and senior management.

- How situations where institutional shareholders and/or agents have a conflict of interest will be minimised or dealt with.

- The strategy on intervention.

- An indication of the type of circumstances when further action will be taken and details of the types of action that may be taken.

- The policy on voting and voting disclosure.

Agents and their institutional shareholder clients should agree by whom these responsibilities are to be discharged and the arrangements for agents reporting back.

3. MONITORING PERFORMANCE

Institutional shareholders and/or agents, either directly or through contracted research providers, will review Annual Reports and Accounts, other circulars, and general meeting resolutions. They may attend company meetings where they may raise questions about investee companies' affairs. Also investee companies will be monitored to determine when it is necessary to enter into an active dialogue with the investee company's board and senior management. This monitoring needs to be regular, and the process needs to be clearly communicable and checked periodically for its effectiveness. Monitoring may require sharing information with other shareholders or agents and agreeing a common course of action.

As part of this monitoring, institutional shareholders and/or agents will:

- seek to satisfy themselves, to the extent possible, that the investee company's board and sub-committee structures are effective, and that independent directors provide adequate oversight; and

- maintain a clear audit trail, for example, records of private meetings held with companies, of votes cast, and of reasons for voting against the investee company's management, for abstaining, or for voting with management in a contentious situation.

In summary, institutional shareholders and/or agents will endeavour to identify problems at an early stage to minimise any loss of shareholder value. If they have concerns and do not propose to sell their holdings, they will seek to ensure that the appropriate members of the investee company's board are made aware of them. It may not be sufficient just to inform the Chairman and/or Chief Executive. However, institutional shareholders and/or agents may not wish to be made insiders. Institutional shareholders and/or agents will expect investee companies and their advisers to ensure that information that could affect their ability to deal in the shares of the company concerned is not conveyed to them without their agreement.

4. INTERVENING WHEN NECESSARY

Institutional shareholders' primary duty is to those on whose behalf they invest, for example, the beneficiaries of a pension scheme or the policyholders in an insurance company, and they must act in their best financial interests. Similarly, agents must act in the best interests of their clients. Effective monitoring will enable institutional shareholders and/or agents to exercise their votes and, where necessary, intervene objectively and in an informed way. Where it would make intervention more effective, they should seek to engage with other shareholders.

Many issues could give rise to concerns about shareholder value. Institutional shareholders and/or agents should set out the circumstances when they will actively intervene and how they propose to measure the effectiveness of doing so. Intervention should be considered by institutional shareholders and/or agents regardless of whether an active or passive investment policy is followed. In addition, being underweight is not, of itself, a reason for not intervening. Instances when institutional shareholders and/or agents may want to intervene include when they have concerns about:

- the company's strategy;

- the company's operational performance;

- the company's acquisition/disposal strategy;

- independent directors failing to hold executive management properly to account;

- internal controls failing;

- inadequate succession planning;

- an unjustifiable failure to comply with the Combined Code;

- inappropriate remuneration levels/incentive packages/severance packages; and

- the company's approach to corporate social responsibility.

If boards do not respond constructively when institutional shareholders and/or agents intervene, then institutional shareholders and/or agents will consider on a case-by-case basis whether to escalate their action, for example, by:

- holding additional meetings with management specifically to discuss concerns;

- expressing concern through the company's advisers;

- meeting with the Chairman, senior independent director, or with all independent directors;

- intervening jointly with other institutions on particular issues;

- making a public statement in advance of the AGM or an EGM;

- submitting resolutions at shareholders' meetings; and

- requisitioning an EGM, possibly to change the board.

Institutional shareholders and/or agents should vote all shares held directly or on behalf of clients wherever practicable to do so. They will not automatically support the board; if they have been unable to reach a satisfactory outcome through active dialogue then they will register an abstention or vote against the resolution. In both instances it is good practice to inform the company in advance of their intention and the reasons why.

5. EVALUATING AND REPORTING

Institutional shareholders and agents have a responsibility for monitoring and assessing the effectiveness of their engagement. Those that act as agents will regularly report to their clients details on how they have discharged their responsibilities. This should include a judgement on the impact and effectiveness of their engagement. Such reports will be likely to comprise both qualitative as well as quantitative information. The particular information reported, including the format in which details of how votes have been cast will be presented, will be a matter for agreement between agents and their principals as clients.

Transparency is an important feature of effective shareholder activism. Institutional shareholders and agents should not however be expected to make disclosures that might be counterproductive. Confidentiality in specific situations may well be crucial to achieving a positive outcome.

6. CONCLUSION

The Institutional Shareholders' Committee believes that adoption of these principles will significantly enhance how effectively institutional shareholders and/or agents discharge their responsibilities in relation to the companies in which they invest. To ensure that this is the case, the Institutional Shareholders' Committee will monitor the impact of this statement with a view to further reviewing and refreshing it, if needs be, in 2007 in the light of experience and market developments.

APPENDIX 19

FURTHER READING

Sir Adrian Cadbury *Corporate Governance and Chairmanship* (Oxford University Press, 2002)

Patrick Dunne *Running Board Meetings* (Kogan Page, 2nd edn, 1999)

John Harvey-Jones *Making It Happen* (Collins, 1988)

Derek Higgs *Review of the Role and Effectiveness of Non-executive Directors* (The Stationery Office, 2003)

Richard Smerdon *A Practical Guide to Corporate Governance* (Sweet & Maxwell, 2nd edn, 2004)

APPENDIX 20

USEFUL WEBSITES

Companies Act 2006

www.opsi.gov.uk/ACTS/acts2006/pdf/ukpga_20060046_en.pdf

Financial Reporting Council

www.frc.org.uk

Foundation for Governance Research and Education

www.foundationgre.com

Institute of Chartered Accountants of Scotland

www.icas.org.uk

Institute of Chartered Secretaries and Administrators

www.icsa.org.uk

Institute of Chartered Secretaries and Administrators Guidance on Terms of Reference – Audit Committee

www.icsa.org.uk/assets/files/pdfs/guidance/071012.pdf

Institute of Chartered Secretaries and Administrators Guidance on Terms of Reference – Nomination Committee

www.icsa.org.uk/assets/files/pdfs/guidance/071013.pdf

Institute of Chartered Secretaries and Administrators Guidance on Terms of Reference – Remuneration Committee

www.icsa.org.uk/assets/files/pdfs/guidance/071014.pdf

Institutional Shareholders' Committee

www.institutionalshareholderscommittee.org.uk

Institutional Shareholders' Committee (Updated June 2007) – The Responsibilities of Institutional Shareholders and Agents, Statement of Principles

http://institutionalshareholderscommittee.org.uk/sitebuildercontent/
sitebuilderfiles/ISCStatementofPrinciplesJun07.pdf

International Corporate Governance Network

www.icgn.org

London Stock Exchange

www.londonstockexchange.com

National Association of Pension Funds

www.napf.co.uk

The Quoted Companies Alliance

www.quotedcompaniesalliance.co.uk

The Revised Turnbull Guidance on Internal Controls (October 2005)

www.frc.org.uk/CORPORATE/internalcontrol.cfm

The Smith Guidance on Audit Committees (October 2005)

www.frc.org.uk/CORPORATE/auditcommittees.cfm

INDEX

References are to paragraph numbers.